How to
Do Groups

How to
Do Groups
Second Edition

William H. Friedman, Ph.D.

JASON ARONSON INC.
Northvale, New Jersey
London

Production Editor: Judith D. Cohen

This book was set in 11 pt. Goudy by Lind Graphics of Upper Saddle River, New Jersey, and printed and bound by Haddon Craftsmen of Scranton, Pennsylvania.

Library of Congress Cataloging-in-Publication Data

Friedman, William H.
    How to do groups / by William H. Friedman. – 2nd ed.
        p.   cm.
    Includes bibliographical references and index.
    ISBN 1-56821-117-1
    1. Group psychotherapy.   I. Title
RC488.F75   1994
616.89′152 – dc20   93-30116

Manufactured in the United States of America. Jason Aronson Inc. offers books and cassettes. For information and catalog write to Jason Aronson Inc., 230 Livingston Street, Northvale, New Jersey 07647.

Contents

Preface to the
Second Edition

This edition is a substantial revision of the first one, though the intent, goals, and target audiences remain the same. So much has changed in the mental health care delivery system and in the theory and practice of group psychotherapy since the first edition that it was difficult to keep from writing an entirely new book. I have tried to retain, in the present edition, those parts of the earlier work that seem to have withstood the test of time, discarding the clearly dated sections, and updating the rest.

Chapter 1 describes the administrative arrangements that go into putting a group together: a room, a co-therapist, patients, a supervisor. In clinical settings where these arrangements are already in place, this chapter will help the student understand and evaluate what has gone into establishing the therapy group. Where they are absent and the student will have primary responsibility for getting a group started, the chapter provides a road map.

Much of Chapter 2 is new. It describes in some detail how to get a patient who has come to the clinic seeking individual therapy to accept a referral for group therapy—whether that referral is to a group that the individual therapist is offering or to a group offered by other therapists. Chapter 3 describes what should be accomplished during the screening interview. Chapter 4 shows you in some detail how to conduct the initial session of a new group.

Chapter 5 begins a digression into theory. Many new clinicians, having spent some years in classrooms and laboratories, are so eager to finally begin learning how to do clinical work—that is, to learn and begin to practice psychotherapeutic techniques—that both the relevance and importance of theory fade into the background. Chapter 5 shows how theory facilitates learning and enhances technical skill. Chapter 6 applies Freud's theory of group psychology to the therapy group. Differing from the psychodynamic theories of group psychotherapy, this chapter helps the student bridge the gap between undergraduate or graduate level course work in personality theory and the realities of how and why people relate as they do during a group therapy session.

Chapter 7 shows how to focus on the factors that make groups therapeutic and how to employ them during group interactions. Copious use of clinical examples guides the student toward fruitful, and away from ineffectual, interventions. Chapter 8 presents a theory of psychopathology anchored in interpersonal interactions rather than in intrapsychic factors. Its purpose is to link intrapsychic events, interpersonal behaviors and the outcomes of interpersonal interactions, and the therapeutic factors in group psychotherapy in a way that has direct relevance to the interpersonal context of the group session. Taken together, these theoretical chapters enable the clinician to make sense of what goes on during a group therapy session and to formulate effective interventions based on that understanding.

Chapters 9 and 10 return to clinical issues. Chapter 9 provides quite specific guidelines about what to pay attention to during the group sessions, while Chapter 10 describes in some detail how to formulate therapeutic interventions during the group sessions, as well as how to determine when to say them.

The remaining chapters are more general. Chapter 11 discusses the co-therapy relationship, bringing together some threads from earlier chapters. Chapter 12 discusses some of the things that can go wrong, in terms of the components of the group therapy service delivery system described in Chapter 1. The final chapter, on brief inpatient group psychotherapy, is a brief road map for doing group on psychiatric wards of medical hospitals and on admissions wards of larger, long-term psychiatric hospitals.

Absent from this edition are the chapter on other theories of group therapy that appeared in the first edition, and on group therapy with chronic schizophrenic patients. Most of those other theories have either vanished entirely, are now practiced in only one or two places, or have transmuted into something else. A new set of theories has now taken their place. I thought it would be more useful to explicate the interpersonal orientation that was all but implicit in the first edition rather than continue to take a relatively atheoretical stance. Times change; so do people.

Anne Alonso told me how to get a task of this magnitude accomplished in a finite period of time while meeting job responsibilities and maintaining family and other relationships. Her implicit assumption that *I could do it* was a very powerful resource when I hit the inevitable dry spells. Laurel Drobits 'minded the store,' enabling me to devote time to writing while maintaining my administrative responsibilities. A number of students, over the years, encouraged me to do a second edition, and I hope that they will forgive me for not naming them individually. I would also like to thank those students I supervised over the years, for it is their stories that gave rise to this book, and to the changes embodied in this edition.

As before, my wife Liz gave unflagging encouragement, support, and editorial help. Indeed, she made the task easier in so many ways that it is clear that nothing would have been accomplished without her; and so it is to her shining spirit and keen mind that readers finding this volume helpful in their work owe thanks.

Chapel Hill, North Carolina
July, 1993

Preface to the First Edition

This book is intended for students in the mental health professions who are just about to begin leading groups. My original intent was to provide a quite slim volume, to be read in the hour or so before the first group session was to begin. However, it seemed prudent to begin this introductory text at an earlier point, namely, the point at which the student decides to lead a group. For the most part, the book addresses the concerns and questions which the student is likely to have at that point and up to the second or third group session. By the time a group has met two or three times, most of what is learned about groups should be coming from supervisory sessions, not from text-books.

The book is intended for practicing clinicians at the graduate or postgraduate level. Thus, graduate students in psychology, education, social work, and nursing who are on internship or field placement, as well as psychiatric residents, should find the present work useful. Except for the last two chapters, which discuss group therapy in mental hospitals, the issues raised here are applicable to groups in a range of nonmedical settings. I have used the terms *group therapist* and *group leader* interchangeably; the terms *group member* and *patient* are similarly interchangeable.

This is, then, a clinical manual. It is not intended as a scholarly work. The bibliography and the references cited are adequate for the limited purpose and emphasis of this work: a *brief* introduction for the clinical student who is harried and hurried. For the preclinical student who is seeking an entry into the literature on groups and who has the time to follow up references, the following bibliographical resources are available: Yalom's *The Theory and Practice of Group Psychotherapy*, 2nd edition (1975); Bednar and Lawlis' chapter on empirical research in group psychotherapy, in Bergin and Garfield's *Handbook of Psychotherapy and Behavior Change* (1971); the annual reviews of the group psychotherapy literature which appear in the *International Journal of Group Psychotherapy*; and Zimpfer's exhaustive *Group Work in the Healing Professions: A Bibliography* (1976).

Much of what is written here is based on my experiences as cotherapist and supervisor over a period of years. I do not think that any student has been without influence on me. I would like to express thanks in particular to Donna Avery, Rich Leventhal, Rich Hanish, Donna Frick, Jim Thompson, and Becca Osborn. Alan Bell provided me the opportunity of supervising his students in group counseling, and that experience was especially fruitful, both in terms of what I learned and the people I met.

Ruth Klein read much of the manuscript, and provided a detailed, line-by-line critique which was funny and enormously helpful; I made virtually all of the changes she suggested, and am grateful to her for the signal improvements she made possible.

Except for one month in the summer of 1976 and one week that fall, the book was written during evenings, weekends, and whatever time I could find during the day. That kind of schedule can put considerable strain on family life, but it didn't. My wife Liz was encouraging throughout the years I worked to complete this task. Sometimes her encouragement was gentle, sometimes vigorous; it was unflagging. She drew on her own background in journalism and her own talent as a writer to provide editorial critique of the manuscript. I sought to write with clarity and simplicity. Where I have achieved that, it has been with her help and because I heeded her advice. The responsibility for turgidity in the prose is mine alone. Liz's help and encouragement has been an act of love carried out with intelligence and skill.

I would also like to thank Patti Fisher, who typed and retyped the manuscript, uncomplainingly, unfailingly cheerful. It was Patti who helped me to find those daytime hours which I devoted to this work. Without her secretarial efficiency the work would not yet be complete.

1

The First Steps

In the beginning, the novice therapist who wants to do a group will have to find a co-therapist, a supervisor, space, time, and patients. Accordingly, the first thing the novice discovers is that it is considerably more difficult and time consuming to put a group together than he or she might have anticipated. How much longer it will take, and how much harder it is than expected, will depend in part on the strength of the group program in the particular setting, the attitude of the therapist staff toward group therapy, the rate of referral, and other factors. In the absence of systematized group referral procedures, eight to ten weeks from conception to first meeting is neither unusual nor a pessimistic estimate. In addition it may take several more weeks before the group achieves a stable membership.

FINDING A CO-THERAPIST

Picking a co-therapist may be somewhat less important than selecting a spouse, but it is probably no less an art. The therapist-to-be is looking for someone with whom he or she will share many hours of heightened emotional experience, hard work, and stress. How can you tell who will work most effectively with you?

There are no hard and fast rules, and you may not have much

choice anyway, depending upon the exigencies of your particular clinical setting. The following are some rather general guidelines, which assume that the co-therapists are of approximately equal status and experience. The supervisor as co-therapist is discussed later, as is co-therapy with members of other disciplines.

1. If at all possible, don't ask strangers to lead groups with you. The better you know someone, the easier time you're likely to have communicating with that person during and about group. Working with a friend, or a colleague whom you know and like, is generally going to be easiest.
2. A co-therapist whose theoretical orientation is similar to yours will probably be easier to work with. Paulson, Burroughs, and Gelb (1976) found that co-therapists of different theoretical beliefs chose not to work together again significantly more frequently than therapists of similar beliefs.
3. A co-therapist who handles emotion in a manner similar to your own will be easier to work with. Commonality in the emotional language you both speak facilitates resolution of problems that invariably arise in any intense relationship over time. Similarity in the handling of emotions will help things go more smoothly. Someone who handles anger and affection in the same general way you do, who is either as open or as closed as you, will make a better *first* co-therapist than someone who is different from you, someone who may have qualities you admire but lack (such as high verbal facility, or a greater cognitive grasp of technique and how to apply it, etc.). There will be enough differences even between co-therapists whose styles are similar; complementarity or noncongruence cannot really be avoided. Similarity does not mean identity.

The issue of complementarity versus similarity in the handling of emotions is somewhat complicated by gender issues. There are data suggesting that along some affective dimensions, same-sex complementarity and opposite-sex similarity mediate successful relationships (Berzins, Friedman, and Ross 1972). That is, you may work best with a same-sex co-therapist who handles affect differently from you, and with an opposite-sex co-therapist who handles affect in a manner similar to your own. However, the data do not address the importance of this factor in the co-therapy relationship; they were collected in research on the patient–therapist relationship.

4. It is not necessary to seek a co-therapist of opposite sex, though there are some potential advantages in such a pairing. Most pertinent at this point is that opposite-sex co-therapists can serve as role models, and their relationship as a model of opposite-sex social relations (in some forms of group therapy). However, if you choose a co-therapist of the same sex, you will find that in the group one of you will assume roles that could be called feminine, and the other, roles which could be called masculine. The role divergence occurs even with co-therapists of the same sex, because people (including therapists) differ in the amount of nurturance (warmth, empathy, and the like) that they are perceived as offering. One of the co-therapists will offer more than the other, and it may therefore seem that he or she will come to assume a more feminine role in the group. It is not unusual for this role to devolve upon a highly nurturant male, with a female co-therapist gradually assuming what some might consider the paternal role model in group. A recent study by Alfred investigated whether male and female co-leaders are perceived differently by group members in terms of influence and effectiveness. Results suggested that the influence and effectiveness of *both* co-leaders increased as the group progressed. However, there were no definitive findings with regard to differences between male and female co-leaders (Alfred 1992). These findings support the idea that therapist characteristics other than gender should be primary in co-therapist selection. The co-therapy relationship is discussed further in Chapters 11 and 12.

SUPERVISORY MODELS

Supervision is an integral part of learning to do groups. Doing a group is, of course, itself a learning experience for the therapist. However, experiential learning cannot, in this context, be more than rudimentary. Supervision is required to help the therapist (1) become aware of the relevant sensory input and (2) interpret and generalize from the experience of doing a particular group. Doing a group does not of itself constitute training. Supervision is training. Training and competence are related. There is some evidence that unsupervised experience decreases therapist effectiveness (Yalom 1985).

The novice therapist should be aware of the various supervisory models and, if possible, should choose a model within which he or she is most likely to learn effectively. In many training settings, however, there are few or no options and the trainee must accept whatever is available.

Groups are usually supervised in one of five ways. These are: (1) the supervisor as co-therapist; (2) the supervisor observing, through a two-way mirror; (3) remote observation, by means of audio- or videotape; (4) in a group consisting of several co-therapist pairs, the supervisor acting as group leader; and (5) verbal report of the co-therapists to the supervisor in the latter's office. Dies (1980) briefly describes other supervisory modes, but these are the most common.

THE SUPERVISOR AS CO-THERAPIST

The great advantage of supervisor as co-therapist is that the student has an opportunity to watch at first hand how an experienced group leader does things. In addition, the supervisor is able to intervene immediately should the need arise (Coche 1977). The shared immediacy of the group experience probably makes the post-group supervisory sessions more meaningful. The supervisor, having been in the room, knows quite well what was going on. Because he or she has shared the experience, the supervisor can more effectively discuss it than if he or she had observed it from behind a two-way mirror or via videotape.

One of the disadvantages of having a supervisor as co-therapist is that the student is not a co-leader but an assistant leader, especially during the early meetings of a group. The assistant leader's task can be construed as knowing or figuring out what the group leader is doing and maintaining readiness to help him or her do it. An assistant's status would seldom involve initiating group interaction, formulating therapeutic interventions, or determining what to say next. The feeling of being in there with a bunch of people, not knowing what to say, but having to say *something*, is not likely to be particularly intense if you are an assistant group leader. This is because you know (1) that it isn't really your group anyway but your supervisor's, and (2) that if you do say something on cue from your supervisor or in response to an interaction initiated by someone else, your supervisor will come to your aid if you get stuck.

At the same time that the assistant therapist status takes some pressure off you in terms of having to say something during the group session, the presence of the supervisor tends to be somewhat intimidating. As a result, you may feel hesitant to offer interventions or observations. Such reluctance and hesitation is natural and quite common in the early sessions. A good supervisor will help you to overcome this intimidation in time, and will also help you to work through the inevitable transference issues that arise in this situation. Berman (1975) has discussed a number of disadvantages in the supervisor-as-therapist model.

It could be said that one disadvantage of the supervisor as co-therapist is that being in there with you, he or she lacks objectivity. This is a nominal disadvantage. In our society, objectivity usually means *without emotion*, and emotion is the stuff of experience, especially in psychotherapy. So a supervisor sitting behind a mirror making cool, detached objective judgments (which aren't objective anyway but may be somewhat less emotional than those of participant leaders) is one step removed from the data of the group. That may be a very big step indeed. Passionate subjectivity that the supervisor can articulate without being defensive can lead to a learning experience at least as meaningful as an objective critique of your technical skills.

A more serious disadvantage of the supervisor as co-therapist

stems from the difference in power or status that obtains between
teacher and student, and which is manifested in the leader–assistant
leader structure. It is highly likely that at some point disagreement or
other passions will arise in the relationship between the two. Because
of the differences in power, in experience, and other factors, the
junior co-therapist is likely to feel considerable pressure to defer. If the
match between co-therapists is poor, the position of the student may
be precarious indeed. The supervisor, coming out of the same
experience as the student but holding very different views or
interpretations of it, may feel that the reasons for the differences in
perception or interpretation of that experience lies in the pathology
rather than the inexperience of the student. The latter, in turn, may
come to feel that group therapy, or perhaps psychotherapy in general,
is a poor professional choice. Problems in supervision are discussed
more fully in Chapter 8.

When strong feelings, either positive or negative, arise between
co-therapists of equal status, these issues can be dealt with more
readily than when the supervisor is directly involved with the therapy
itself, for he or she can then function as a mediator.

Despite its disadvantages, having the supervisor as co-therapist
probably provides the best learning opportunities for the novice
clinician. The structure of the group therapy session allows the
student therapist to attend closely, moment by moment, to what the
supervisor therapist is doing, to seek to understand the underlying
strategies, and to develop interventions consistent with what the
supervisor is trying to do. In addition, the structure of the session
more or less requires that the supervisor attend to what the trainee is
doing. While such close observation can have its disadvantageous
aspects, it allows for feedback both about the major dimensions of
therapeutic intervention and about the minutiae of interpersonal cues
(tone of voice, gesture, timing), which are more difficult to learn about
in other models. In clinical settings where the administrators may be
reluctant to allow experienced clinicians to do training rather than
provide service to clients, this supervisory model may be more readily
available than some of the others.

THE SUPERVISOR OBSERVING THROUGH A TWO-WAY MIRROR

One advantage of this model is that the supervisor, being detached from the action, can more readily observe the entirety of the session, formulate some hypotheses about what is really going on, and facilitate the development of the therapists' intervention-formulating skills during the supervisory sessions. The supervisor can sometimes see things that neither co-therapist has observed—in part because of the different viewing angle—and has more opportunity to reflect about underlying themes than do the therapists, who must attend to the action as it unfolds. A second advantage is that the novice therapist can be paired with a more experienced co-therapist, and so obtain the benefit of working with two more experienced clinicians.

There are a number of practical limitations. One is that the model cannot even be considered unless the clinic has an observation room equipped with a two-way mirror and a decent sound system. Another is that it represents a considerable investment of supervisor time and is therefore not usually an option in clinical settings where supervisors are required to deliver clinical services directly.

If a group is to be observed, whether by a supervisor or others, the informed consent of the group members must be obtained. This is not usually difficult. The supervisor might sit in on the pregroup screening interviews, introduce himself or herself to the group at its first meeting, or remain anonymous—but the group *must* be made aware of the fact that he or she is there.

Whenever there is observation of a group, the possibility exists that group members' awareness of observation by unseen others constitutes an intrusion into the group room and influences the interaction. One disadvantage of this supervisory model is that it may make novice (and more experienced) therapists nervous, and their nervousness may be transmitted to the group members, making the work of therapy more difficult. However, as the relationship between therapists and supervisor becomes more comfortable (assuming that it does), this particular problem is likely to diminish.

The loss of immediacy that comes from being outside the room and not engaged in the interactions is seldom seen as a disadvantage by participants in this model of learning how to do groups. Any such loss is outweighed by the advantages stemming from the broader view of the actions afforded by the external observation point. However, the meeting between supervisor and co-therapists is best held immediately after the group meeting, while events are still relatively fresh in everyone's mind.

When it is available, this model tends to be preferred by students and trainees, though not always by supervisors or clinic administrators. The student or trainee who can choose from among several different clinical sites for therapy training should consider the availability of direct observation, sometimes called live or in vivo supervision, a major advantage in determining which setting is likely to offer the best learning opportunities.

SUPERVISION WITH AUDIO- OR VIDEOTAPE

When audiotape is used, the supervisor is blind, so to speak, and usually hard of hearing. His or her comments will therefore be less helpful than if he or she were able to pick up the visual cues and to hear the people mumbling in the background while someone else is talking. But sometimes this is the only way you can get supervision.

By comparison, videotape is infinitely better. However, it has some problems. Primary among these is the question of who runs the equipment. Stationary cameras are not generally satisfactory because in order to get the whole group into the picture, the vantage point offered by the camera lens is too far away to pick up many of the smaller behavioral cues emitted by the group members and the therapists. In addition, the unchanging view is visually boring. Arranging for a camera operator can be cumbersome, and clinic administrators may be reluctant to commit so many resources to a single group unless the clinic's primary mission is training. Asking a group member to run the camera can provide some *very* interesting pictures indeed, but it effectively removes that client from the group session. Having the camera and operator in the room rather than behind a mirror can be distracting, but most groups seem to quickly forget the camera's presence.

The advantages offered by videotape are therefore to some extent counterbalanced by the disadvantages inherent in the requirements of equipment and operators and the increased time likely to be spent during the supervisory session searching the videotape for the desired segments of the therapy session. Unless videotape is routinely used for supervision in your setting, the time and effort it takes are not likely to be worth the additional effort.

GROUP SUPERVISION

In this model, several co-therapist pairs meet jointly with the supervisor. The advantages of this model are:

1. It is most economical of the supervisor's time, and is an efficient way to utilize his or her expertise, especially if the supervisor is a consultant or part-time employee of the clinic.
2. There is a sharing of problems and a pooling of experiences that can, in sum, broaden the student therapist's acquaintance with or exposure to doing groups. There is probably no better way to experience both the commonalities and the idiosyncrasies of groups than this.
3. In the process of dealing with particular problems in the student's group, the supervisory group can provide the opportunity for role playing. The therapist who comes to the supervisory session with the question, How is this patient's behavior to be understood? or How might I have handled this situation differently? can play the role of his or her own patient. The supervisor, and other members of the supervisory group, can take the role of group leader. Thus

the therapist may not only gain greater understanding of what it must have been like for that patient in his or her group, but may also experience the effect of different leadership styles upon what the patient is doing and upon the interaction between patient and group.

4. Through the phenomenon of *parallel process*, the supervisory group can re-create the interpersonal context of the therapy group under discussion. The interpersonal context includes the affective tone or feeling in the group, the pattern of communication among members (patient to patient, patient to therapist, therapist to patient), and the affect with which the words are being conveyed. Listening to a therapist describe a group that feels stuck or in which, for instance, there are long unproductive silences, the supervisory group comes to feel stuck itself. A potentially long and unproductive silence may follow the student's description, just as the silence in that student's therapy group followed something one of the group members had said. What is occurring at that point in the supervisory group is parallel to what happened in the therapy group. The supervisory group can then explore the phenomenon, facilitate understanding on the part of the therapists as to what is going on and what it probably feels like to the therapy group members, and propose some alternative ways of handling the situation.

The problems of this supervisory model are magnifications of those stemming from the supervisor's distance from the therapy group experience. Here the supervisor has no direct access, either in person or via tape, to the data of the group. It is therefore not possible to do the kind of detailed, meticulous examination of what happened that is the best learning experience in both individual and group therapy. Such an examination involves discussion of several cue dimensions that comprise a single comment or brief series of comments. Tone of voice, facial expression, and posture, as well as what preceded and followed the comment(s), are explored and may be interpreted. Thus, when the supervisor can see as well as hear what is going on, it is possible to attend to the non-verbal minutiae of interpersonal communication and the nuances of interaction that influence both the meaning and the effect of the verbal message.

Just as in the therapy group itself, in a supervisory group not every co-therapist pair may be in the spotlight at every meeting. You may come to the supervisory group meeting with some questions of (in your judgment) fair-to-middlin' importance, and one of your colleagues may present a problem the supervisory group spends most of its time on, never getting to you at all. There are some issues that survive postponement, and problems of at least moderate significance tend to recur in therapy groups (and individual therapy as well). But when you bring a problem to supervisory group and then don't have an opportunity to discuss it, the immediacy of that particular situation is lost, and with it a genuine opportunity. This is one of the disadvantages of supervisory groups.

Supervision cannot be as close as in the supervisor–co-therapist pair situation. At the same time that you learn more about how others do groups and about the problems that arise in other groups, you learn rather less about you and groups. This model is therefore not recommended for people who are doing their first groups, unless it is in addition to individual supervision. It is better for people doing their fourth or fifth groups (or who are in their second year with their first group), who are therefore less in need of the kind of detailed examination of events that individual supervision can afford.

VERBAL REPORT

In this model, a co-therapist pair meets with the supervisor, usually in the latter's office, at some time during the week between group sessions. The co-therapists describe what happened in the group, either from notes or (more frequently) from memory, and the supervisor comments on the verbal report. There is some evidence that this is the most common (Hess and Hess 1983) and least satisfactory (Dies 1980) of the supervisory models.

It is the most common model perhaps because it is the most convenient, at least for the supervisor. It is least satisfactory because the novice therapist may not yet know what is of critical importance during the group session and may fail to present it, focusing instead on aspects of the session that may be more familiar or more comfortable to describe. Supervisors, not therapists, should determine what to attend to in the complex group interaction and cannot do so without some kind of first-hand data. This model is therefore to be avoided wherever possible.

SUPERVISORY MODELS: CONCLUDING COMMENT

Having discussed the various supervisory models, we come to the question of which is best for the novice therapist. The exigencies of any particular clinical setting will probably lead toward answering that question one way or another: you have to start with what's available. But if the opportunities are there and you have a genuine choice, do a short-term group with an experienced leader first, and then a longer one with a colleague, with the supervisor observing. Group therapy is an art, and modeling is frequently a highly effective teaching device that can help students recognize their own potential for artistry.

2

Referral of Patients for Group Therapy

Referral of patients for group therapy is a highly complex process because of the many issues and people involved. These include: (1) the referring therapist and those reasons for referral that stem from individual patient–therapist interaction; (2) the interest or need, on the part of the training facility, to provide group therapy as a training experience for its students; (3) the interest or need of the facility to provide group therapy as a means of efficiently providing services to larger numbers of clients than could be accommodated by the therapist staff seeing clients one at a time; and (4) the potential benefit to patients in terms of group as treatment of choice or as a weekly alternative to monthly or bimonthly individual therapy sessions.

A number of authors have described attributes or characteristics of patients that render the patient more or less suitable for therapy. Our focus in this chapter is not upon these intra-individual attributes, but upon the referral process and what constitutes a good group referral from the standpoint of the group therapist.

REASONS FOR REFERRAL

There is only one legitimate reason for referral of a patient for group therapy. That is the expectation on the part of both patient and therapist that the patient will benefit from the experience, and the judgment on the part of the therapist that group therapy is the treatment of choice, the best possible therapy for this patient at this time.

There are a number of reasons for referral that might be classified as nonlegitimate, and a few that are illegitimate.

Nonlegitimate referrals are those made primarily for the benefit of someone other than the patient, but from which the patient can reasonably be expected to benefit. One type of nonlegitimate referral is that made because of the lack of availability of individual therapy for patients for whom this technique would be the treatment of choice. Individual therapy may not be available because the demand exceeds the supply of therapists and there is a waiting list; because no extended individual therapy is offered in the clinic; or because the patient is for whatever reason ineligible for individual therapy in the clinic and cannot (or will not) afford individual therapy on a private basis. In these instances, group therapy might be offered to the patient primarily for reasons of convenience and cost, even though as a treatment modality it is regarded by the referring therapist as second best. Patients referred in these circumstances are, understandably enough, going to be difficult to work with during the initial group sessions.

A second nonlegitimate reason for referral involves the clinic's need to provide a group therapy experience as part of its training function. The individual therapist's knowledge that group referrals are needed may influence his or her clinical judgment as to disposition in some cases, and perhaps more so if a couple of the referring therapist's friends are trying to get a group going. The situation is no different in purely service-oriented clinical facilities that offer group therapy. Informal peer pressure exists for the individual therapist to make group referrals. It should be emphasized that we are discussing here a situation that is reasonably expected to benefit the patient. It is listed as non-legitimate because it is of primary benefit to the clinic rather than to the patient.

Illegitimate referrals involve, in effect, rejection of the patient by his or her individual therapist. Such a rejection may occur for a wide variety of reasons. The therapist may abandon hope, lose interest, feel that the patient is getting too involved (transference) or that the therapist is getting too involved (countertransference). Such therapist involvement may involve positive feelings, but anger is more frequent. When patients seem demanding and insatiably needy, the therapist may come to feel that he or she cannot meet those demands and may hope to dilute their impact by sharing the patient with a group.

A successful illegitimate referral involves (1) a change of attitude on the part of the therapist such that he or she desires to abrogate the original contract with the patient; (2) the therapist's decision not to inform the patient of his or her change in attitude (this is what makes the referral illegitimate); and (3) convincing the patient (and perhaps himself or herself as well) that such a referral for group therapy is appropriate.

Neither the nonlegitimate nor the illegitimate reasons for referral necessarily preclude admitting a patient into group. However, the group therapists will probably find it prudent to be aware of the factors involved in the primary therapist's decision to refer the patient. Unless you know the referring therapist well, some direct contact prior to the screening interview with the patient may save both of you, and the patient, some difficulties later on.

MAKING THE REFERRAL

Referring an individual therapy patient or client for group therapy takes some skill. You have to determine that the patient or client would be suitable for group, or recognize that group therapy might be a desirable alternative. Then you have to persuade the patient or client that group therapy would be of benefit to him or her, help the client work through the doubts that most people have about discussing very personal matters in a group context, and attempt to identify and dispel any misconceptions the client may have about what group therapy involves and what the potential benefits may be. An effective referral results in the patient becoming a member of a therapy group.

Recognizing that group therapy might be a desirable alternative involves some familiarity with the personal characteristics of good group members and sufficient familiarity with your client to compare his or her characteristics with the criteria, some of which are discussed in the following section. It is difficult to know what a good group member looks like until you've had some group experience yourself, either as a member or as a co-leader. This presents a bit of a chicken-and-egg problem because it's difficult to refer someone for group unless you have some experience of group, and training in individual therapy usually precedes training in group therapy. In clinical settings that offer good group therapy training, new clinicians are offered the opportunity to participate as members in a group experience, and there may be some didactic work as well. Where these opportunities are absent, you may have to rely on your group therapy supervisor (supervisors of individual therapy may not have the skills) for advice or instruction on how to make a referral from individual to group therapy.

Few people come to a mental health facility seeking group therapy. What most people are seeking is relief from some symptom(s) or help in resolving some problem(s). Usually what they are seeking, and get, is individual counseling or therapy, with or without additional psychological testing or prescriptions for medication. Both testing and the proffering of prescriptions are usually done by an individual clinician meeting with the individual client or patient. Group therapy has virtually no constituency of its own. Therefore, the clinician seeking to make a referral for group therapy has the task of educating the client about this treatment modality, persuading the client that it is likely to be of benefit, and then also dealing with the relationship issues that arise if the client feels that he or she is being rejected by the individual therapist.

The best time to introduce the *idea* of group therapy as a possible treatment is in the initial interview. If you are working in a clinic where someone else does the initial intake or screening interviews and then refers the patient for additional workup or therapy, then it is important for you to know what this intake person has said to the patient about clinic services. Ideally the intake worker will mention group as a possibility, so that when you do so it is not a totally new idea to the patient. Whether or not this happens depends on the salience of the group therapy program to the clinic and to the intake worker. In clinics where all clients are seen by an intake worker and then referred to a treating clinician, it is difficult for a group therapy program to thrive unless the intake workers understand and accept the importance of their role in facilitating later referrals.

Whether the proffering of services is done by an intake worker or by the treating clinician, there is usually some point in the patient's initial contact with the clinic where a mental health professional says to a (prospective) patient, *This is what is available* or *I think you might benefit from* _____ or something of the sort. That is the point at which group therapy should be mentioned as a possibility unless the mental health worker has already decided that the patient should be referred for group therapy. In that case the task of persuading the patient to accept the referral should begin.

In introducing the idea of group therapy, there are some things which it is important not to say. One is, "There's a waiting list for individual therapy but we can offer you group therapy right away." A variant of that is, "You can be in group therapy until an appointment for individual therapy is available." Such suggestions indicate that group therapy is second choice and second class and make acceptance of the referral less likely.

There are some clinicians who in fact regard group therapy as second best, or even less than that. These workers regard individual therapy as the sine qua non of mental health services. The belief is sometimes so strongly held that clinicians may prefer to see individual clients twice monthly for half an hour, or less frequently, rather than to see them weekly for an hour and a half in group therapy.

Toseland and Siporin (1986) reviewed the clinical and research literature comparing the effectiveness of group and individual therapy. They found no evidence in the studies they reviewed that individual therapy is superior to group therapy. They found some evidence that in some instances group therapy may be superior to individual therapy, though they acknowledge methodological weaknesses in some of the studies reviewed. It may be concluded with some confidence that group therapy is not, and therefore should not be presented as, a second-best treatment alternative.

Group therapists seeking referrals for their groups are likely to hear the comment from clinicians, "I have a patient who may be ready for group later on but nobody who's ready right now." The data reviewed by Toseland and Siporin are at some variance with such statements. One might conclude that it is the clinician, rather than the patient, who is not ready for the referral to group therapy.

This bias against groups may surprise and dismay the novice clinician seeking referrals for group therapy from other clinicians. If you encounter such bias, consult with your supervisor about ways to overcome it. But if you are the referring clinician and you yourself feel such a bias, then it may be premature for you to become involved in the clinic's group therapy program. You can't sell something you don't believe in, and you can't persuade a client to accept referral to something you yourself believe is second best.

On the other hand, group therapy occupies an important place in many mental health care delivery systems. You may find that there is ample support for group therapy, and the major initial obstacle to starting a group may be your own skill in making an effective referral.

As indicated above, the best time to introduce the possibility of group therapy is during your first interview with a patient or client. If after further discussion with the patient (and, presumably, with your supervisor) you decide that you'd like to make the referral, you have to decide when to broach the subject and what to say. Referrals are generally easier to make very early in a therapy relationship and again toward the end. Referrals made in the middle of a course of individual therapy may be, or be misconstrued as, reflecting resistance or countertransference issues in the therapy relationship. Patients are more likely to accept referral if they understand the potential benefits offered by group therapy, and how those benefits will help the patients reach the goals of therapy agreed on by both patient and therapist. Patients, as well as clinicians, have some common misconceptions about group therapy, and it will be helpful if you are prepared to dispel them.

The benefits of group therapy are not necessarily obvious either to patients or to clinicians unfamiliar with this treatment modality. The task of the referring clinician is to explain those benefits briefly, clearly, and persuasively. In order to do so, the clinician should have a good grasp of what those benefits are, based preferably on personal experience. The therapeutic factors (Bloch and Crouch 1985, Yalom 1985) associated with good outcome in group therapy are discussed in Chapter 7. It is difficult to describe them briefly and succinctly. In addition, the therapeutic factors are somewhat theory-based (Weiner 1974), which makes them more difficult to explain clearly if you are not using an interpersonal theory in your therapy. The best way to approach a discussion of the potential benefits of group therapy is in terms of the goals the patient was seeking when he or she initiated contact with the clinic. The referral is most readily made when the patient's initial formulation of his or her difficulties involves relationship problems. Put most simply, group therapy is an interpersonal context for the resolution of interpersonal difficulties, the development or enhancement of interpersonal skills, and the facilitation of change in characteristically unsuccessful interpersonal coping strategies. There are many ways of translating that definition into simpler language. One is, "Group therapy helps you to look at what you're doing with other people, gives you information on how you look to others (which may be different from how you think you look), and helps you figure out what to do that will work better for you." Other ways to phrase the definition depend on the theory of therapy that you're using, or your supervisor's theory. They might involve comments like "Group therapy helps you to see the connections between how you related with people in the past and how you relate with people now. Understanding those connections makes it easier for you to change some of the ways that you relate with people now and in the future."

It is prudent for a referring therapist not to be too specific about what will happen in the group or what the group leaders will do. Leave that to them. If you are referring a patient into your own therapy group, some description of typical group interactions would not be inappropriate.

Perhaps the most common misconception on the part of patients and others unfamiliar with group therapy is that there is some requirement to discuss intimate matters in the presence of strangers. Most people are naturally reluctant to get into a situation where they anticipate such a requirement. Those who lack such reluctance tend to engage in premature and inappropriate self-disclosure in group sessions and then drop out. This natural reluctance is most often expressed as reluctance to talk at all in front of groups. Patients should be reassured at the outset, whether they voice such reluctance or not, that there is no requirement that they reveal intimate secrets in group therapy. That is not what group therapy is about. Rather, group therapy focuses on the relationships among the members present. Depending on the theoretical orientation of the therapists (and their supervisors), the group may also focus on the relationship between the members and the therapists, or on the connections between present ways of relating in the group and other patterns of behavior usually stemming from the individual's past. But group therapy is not the place to reveal intimate secrets.

Indeed, there is some evidence that group members need not talk at all in order to benefit from group therapy. *Vicarious learning* is one of the factors identified by Yalom (1985) and by Bloch and Crouch (1985) as being therapeutic The factor describes group members who attend regularly and follow the group interactions closely but say little or nothing during the sessions. These members report benefit from what is, in effect, empathic participation. Although it is likely that members who are more active benefit more from group therapy than those who are less active, it can be made clear to prospective group members that being in group therapy does not involve an obligation to talk at all. If you are relying on referral from other clinicians for your group members, the point should be made to the referral sources as well.

Having described some of the benefits of group therapy and discussed some of the more common misconceptions, the next step in making the referral is to describe to the patient the procedure to follow in gaining access to the group. If you are referring into your own group, tell the patient when and where the group meets, how many people will be there, and the cost. If you are referring to someone else's group, be as specific as possible about when and how to contact the therapist(s). Ideally, if the patient agrees to a screening interview, you would help him or her to make the appointment right there, or ask the appointment secretary to do so. In many clinics this is not possible, and there is some delay between the time you make the referral and the time that the group therapists interview the patient. If a new group is starting up, or if there are no openings in the group, there may be some further delay before the patient actually begins group therapy.

Referral Facilitation

In order to make an effective referral, that is, one which results in the patient becoming a member of a therapy group, the procedural path from individual to group therapy has to be well paved. The more convenient it is for the patient to go through the referral and screening procedures, the more likely it is that he or she will become a group member. Handing the patient the name and telephone number of one of the group therapists is one way of facilitating the referral. This procedure assumes a highly motivated patient who is nonetheless willing to wait for some months before entering a therapy group. Most therapists are available by phone only a few minutes each hour. The patient must call the clinic and leave a message. A game of telephone tag follows: The therapist returns the call, but the patient is out. The patient returns, gets the message that the therapist has called, and calls the clinic again. The therapist is not available but returns the call later that day or that week. Again the patient is out, and so on. Depending on the level of motivation of the players, telephone tag can go on for weeks. Then the therapist has to arrange with his or her co-therapist for a time to meet the client. It is usually no easier for therapists to reach each other than it is for clients to do so. Another game of telephone tag can easily ensue. If the therapists are already leading a group, then arrangements can be made at the next group session to offer the prospective group member a screening interview. Again, telephone tag with the patient. By the time the screening interview takes place, a month can easily have elapsed. Experience suggests that novice clinicians will lose up to two-thirds of the patients referred to them for group therapy (Alonso 1992). Some of the loss may be related to the length of the time interval between referral and screening.

Some clinics provide referral facilitation. The facilitator provides a bridge between the referral source and the group therapists. Referrals for group therapy are made to the facilitator rather than to the group therapists. The facilitator contacts the patient and conducts an interview, either in person or by telephone. The facilitator determines which of the various therapy groups the patient would fit best in, contacts the group therapists, and briefs them. He or she also arranges screening interview times and maintains contact with the patient until the screening interview takes place. Because contacting people is a primary part of the facilitator's job, he or she is much more available by phone than the clinicians and frequently more than the patient. This increased availability tends to result in a significant reduction of telephone tag and reduces the burden of that game on clinicians. As a result, the time between referral for group and the screening interview can be reduced to a week or less.

Because referral facilitation requires the employment of clinical skills and judgments of working with patients, and professional-level skills in both eliciting relevant information from the referral source and providing it to the group therapists, it is not a task that can be assigned to the secretarial staff, no matter how gifted an individual secretary may be in interviewing and in scheduling appointments. The program of group therapy referral facilitation established by Elaine Lonergan at the Langley Porter Clinic in San Francisco is perhaps the best known of these resources (Lonergan 1982). My own program at the University of North Carolina Hospitals is another. The clinician seeking to develop competence in group therapy during his or her training should ask about referral facilitation resources at prospective internship or residency sites before making a training commitment. The presence of such a program usually indicates quite good support for group therapy and for the therapist seeking to develop or sharpen group therapy skills.

CRITERIA FOR SELECTION OF GROUP MEMBERS

In the screening interview, you will be evaluating the patient based upon certain criteria. These include your general and perhaps idealized concept of what a "good" group member is, and how well this particular patient might fit into your group. Trying to define criteria for the "good" group member is rather like trying to define mental health. It is easier to say what it isn't and to describe exclusive rather than inclusive criteria for group membership.

Group therapy has been offered to patients exhibiting a wide range of psychopathological behaviors (Berman 1975, Toseland and Siporin 1986). Outcome studies suggest, in the main, the efficacy of group therapy across the entire range of pathology (Battegay and von Marschall 1978, Yalom 1985). On one hand, these data suggest that in selecting group members, you cannot go wrong. On the other hand, the data are so general as to offer little specific guidance to clinicians. Under these circumstances common sense, clinical judgment, and consultation with your supervisor may offer the surest guidelines.

Novice therapists should, then, select patients with whom they feel it would be easy to work. There will be time and opportunity enough later on to work with more difficult patients. Although there is some individual variation, you will find that a good group member (that is, one who is easy to work with) is one who (1) defines his or her problem as interpersonal; (2) is committed to change in interpersonal behavior but is unsure of what or how to change; (3) is willing to allow himself or herself to become susceptible to the influence of the group; (4) is willing to report the fact and effect of change, or efforts to change, to the group; and (5) is willing to be of help to others during the group sessions.

It is quite possible that individuals meeting *none* of these criteria would be good group members. In clinical settings where service needs are great and resources limited, group therapy may be not so much a treatment of choice as a treatment of necessity. In such circumstances, group therapy may be offered to people who would not be referred for group under more favorable circumstances. Such people tend to benefit less from group, and probably also from individual therapy, and are more challenging to work with.

The attributes that make a patient a good group member may not be the same attributes that make benefit from group likely. Highly manipulative, articulate individuals, with a flair for the dramatic and a penchant for the spotlight, can help get a group going and may at times oil the silences. However, they may be able to do these things without ever letting the group touch them or without learning from the group experience. For the most part, however, good group members are probably also those who are most likely to benefit from group.

Exclusionary Criteria

As noted above, the empirical literature offers little guidance as to whom to exclude from group therapy. Common sense, clinical lore, and personal preference can, however, provide some clues. The following discussion assumes that the therapy groups being assembled are not what might be called special-purpose or topic groups. Such groups, which are limited to patients with some specified problem or status, might be restricted to those manifesting depression, substance abuse, or serious and persistent mental illness; or to women; or to adults who regard their parents as having had some defect such as alcoholism. The groups discussed here are *general* therapy groups, open to individuals with few personal characteristics in common other than level of pathology. This aspect of group composition is discussed below.

In general in outpatient therapy groups in which one or both co-therapists have little or no experience, it is best to exclude patients who are suicidal, acutely psychotic (delusional or manifesting hallucinations), suspicious of others to the point of being paranoid, or who indicate with some vehemence that they are not likely to be influenced by others. "I don't care what anybody thinks, this is the way it is," is the kind of statement that is a clear contraindication for group therapy.

Pathological narcissism is another contraindicator. Individuals manifesting very strong narcissism tend to monopolize the group's attention, generate considerable anger on the part of other group members, and then withdraw without notice—usually to the relief of the therapists and the other group members. Although it is possible for narcissistic individuals to benefit from group therapy, the challenges they pose seem more appropriate for experienced rather than novice group therapists.

The evidence that patients with borderline personality disorder can benefit from group therapy is somewhat mixed. The literature has recently been reviewed by Monroe-Bloom (1992). She reports only one study which meets her rather stringent criteria for methodological adequacy (Linehan 1987a,b) and describes a study of her own still in progress. She concludes that "both time-limited and longer-term approaches may contribute positively to clinical and social outcomes for borderline patients" (p. 297).

Patients with borderline personality disorder pose considerable challenge for the mental health care delivery system. The magnitude of the challenge is itself pathognomic and has been amply described in the literature, of which the recent book by Clarkin, Marziali, and Monroe-Bloom (1991) is an excellent example. The problems posed by these most difficult patients are formidable for seasoned clinicians, and novices should not be exposed to them unless there is ample clinical support and constant access to plentiful supervision.

With these exceptions in mind, your general approach to selection should be inclusive rather than exclusive, and to accept an individual unless there is some clear indication that group would not be appropriate or beneficial. The most important operational criterion is likely to be whether or not the patient is available for meeting at the time you are planning to schedule the group.

A Referral Declined

Lucille is a 30-year-old college graduate, an attractive, slim, blue-eyed brunette, who came to the walk-in clinic with a presenting complaint of depression, which she attributed to difficulties in her relationship with her married lover. The screening psychiatrist decided that she was suicidal and offered admission to the inpatient psychiatric ward, which Lucille immediately accepted. Articulate and engaging, she responded well to individual and group therapy. Discharge planning was soon initiated and she was referred for outpatient group therapy—a referral in which she expressed considerable interest.

Lucille was unemployed, living at home with her divorced father, a self-employed professional. She was making some apparently desultory attempts to study for admission to graduate school. She had been in and out of individual therapy for some years with more than a dozen different therapists. Despite her attractive appearance and obvious intelligence, she had few friends and had very low self-evaluation and self-esteem. Her mother had not been in the picture for some time, and Lucille reported that both her father and her lover derided her for underachieving and failing to live up to their standards.

No other information was readily available to the Group Therapy Service. A Millon Multiaxial Clinical Inventory—II (MCMI-II) was administered and a narrative report obtained through the Microtest system of National Computer Services. Findings were consistent with the treating psychiatrist's diagnostic impression of avoidant personality. Lucille's responses to the test suggested the presence of more thought disorder than was apparent during her brief hospitalization, though not quite enough to support a primary diagnosis of schizoid personality or one of the schizophrenias. By the time she took the test, the depression precipitating the hospitalization had cleared considerably (though it was still present) and she was no longer reporting suicidal ideation; neither the test results nor her course in the hospital supported an Axis I *DSM III-R* diagnosis.

Both her history and the MCMI-II narrative report indicated that she was unlikely to remain in therapy long enough to experience significant benefit. Rather, her pattern of withdrawing instead of doing the psychological work and modifying unsuccessful behavior patterns appeared likely to persist. Because of the high probability of premature unilateral termination, referral for group therapy was declined, and the patient was not offered a screening interview.

3

Screening Patients
for Group Therapy

PREGROUP SCREENING INTERVIEWS

Screening interviews are seldom desirable and frequently necessary. They are seldom desirable because they are quite expensive of the therapist's time and the patient's. They give both patient and therapist very little information about how each will act during the group meetings, and they constitute a test or examination for the patient, who, if he or she is not accepted for group, must add yet another failure experience to a list that is already long enough to have brought him or her to the clinic for help. Rejection is always painful, and rejection by those from whom one seeks help is especially so.

In rejecting a patient for your own group during a screening interview, it is sometimes possible to suggest to the patient that another group offered in your clinic might be more appropriate. Experience suggests that the magnitude of rejection by the screening therapist is such that patients seldom follow through by seeking a second screening. If you reject them for group, they are generally not going to seek admission to other groups, at least not in your setting.

Screening interviews are frequently necessary because in a training clinic, referrals for group therapy are usually made by therapists who are inexperienced in group therapy and thus uncertain as to what constitutes an inappropriate group referral. Novice therapists may also have a somewhat greater general propensity for making illegitimate referrals than do experienced therapists. However, countertransference issues are not unknown among more experienced therapists as well.

A screening interview reflects the group leader's (and supervisor's) uncertainty about the ability of the referring therapist to avoid an inappropriate referral. In a training clinic, where the referring therapist is a trainee, he or she is learning how to make referrals as part of learning how to be a therapist. In clinics where group leaders and referring therapists know each other fairly well, there is much less need for screening interviews. In such instances, the referral source will have some idea of the kind of person the group leader is looking for, and the group leader will be familiar with how the referring therapist uses technical language to describe patient characteristics.

The specific manner in which the screening interview is conducted will depend on the theoretical preferences, personality styles, and prior experience of the therapists; the needs and expectations of the patient; and the interaction between these patient and therapist factors. In the ideal situation, the therapists will have discussed with the supervisor the type of patient or kind of patient characteristics they are looking for and will have obtained some guidance in how to conduct the screening interview. Similarly, the patient will be either clearly appropriate or clearly inappropriate for group, and that fact will emerge and be agreed upon by the end of the interview.

In the more typical situation, the group therapists are likely to have only a general, vague notion of what patient characteristics to look for and no notion of how these characteristics might manifest themselves in group. Some supervisors may not conceive of the supervisory process as starting before the selection of patients for screening, viewing it instead as beginning with the first group session. In those instances, the novice group therapist may not get much pertinent and needed assistance in the conduct of screening interviews and the selection of patients. And finally, in the real situation as distinct from the ideal, it will be found that very few patients are clearly inappropriate for group, some are almost certainly good risks, and the majority fall into the category of uncertainty.

Under these more typical circumstances, there is a very strong tendency for novice group therapists to conduct screening or initial interviews for *individual* psychotherapy. The strength of this tendency seems, naturally enough, to be related to the amount of experience the therapists have had with individual therapy. Because experience as a group therapist is seldom offered to practicum students (predoctoral clinical or medical students, for example) and training in individual therapy is usually initiated prior to training in group therapy, most new clinicians come to the group therapy enterprise with at least some experience in individual therapy. In addition, the pressures of increasing need for services in the context of diminishing resources is generating or renewing the interest in group therapy on the part of experienced clinicians, especially in the public sector. When you have been doing screening interviews for individual therapy for ten or more years, it is difficult to shift to the different mind-set and different paths of inquiry appropriate to the screening interview for group therapy.

To overcome this tendency, it will be helpful to observe your supervisor or an experienced colleague conduct some screening interviews for group therapy before attempting it yourself. If that is not possible, then role-play practice with other clinicians, under the direction of your supervisor, or some other training prior to initiating the actual screenings with real patients is advisable. The screening interviews for group therapy should be as closely monitored by supervisors as were the student's initial therapy interviews. In the absence of such training and supervision, students tend to reject good group candidates, recommending additional or continued individual therapy instead.

The Contract Made during the Screening Interview

There are two contracts made during the screening interview. One pertains to the interview itself. This contract between patient and therapists is that some conclusion will be reached by the end of the interview about whether or not the patient should attend group therapy. For the therapists, this contract involves structuring and defining the task of the screening interview and should be made as early as possible during the interview.

Implicit in this contract is the notion that the determination of the patient's suitability for membership in this particular therapy group can be made in a single session. There are some instances where such a rapid determination is difficult. These include those settings in which there has been little contact between the group therapists and the referring therapist, or where the referring therapist has made the referral without having much information about the patient. Other instances include those where the interviewing therapists come to some conclusions about the patient fairly quickly but then are reluctant to trust their own judgment. However, most clinicians, even new ones, come to some intuitive conclusions about people they encounter within a matter of minutes. Such conclusions are not usually far from those reached by most people based on initial impressions, conclusions that are typically mostly accurate but in need of some later revision. Usually these conclusions comprise all the data that clinicians really need in order to determine the patient's initial suitability for group. Decisions about whether or not to accept the patient into your group should be made by the end of one screening interview and communicated to the patient at that time. A screening interview with an inconclusive or noncommittal ending is analogous to a classroom situation in which the instructor gives an oral exam and then announces that he or she won't tell you until next week whether or not you passed. Patients should not be put through that kind of anxiety unless it is unavoidable.

The second contract made during the screening interview involves what kind of group experience the therapists will undertake to provide, some delineation of the problems the patient wants to work on, and the magnitude of the commitment the patient makes to the group and to group interaction. The therapists should describe, as specifically as possible, what they expect will happen during the group sessions, at least in the early stages. What is predictable about virtually any therapy group is that people will be tense, anxious, and possibly hostile. These phenomena are sufficiently ubiquitous that telling a patient about them in a screening interview does not constitute a self-fulfilling prediction. What is usually not predictable is how the tension, anxiety, and hostility will become manifest in early group interactions, or how much there will be.

Whether or not the problems the patient wants to work on will emerge in the screening interview may be open to question. How truthful the patient will be depends on many factors, including his or her fear of rejection, ability to be open, and trust of the interviewers. In general, patients *are* truthful at this point, and what they describe in terms of problem areas to be worked on can be taken pretty much at face value. The accuracy of a patient's assessment of his or her problem may be questionable, however, which is one reason that adequate diagnostic work should precede referral.

The surprises come later on, during the initial group meetings, when the problems discussed in the screening interview fail to surface and the patient takes an interpersonal position that has no apparent relevance to the problems discussed in that interview. The problems and issues discussed in the screening interview (and before that, in individual therapy or evaluation) may not surface in group until the patient feels comfortable or safe enough to reveal them in the larger interpersonal context of the group therapy session.

Not all patients come to the screening interview with a clear idea of what they want to work on in group therapy. Their uncertainty about how they might benefit from group therapy may persist even though the referring therapist has spent some time discussing this topic with the patient. The therapists' task in such situations is to help the patient identify problems or issues that the group therapy experience may help him or her to handle in ways that are more satisfactory or effective or healthy. Most patients have not previously been in group therapy and have little or no idea of how a group works or what kinds of benefit the group therapy experience may bring.

It seems fairly natural, especially for the inexperienced group therapist, to ask the patient during the screening interview, "How do you think group can help you?" The most common response to such a question, from an even more inexperienced patient, is likely to be, "I have no idea." At that point it is necessary to ask the patient what brought him or her to the clinic in the first place. Some patients will indicate that they came because they were referred, or required, or urged by relatives or others to do so. It takes more work with such people to identify specific interpersonal issues likely to respond beneficially to the patient's attendance at group therapy sessions. The task is more difficult if you yourself are not altogether clear about what those benefits might be. Sometimes the extra effort is worthwhile; sometimes it is not. However, telling the patient to go away and to return when he or she has figured out what she wants from the group, or the clinic, or you, is a technical error. If the patient were skilled enough at evaluating interpersonal strategies to have figured that out, perhaps he or she would not have come to the clinic in the first place. What may be needed is *help in identifying problem areas*. Sometimes group can offer such help.

Although each contract between patient and therapists can (and should) be negotiated on a very individualized basis, there are some clauses that should be included in most group contracts. These are:

1. *Specification, by the therapists, of what they expect from the patient.* Therapists can reasonably expect the patient to (a) come to the group meetings, (b) pay the bill, and (c) make a commitment to change in behavior, attitude, life situation, or all three. People who are unable or unwilling to make such a commitment may be looking for some other type of activity, such as a support group.

   Note that the list of what the therapists can expect of the patient is not long, nor should it be. We cannot ask much more of the patient than that he or she comes to the group sessions and that he or she pay the bills. If we expect patients to have a high level of psychological sophistication, or insight, or the ability to formulate their problems in such a manner that they are rapidly susceptible of resolution, we are asking of patients the level of expertise which they pay us to make available to them.

2. *Specification, as much as possible, of what the patient expects or hopes to gain from the group therapy experience.* If specificity is not achieved and the patient has a generalized expectancy of benefit, it will be difficult for both patient and therapists to recognize the point at which such benefit is clearly manifest.

Not all of a patient's problems will be amenable to group influence. One of the few genuine advantages of the screening interview is that such problems areas can be defined and their later avoidance in group legitimized. For example, problems of physical intimacy in relationships with others are not usually fruitfully discussed in group. A therapy group may become open and honest, but it is seldom intimate. Problems of dependence and counterdependence are, on the other hand, more readily discussed. Thus, a patient's need for and fear of sexual tenderness from a spouse is a less appropriate problem area for group therapy than that same patient's conflicts about the spouse's helping with household chores. In a screening interview, the patient can be reassured that the former need not be dwelt upon during the group sessions.

Whether or not the issue of self-disclosure has been discussed by the referring therapist (and usually the interviewing therapists will not know this), it should be at least mentioned during the screening interview. Self-disclosure is but one of the therapeutic factors in group therapy (Bloch and Crouch 1985, Yalom 1985), and the patient can be reassured that he or she need not talk at all in order to benefit from the group therapy experience. Attendance, payment of bills, and commitment to change are the only requirements.

What a group contract boils down to is that the therapists offer to make their expertise available in the group setting. The patient, in turn, offers to come to group, to participate in the interactions (verbally or nonverbally), and to avail himself or herself of the expertise of the therapists and the wisdom of the group.

Individual versus Group

Early in the screening process, the therapists will not have a good idea of the type of people who are going to be in their group, and thus can be rather more open and broad in their selection criteria. At some point, usually at the third or fourth screening interview, the therapists will begin to ask themselves, "How will this patient fit in with those we have already accepted into the group?"

This is the starting point of a balancing act of individual versus group interests with which the therapists will be wrestling through much of the group's life. At this very early stage in group formation, the therapists' concerns will be about group interaction, as distinct from and sometimes opposed to the individual's need for group therapy, the amount of benefit he or she is likely to derive from it, and so on. Later in the life of the group, the problems or issues which constitute the individual-versus-group balancing act will be different.

At this point, the polar conflicts involve the patient who needs group but is not likely to contribute much to it, as contrasted with the individual who does not much need it but is likely to make some major contributions to group interaction. These are conflicts experienced by the therapist, who has rather less of an opportunity to discuss them during the screening interviews than does the patient.

Although it is generally true that effective psychotherapy constitutes a peak emotional experience in the life of the patient (and the therapist!), it may also be true that the novice therapist tends to greatly overestimate the magnitude of his or her impact upon the patient, and to underestimate the patient's ability to escape a difficult or taxing situation by simply dropping out of group. If the group experience does not prove itself to be worth the patient's time, effort, and money, he or she will drop out. Making a bad guess about how a particular patient will work out in a particular group does not have the same kind of consequences for that patient that a bad guess by a surgeon or internist might have. If a patient whose emotional life is sparse ends up in a group that demands a high level of emotional interchange, he or she may very well withdraw from group. Such a withdrawal may be viewed as a protective mechanism and, given the circumstances, perhaps healthy. By the same token, an individual who is accepted into group primarily because of group needs, and who stands to benefit little or not at all, may withdraw because of a sense of being taken advantage of or used by the group.

Somewhere between these two extremes is the individual who can both contribute to and benefit from group. This is where most people will be found: group and individual interests usually coincide. Even where there is conflict between group and individual interests (and the therapist is in conflict, facing a choice between individual and group benefit), it is sometimes possible during the screening interview for a skilled and experienced therapist to make a contract that involves *reconciliation of individual and group interests as one of the goals* for that individual. But the novice therapist who is not experienced in group *or* individual therapy may lack confidence in his or her skill regardless of whether it is great or small. Therefore, if the novice therapist comes to feel, during the screening interview, that there is or might be conflict between the best interests of the individual and those of the group, the following guidelines are offered for resolution of the dilemma:

1. If the individual would benefit from inclusion in the group but seems likely to impair the effectiveness of the group experience for some or most others, he or she should be excluded. It is not that group needs have primacy over individual needs, but the needs (and rights) of each of several people should in this instance prevail.

2. If the group would benefit from inclusion of an individual for whom such an experience would be of dubious benefit at best, the interests of the individual should prevail. In this case, responsibility for the decision may be shared with the patient, who after all has a right to choose how to spend his or her time and money.

3. When there is considerable ambiguity in the conflict between individual and group needs, and it is not clear that an individual's inclusion would harm the group or exclusion would impair the group but not affect the patient, include the patient. A tie or

balance between positive and negative factors should almost always be resolved in favor of inclusivity.

The conflict between individual and group interests is probably most difficult for the therapists to resolve during the formative stage of group: the screening interviews. This is because of the nature of the decision to be made about entry or non-entry into group. It is an all-or-nothing decision, either way: the patient is either accepted or not. The consequences of the decision are therefore greater than later on, when decisions about individual versus group interests are made in the context of a continuing commitment to come to group, and imbalances can be redressed at subsequent meetings.

SCHEDULING SCREENING INTERVIEWS

Unless you are handed, all at once, a sufficient number of referrals to be able to start the group as soon as screenings are completed, it will probably be difficult to set a definite date for the beginning of the new group. You then have the problem of what to tell the first few patients who are accepted about when the group will begin. If the rate of referral is slow, so that there is some possibility of a lapse of several weeks between referral and first group meeting, it is generally better to set the appointment for screening no more than two weeks before you expect the group sessions might begin.

In some instances the appointment for the screening interview might have to be made a month or so in advance. You will lose some patients that way; interest declines, problems resolve themselves, people seek service at other clinics. But you will also lose patients if they come in for a screening interview, are accepted, and then have to wait for several weeks before the group starts. If people are going to drop out of the referral pipeline, it is better for them to do so prior to screening, because then that time will not have been wasted and you won't be planning on their coming. The longer the interval between referral and the beginning of group, the more people you will lose.

It is generally best to do the screening interviews one or two weeks before beginning the group, if possible. That means setting the date for starting the group before doing the first screening interview. That way, you can tell the prospective patients the time, place, and date the group is to begin, without ambiguity. Group members are more likely to appear for the first session if things are firmed up during the screening interview.

Scheduling the screening interviews during the time that the group will meet may save some trouble. If people can't come for a screening interview at 5 P.M. on Wednesday, then probably they can't come for a group that begins at that time either. It is disheartening to get clear through a screening interview only to find the patient can't come at the time the group is scheduled. Restricting screening interviews to those hours minimizes that problem.

In the ideal situation, you will screen and accept a sufficient number of patients to begin the group on schedule. In the more typical situation, you may experience some uncertainty as to whether to go ahead and start the group because only three or four people have indicated that they will come. It is better to go ahead and meet with those few than to cancel or postpone the group meeting. The clients have set the time aside and have geared themselves up to come to group; they are entitled to some service. It isn't possible to do as much with a group of three as with four or five; but cancellation or postponement of a group meeting tends to lessen the group members' commitment to coming and may make your referral sources even more hesitant to refer. So it is better to meet with those three or four, and perhaps talk with them about their expectations of group. In this instance, the fact that the meeting is held may be more important than what transpires during the meeting.

4

Starting the Group

Groups start in silence and solitude. There may be six or eight or ten people sitting in the room waiting. There is tension, nervousness. Usually there is little movement, little fidgeting. What motion there is, is mostly in the hands and fingers; small, incessant, repetitive. Twisting strands of hair, rubbing the arms of chairs, running back and forth lightly over the fabric of skirt or shirt or coat. Scarcely perceptible, yet constant. The background motion of anxiety.

No one is likely to be looking directly at the group leaders, lest such a glance draw attention and result in being called upon. Nor are people likely to be doing a great deal of looking at each other. They are, usually, quite cautious initially about giving off nonverbal cues that might be taken as an expression of interest in other group members, or in the group leaders, or as an expression of willingness to initiate the group interaction.

When you do a group, this is the atmosphere that you find yourself in at first. The knowledge that you are supposed to somehow help these anxious, isolated, and awkwardly silent individuals to become a group, and to establish the warm and supportive atmosphere in which the therapeutic work of the group will occur—this knowledge is likely to contribute to your own anxiety. Like your group members, your own defenses will probably be operating at full throttle.

It is usually of considerable help to know what your defensive style is: the kinds of things you say or do when you are anxious, uncertain, a little or very scared and trying not to show it. Your defensive style is how you act to ward off anxiety or to reduce its debilitating effect on you. It helps to know what you look like and how you come across to others when you are feeling defensive and trying not to show it. This is one reason why some experience as a group member is particularly useful for the novice therapist—especially a training group where the focus is on how you come through to others, how you are perceived by others, and on the discrepancy, if any, between how you think you are coming through and how you are perceived by other group members. This knowledge of how you come through at such times may help you to modulate your responses so that you are perceived as you intend and not merely as you assume.

It is also likely to be helpful to you if you are aware of what you do when you perceive that other people are anxious. Before you ever reach the group therapy room, you will have been in many situations where you have sought to reduce or alleviate someone else's anxiety. The situation in that group room full of silent, nervous people will tend to evoke behavior from you that is similar to what you have done in those other situations.

These two vectors—your defensive style and your need, desire, or intent to reduce interpersonal anxiety in others—will influence the way you begin to interact with the group. Other factors influencing how you start will include what your supervisor has told you, your own assessment of the interpersonal situation in the room at that moment, and how helpful you find the following sections of this chapter.

What you are facing is probably the most awkward, most delicate, and most anxious moment in the life of the group: the moment when you begin to lead. What follows can be beautiful or disastrous. There is nothing in any book that can tell you precisely what to do.

There are, however, some guidelines. Your first tasks are to reduce anxiety and facilitate interaction. Those are the first steps toward the establishment of group cohesiveness and an atmosphere of warmth and supportiveness. In beginning a group, you will reduce anxiety if you, as group leader, appear to be in charge and appear to know what you are doing, and if you provide the group members with some instruction about what to do and information about what will happen. Your own anxiety is not likely to be perceived by the group members. The probability is that you will appear remarkably calm and confident, both to the group and to your co-therapist. Your defensive style is likely to be taken (or mistaken) by them as a manifestation of your technical approach.

Nonetheless, the first thing to do is to reduce your own anxiety. It is difficult to help people lower their anxieties when yours is very high, whether or not your anxiety is perceptible to others. Knowing that you are likely to be in a situation where you are feeling at least nervous if not anxious, uncertain about what to say, and feeling some need or expectation to say something—that is, some performance anxiety—think back to similar situations in the past, and ask yourself how you handled those situations then and how you might handle them differently today. The situations most closely resembling the opening moments of a first group session are likely to be social gatherings where most people don't know each other and where there is some general commitment to interaction: events at college or university offered for freshmen during orientation week, for example.

If your tendency in a situation like that is to remain silent and observe for a while, until you get some feel for what is going on, then it is important to select a co-therapist who reduces interpersonal anxiety by taking some action, like talking. Joining the initial silence is not likely to decrease either your anxiety or the group's. Doing something interpersonally that is distinctly not your style is likely to be so stiff and awkward as to increase anxiety as well, unless you have considerable practice at it. What is needed here is an ability to plunge into the frozen silence and to begin to thaw it. If you don't have this ability, look for a co-therapist who does.

The initial anxiety of the group is probably related to the ambiguity of the new interpersonal context. People are uncertain about what is appropriate, what is expected, what will happen. What one is supposed to do in a therapy group is not likely to be clear to them; whatever anxiety you are feeling about how to proceed is probably magnified in the group. Under these circumstances, providing some structure frequently reduces anxiety: yours because you are doing something, theirs because you are providing cues about what to expect and how to relate.

In the screening interview, you will (ideally) have given the prospective group member some idea of how the group works. Now, however, is a good time to remind the group of the procedural guidelines discussed during the screening interview, to establish some common ground rules. What the rules are is probably less important than the fact that you are setting out *some* rules that all can agree on as given, the common basis for beginning to relate in that setting.

PROCEDURAL RULES

The procedural guidelines cover three general areas: confidentiality, respect for privacy, and the development of relationships among group members. In some groups, a fourth guideline, pertaining to absences and payments of fees, may also be discussed.

Confidentiality

In individual psychotherapy, you are prohibited from talking to others except your supervisor, about your patient. If you talk with your colleagues about your patient, you will (or should, at any rate) generally do so in such a manner as to make identification of the patient impossible. The patient, however, is not bound by any such prohibition: he or she is perfectly free to report anything that you say to his or her friends, parents, spouse, the public. In group psychotherapy, the patient should be asked to accept some of the limitations that are characteristic of the therapist role in individual psychotherapy: that is, to refrain from discussing other group members in such a way that they could be identified by people outside the group.

How you word this request will depend on your verbal style, your leadership style, and the assessment you make of the characteristics of the group members. You can tell the group, for instance, that talking about group outside of group is forbidden. You have no way of enforcing this prohibition, nor any reliable method of determining whether or not it has been broken. An important principle to follow here, as in other areas involving rules or guidelines, is, *do not prohibit what you cannot prevent*. The principle is not limited to the formulation of group guidelines. If you prohibit behavior that you cannot prevent and that has some fairly high probability of occurring, then you will simply not hear about it. This problem is discussed below in the context of sexualized relationships among group members.

A more workable alternative rests on the assumption that people are going to talk about what goes on in group whether you forbid them to or not. Couched as a request, the guideline that group members should talk about others in such a way that people not in the group would not recognize them has a greater chance of being followed than a stern, blanket prohibition. Anonymity is what we offer our individual patients, not confidentiality. Anonymity is all we can hope that our group members, who are not bound by professional ethics, will grant each other.

Here are three ways of presenting this issue to the group. The first two I heard at an American Group Psychotherapy Association AGPA Institute from people I did not know, saw only once, and whose names I no longer remember; the third is my own, though on occasion I use one of the others as well.

> What I say to you in this group, I give to you: it is yours. Do with it whatever you like. What you say to me is also yours. What I say to others in the group, and what they say to me, belongs to them. Do not take from this room something that belongs to another person.

> What is said here in this room, among us, is private. In talking to others outside the group about what happens in here, I ask that you respect the privacy of the other group members.

> In talking with people who are important to you outside the group, please don't talk about the other group members, or what they say in

such a way that they could be later identified by people who are not in the group. For example, the people you talk with about your group experiences should be able to talk with another group member at a party or social event six months from now, and have no clue that the person he or she is talking with is a member of this group.

Respect for Privacy

A very common fear among patients who have been referred for group is that they will be required, during the group sessions, to reveal their most intimate secrets to other group members, who will respond with criticism, revulsion, or ridicule. It is not an unrealistic fear: a group is capable of putting considerable pressure on one of its members to reveal what he or she really does not want to reveal, to discuss matters he or she does not want to discuss, and to provide feedback to other members that he or she would strongly prefer not to provide. All of these things have happened.

The fear that group therapy sanctions such activities should be dealt with during the screening interview, and further reassurances should be given to the entire group at the beginning of the first session. There are not many things that the group therapists can guarantee: they cannot guarantee patient improvement, or that the group will be exciting or interesting or fruitful. But the therapists can guarantee that a patient's privacy will be respected. Unlike the issue of confidentiality, this is a rule that the therapists can enforce. The principle is simple: if a patient indicates that he or she does not wish to pursue a particular topic or exercise further, the matter is dropped, without question and without penalty (e.g., making the patient feel bad or guilty for refusing to continue). Efforts on the part of other patients to cross the line, once it is drawn, must be thwarted by the therapists, as gently as possible but with vehemence if necessary. And once a patient has closed the door on a particular topic, the therapists as well as the other group members must refrain from breaking it down.

There is a difference between a door that is locked and one that has rusty hinges. Some things are difficult to talk about, in group or in individual therapy. When the door to those things is not locked but the hinges are rusty, the therapists and the group sometimes can provide oil, making it easier to give voice to things long unspoken. The therapists' task is to help the patient make clear to the group whether or not the topic should be pursued, and to stop or facilitate the pursuit depending on the patient's wishes.

Development of Relationships among Group Members

Some therapists forbid group members who do not already know each other to see each other socially outside the group. The development of friendships among group members is regarded as undesirable. Such relationships draw energy away from the group, provide an alternate forum in which issues better explored in group might arise, and support the maintenance of unsuccessful relationship strategies. In addition, there is unanimity among group theorists that the development of sexual relationships between group members[1] is virulently destructive to group cohesiveness and to the therapeutic efficacy of group. Therefore it is better not to let relationships get started that might turn into friendships and/or seductions.

The injunction against patients seeing each other socially outside of group is, like confidentiality, unenforceable. If a prohibited relationship should develop, it will almost certainly not be reported in group. The main reason for the injunction is that such relationships will influence how people relate to each other and to the group during the therapy sessions. The purpose of the injunction against forming new friendships with group members can be accomplished at least as well, and perhaps more effectively, by asking the group members to report to the group if a social relationship does arise. The justification

---

[1]Commonly known, in the mental health professions, as "sexual acting out." The term *acting out* refers to behaviors of which the therapist disapproves, and which are defined by the therapist (but not the patient) as being not in the patient's best interests.

for this request should also be made explicit: friendships outside group influence behavior in group, and the other group members can better understand what is happening in group if they are aware that the friendship exists.

There is also little point in forbidding patients to go to bed with each other. At the beginning of a group, such an injunction is likely to prove more frightening than reassuring. If affiliative passions develop later on, the therapists' rules aren't going to keep people out of bed anyway. Sexual alliances are a type of special problem for the group leaders and for the group. They are extremely rare during the early stages of group—the first four or six weeks—and are never very common. (This problem is discussed further in Chapter 12.) Here, my point is only that the prohibition of sexual or social liaisons should not be a procedural rule laid down by the therapists at the first group meeting.

A number of other procedural guidelines can be introduced at this very early point in the group's life. One is a prohibition against physical violence. But the time to tell your patients not to hit each other is not during the first session. Such a statement presumes that the group will reach a level of intensity and involvement that is likely to be inconceivable to people attending their first group meeting. The effect of this prohibition is likely to be frightening, to make people even more cautious about interacting in group than they already were when they arrived, and to further slow the development of group cohesiveness.

The prohibition against violence may seem more salient in hospital inpatient settings, especially on admissions wards. However, potentially violent patients should be excluded from group therapy sessions even in such settings. It is difficult for patients to benefit from group therapy when they are worried about getting hit.

There are two general principles to follow in laying down procedural or ground rules at the beginning of a group. One is to keep the list short and concise. You will be talking to a group of very anxious people. They are not likely to perceive nuances in meaning nor to retain very much information about events that may not occur at all and that have little salience for them at the moment. The other general principle is that the procedural rules should pertain primarily to rational, unemotional behavior and not to potentially intense interactions or relationships in group. Comments about intensity should await the development of intensity.

Following is another example of an initial guideline situation, drawing together the issues discussed above.

There are three things I'd like for you to remember about how the group is going to work together. One, respect the privacy of the other people in here. Don't talk outside the group about who's here or who said what. It's better not to talk at all to people outside the group about what you hear from other group members. Second, you don't have to talk about anything you don't want to. If something comes up that you don't want to talk about, just let us know and that will be the end of it. Third, if you start getting together outside the group during the week, let us know what's going on. It helps us understand how you act with each other in here. Are there any questions?

Usually there aren't any questions. If there are, it is important to answer them rather than to put them off or to respond with another question. When you have responded to the questions, the group is ready for the next step, which involves the further reduction of anxiety; and to the extent that talking helps to reduce your own anxiety, you're not quite as anxious as you were when you started.

The second person's anxiety to reduce is your co-therapist's. It is important to know, prior to the first group session (and preferably prior to making the commitment to work together) what your co-therapist's defensive style is, and what he or she is likely to do in anxiety-generating ambiguous interpersonal situations. Working with a co-therapist whose interpersonal style is very different from your own, or very similar, poses some challenges and perhaps eventually some strain on the co-therapist relationship. A co-therapist whose style is moderately different is probably the easiest to begin working with initially. This point is more fully discussed in Chapter 11.

After dealing with your own anxiety and that of your co-therapist and providing the group with reminders about the procedural guidelines, you are ready to go on to the next step, which involves the initial silence likely to have both preceded and followed your presentation of guidelines.

DEALING WITH THE INITIAL SILENCE

The group leaders can wait until the silence is broken by a group member; they can break the silence themselves; or, foreseeing that the silence is quite likely to occur, they can in effect seize control of it and use it to assert and exercise their power. If the group leaders choose to wait, the silence will be broken by the most anxious group member. The level of group anxiety, initially high, tends to increase. Frustration and hostility are at a peak. Sometimes the member who first breaks the silence serves as an initial focus for hostile attacks from other members; or the hostility will turn at the group leaders or at the clinic. The point here is that an initial impassive silence by the group leaders will generally lead to hostile opening interactions in the group. If the hostility reaches too great an intensity, it will frighten patients away, and those who remain will tread cautiously for a very long time—months, in a weekly group—before entering into significant interactions on risky topics. If the group leaders prefer to function in an initially hostile atmosphere, they can create for themselves the task of conflict resolution and the role of peacemaker or neutral intermediary by waiting until a group member breaks the initial silence.

Waiting until that happens has a lot of tradition behind it (Powdermaker and Frank 1953) and may stem from therapist (or supervisor) misapplication of psychodynamic principles that—whatever their value in individual psychotherapy—are not advocated by psychodynamic group therapists (Fried 1971, Kadis et al. 1974, Rosenbaum 1978, Rutan and Stone 1984, Wolf and Schwartz 1972). Even Bion (1961), who warns explicitly against attempting to meet group needs, would break the initial silence if it lasted more than a few moments , and Lakin (1985), writing from the point of view of group dynamics, suggests initial interventions lest the silence become oppressively prolonged. Yalom (1985) takes a similar view.

I am stressing this point—breaking the initial silence rather than waiting for a group member to do so—because I have seen its opposite so frequently adopted by novice group therapists and, I suppose, their supervisors. In addition, virtually complete nonresponsiveness is sometimes adopted by senior therapists offering training group experiences to their students. It is the stance most frequently taken by instructors in the Annual Institutes of the American Group Psychotherapy Association, and the student seeking group experiences may encounter such an approach elsewhere as well. Common sense would suggest that a technique appropriate for a group consisting of novice (or more experienced) therapists seeking training might not be appropriate for a group of patients seeking relief from intrapsychic or interpersonal distress, but experience indicates that the point needs to be made explicit.

The problem confronting the group leader, then, is how to break the initial silence. One way is to ask group members to tell something about themselves. If you choose this course, what follows is a series of patient–therapist interactions, one-to-one but in public, since the other members of the group will be watching closely.

At this point it is unlikely that the group leaders will elicit any meaningful information whatsoever. As a group begins, the conditions for genuine—let alone intimate—self-disclosure are simply not present. Indeed, the occasional group member who announces that he or she is going to be open and/or honest, or who begins by revealing apparently highly personal and intimate information, is likely to turn out to be closed but able to fake rather well. What is disclosed in terms of case history facts is relatively unimportant. The initially open/honest group member is staking a claim to a particular interpersonal position, and if the group leaders respond at this point to content rather than to process, they may be making a serious error.[2]

---

[2]Content refers to what is being said; process, to what is being done, what is happening. Process includes the nonverbal metacommunications about how the content is to be understood, and the flow and play of interpersonal maneuvers and manipulations within group or dyadic interactions.

Prodding group members to respond, as a means of breaking the initial silence, is sometimes like trying to start a wood fire with a propane torch and no kindling: as soon as the heat is turned off, the fire goes out. You ask a question, the patient responds, and then there is silence again. A question–answer, teacher–pupil relationship is established. Patients, who may not have been in group therapy before but almost certainly have been pupils, may conclude that the group therapy session is like a class and that what they are supposed to do is wait politely until called upon by the therapist. It takes both time and skill on the part of the therapists to modify such conclusions.

Taking control of the initial silence may not always be easy to do, but it is usually worth trying. The group leaders, knowing that the initial silence will occur anyway, can lay claim to it by asking the group members to be silent for a few minutes, to focus or concentrate on their feelings. The group leaders should then add that they will ask each group member to report his or her feelings to the group. Or the group leaders might ask the members to tell the group something, one thing, about themselves that they would like the other members to know, or some similar disclosure following brief reflection. The more important disclosures come later on.

An important function of the request to reflect and then report is to reduce anxiety. The initial anxiety is produced in part by the lack of structure inherent in any new situation. As the leaders begin to provide structure, anxiety begins to decrease.

Some group therapists, and perhaps some theorists, are opposed to the reduction of anxiety or tension in a group session. The rationale offered is that people work harder in group if they are more anxious or more tense (Armstrong and Rouselin 1963). The assumption appears to be that the therapists can help the patients channel the psychic energy generated by anxiety into more fruitful paths, or that in the absence of anxiety there is little motivation for change. The net effect is supposed to be the reduction of anxiety and the learning of new and more effective ways to deal with anxiety and with anxiety-provoking interpersonal situations.

Yet, the patients in a therapy group have come for therapy and have accepted referral for group because something in their lives is intolerable: anxiety, depression, rage, guilt, grief, and so on; it is the litany of pain and despair and fear that we call presenting complaints and symptoms. Patients come for therapy seeking relief. To deliberately increase, or deliberately avoid decreasing, anxiety is cruel. The first task of the group leaders is to reduce anxiety, not to nurture it. No theory of therapy regards compassion as a technical error.

Providing structure by asking group members to report how they feel gives them an opportunity to express anxiety without taking any particular interpersonal position within the group, without losing self-esteem and self-respect, and without revealing more about themselves than a willingness to cooperate with the group leaders. The leaders know that anxiety is likely to be both high and ubiquitous; hence, what they are doing in effect is asking each individual to report his or her anxiety. Getting the group started in this way relieves that anxiety to some extent. The admission or acknowledgement helps, and each member discovers that he or she is not the only one who is anxious. This discovery is the first instance of the operation of the therapeutic factor of *universality*, which has been shown to be related to positive outcome in group therapy (Bloch and Crouch 1985, Yalom 1985).

The exact wording used by the leaders when they ask the group members first to introspect and then to report is not important. Jargon like *introspection* and *selfness* is best avoided. If you're worried about how you will sound, try your introductory speech out on your co-therapist or supervisor before the initial group meeting.

The following is an example of how to start a group in this manner. If you are about to do your first group, you may feel some impulse to memorize this example. The feeling of, "Aha! Here's what to do!" can be reassuring or anxiety-reducing. The danger in memorizing someone else's words, however, is that you perform for, rather than interact with, the other people in the room. It's better to do it in your own words, and to memorize someone else's words only as a last resort, if by doing so you reduce your own anxiety to the point where you're at least functional.

Well, it's time to start. The way I'd like to begin is to ask you to take a moment or two, and turn your attention inward. Pay attention to how you are feeling right now: what your emotions are, but also what's going on inside of you—how your stomach feels, and your head and your arms. Also I'd like for you to pay attention to the feelings that you have, the sense impressions from the environment: how the chair feels against your back, the way your clothes feel against your skin, the temperature of the room, that sort of thing. Take a moment or two to look inside yourself this way and then I will ask each person to tell us how you are feeling at this moment, how it feels to you to be here now.

When people have completed the task of looking into themselves, gathering their feelings at this moment, they will generally stir, change position, raise their heads, but the room will still be silent. When people are ready to respond, the nonverbal cues they emit resemble the cues given in church or synagogue when the congregation finishes a silent prayer. Generally, after a couple of minutes, more than half the group will have finished, and you can ask someone to begin the reporting process.

Look around the room. Some people will still be looking down, eyes closed perhaps, lost in thought. Others may be looking into the distance or working hard at avoiding your gaze. Usually one or two people will look like they're ready to go on, ready to respond. In deciding who to ask, *look for the person who seems readiest to respond.* Do *not* start with the person sitting next to you, unless that is the person who looks readiest to respond. If no one looks really ready, as sometimes happens, then start with the person who looks *least unready.* From that point, go around the circle in order, either left or right, it does not matter.

As soon as you have cued the second person, either by nodding or looking or calling on him or her, the order of speaking will be obvious to the group; each person will know when his or her turn is coming. This is an additional provision of structure, which further serves to reduce the anxiety stemming from uncertainty that is so characteristic of the opening moments of a new group.

Getting the group started in this way will not necessarily set up the question–answer, teacher–pupil structure mentioned above, one reason being that the patients talk in turn after the initial cue from the leader. Whether to join in the circle yourself or not is really a matter of personal preference. Some group leaders prefer not to do so. It is a simple matter: when the person on your left finishes speaking, you simply turn and look at the person on your right, saying "Go ahead" or some such thing if necessary, and the spotlight of the group's attention passes right over you as you turn. Other group leaders include themselves in the process, saying something about how they feel.

Therapist Self-disclosure

It is perfectly all right for a group leader to admit that he or she is nervous or anxious in the opening session of a group. Admitting panic, however, or uncertainty about what to do is wrong, for it is likely to further increase group anxiety. The leader may admit uncertainty about what is going to happen, but only in terms of how this particular group, which at this point is still a gathering of individuals, will respond in this situation. Uncertainty about what is going to happen is not the same as uncertainty about what to do. The latter is a reflection on the technical competence of the therapist. You may feel incompetent, but it is a mistake to admit it to the group.

The important thing to remember here is that there is no single correct way of doing group therapy. Interventions that are technically correct and that have the intended effect of being helpful or therapeutic to the group members are those that are consistent with who you are, with your interpersonal style, and with your own immediate and direct experience of what is going on in the room. If you tend to be self-disclosing in other situations, then it is better to be self-disclosing here. Similarly, if you tend not to talk much about yourself, or your personal reactions to other people, it is best not to do so here.

The therapist self-disclosure to which I am referring here pertains only to your assessment of and reaction to what is going on in the room at the moment. In a therapy group, it is almost always inappropriate to talk with patients about your personal reactions to issues in your own life having nothing to do with the patients in the room or with their purposes in coming to group therapy. Hence, a statement like "I'm Bill and I'm really glad to be here and to get started with the group" involves a report of a subjective reaction to the immediate situation, while "I'm Bill and I'm glad to finally get here because I've been really hassled today" contains information not germane to the group or the task at hand. Most patients have at least some interest in your reaction to them, but they may react negatively to information about your own life, personal or professional, outside the group.

The literature on therapist self-disclosure in group therapy has been reviewed by Dies (1983b). He cites earlier work (Dies and Cohen 1976) suggesting that

> group members preferred therapists who were confident in their leadership abilities and in their own emotional stability and who were willing to share positive strivings (personal and professional goals) and normal emotional experiences (e.g., loneliness, sadness, anxiety). In contrast, group members expressed reservations about the appropriateness of therapists' confronting individual members with such negative feelings as distrust, anger, and disdain, and criticizing the group experience by admitting feelings of frustration, boredom, or isolation. [Dies 1983b, p. 42]

Dies draws two conclusions from his review of the literature on therapist self-disclosure in group therapy:

> As the client population becomes more psychologically impaired, group therapist self-disclosure becomes increasingly less appropriate. [p. 41, emphasis in original]

and

> Most clients will expect the group therapist to convey a certain amount of competence and confidence and to provide some initial structuring of the treatment situation, and . . . clients will neither anticipate nor desire the

> *therapist to be too revealing of her or his own feelings, experiences, or conflicts*
> *early in therapy.* [p. 41, emphasis in original]

Thus, as Dies notes, the amount of self-disclosure you choose to engage in at this very early point in the group's life must be tempered not only by your own preferences and personal style but also by the characteristics of the patients you are working with. In inpatient settings, where the level of psychological impairment is presumably higher than in outpatient groups, saying less about yourself, at least initially, may be more effective in reducing initial group anxiety than saying more.

After the Opening Survey

The opening survey provides you with a great deal of information about how and to what extent the people in the group are prepared to begin interacting with each other. That information is conveyed in a number of ways: (1) body posture, tone of voice, and gaze, and all of these combining to yield an overall impression of the patient's interpersonal presentation; (2) and what is said, how long it takes the patient to say it, how loudly it is said, and how many words and the kind of language the patient uses to convey the information. All of these interpersonal data combine to provide you with information about how ready the patient is to initiate or respond to interactions, to engage in self-disclosure, and to help get the group going.

The patients' responses, in the opening survey, can be understood as bids for the group's attention, or the therapists', or both. When the circle has been completed, turn to the patient who has made the most urgent bid and invite him or her to continue. Most of the time, it will not be difficult to determine whom to turn to. Following is an example of an opening survey from a group consisting of three men and three women, college and graduate students ranging in age from 23 to 30, with presenting problems of anxiety, depression, or difficulties in interpersonal relations.

Bob: My name's Bob, and I'm feeling fine right now.

Charles: I'm Charles, and I'm feeling a little nervous, not sure how to start.

Francine: My name is Francine. I've got a lot on my mind right now. Sometimes it's hard for me to talk or even think. I'm not sure what's happening and I hope the group can help.

Halsey: My name is Halsey? And I'm here because I'm not getting along with my boyfriends? And the same thing keeps happening with different boyfriends? So my therapist said that group therapy could help? That's all.

Alex: I'm kind of anxious, you know? I get so anxious sometimes I can't study, which is why I'm here.

Roberta: My name is Roberta, and I'm feeling OK, I guess.

The therapist must now determine which of these comments should be followed up. There are three criteria for making that determination.

1. Patient report of present distress or anguish takes precedence and should be responded to first. In the above example, no one is reporting anguish. Charles's report of nervousness seems to indicate some distress, and Alex mentions anxiety in this and other situations. Francine's statement that she has a lot on her mind "right now" followed by reporting that it is hard to *even think* and that she is *not sure what is happening* appears to reflect a higher level of distress because it may be related to some impairment in functioning.

2. Patient report of anything that would impair communication or inhibit the patient's ability to engage fully with the group at this time should be attended to next. In the above example, Alex's reference to anxiety is the only comment that might indicate such impairment, but it is not particularly striking. Statements like "I can't stop thinking about the exam I just had" or "I'm really very sleepy tonight and hope I can stay awake during group" are clearer

indications of potential interruptions in communication and in the sharing of the group experience. These should be attended to just after any significant expressions of distress.

3. People differ in the amount of energy that they put into communicating. In the early stages of group, interactions are facilitated and long, dead silences can be avoided by encouraging the people with the highest energy to talk. In the above example, Bob and Roberta appear to have little energy for interaction. Charles seems a bit more energetic but *not sure how to start.* Both Francine and Halsey refer to the group helping, which suggests a readiness for interaction. Alex says that he is here because of his distress (anxiety) but gives no indication that he is looking for interaction. His opening statement is, in essence, *I'm here because of anxiety* and indicates a lower readiness to interact than the messages of both women, which include the concept *I think or hope that you can help.*

In this example, Francine has clearly made the strongest bid for the group's attention, followed by Alex, Charles, and Halsey, with both Bob and Roberta offering minimal bids. Francine's opening statement indicates (1) present distress, (2) at least potential impairment in functioning ("It's hard for me to . . . even think") and (3) a willingness to engage with the group ("I hope the group can help"). Alex has indicated both present distress ("I'm kind of anxious, you know?") and some impairment in function ("I get so anxious sometimes I can't study") but not such a strong commitment to initiating interaction within the group. Charles reports some minimal situational anxiety but no other distress. Halsey, who raises rather than drops her voice at the end of her sentences, so that it sounds like nearly every sentence ends with a question mark, describes her presenting problem in interpersonal terms but does not indicate either present distress or impairment in functioning.

In turning to Francine, it might seem tempting to the therapist to say, "How do you think the group can help?" However, unless Francine has been in group therapy before—a fact that would have emerged in the screening interview—it is not likely that she will have any idea of how the group can help, though she may have some unrealistic or fantasy expectations. The most common answer to the question "How can the group help?" is, "I don't know."

Although Francine said "I've got a lot on my mind right now," she gave no indication of what that might be. That's where to start. You could ask, for example, "Would you like to tell us what's on your mind?" This is a reasonable question, and it might work. However, questions should not be framed in a way that allows for a yes or no answer. Hence, "Francine, what's on your mind?" would be better because it is likely to elicit more than a monosyllabic response.

What is most likely to occur at this point is that Francine will tell her story, or some part of it. In so doing, she takes an initial position relative to the other group members: she provides them (and the group leaders) with information about how to relate to her, about how she appears (or intends or would like to appear) to others, how open or disclosing she is likely to be initially, and other information. None of these data pertain to what she is saying, to the *verbal content*. Rather, they pertain to how she is saying it, to how the message is being sent, that is, to the *process* of communication. The most common error of the novice group therapist is to respond to content rather than process. This issue is discussed further in Chapter 9.

As Francine talks, you are, as a novice group therapist, probably trying to figure out what to say and whether or not to say it. Ask yourself what the client (in this instance, Francine) is *doing*. If the intervention you're thinking about pertains to what she is saying, wait. If it pertains to what she is doing, go ahead and say it. Of course, she is doing several things at once. Pick the one that is most obvious to you or that is easiest or safest or most comfortable for you to say. If she tells a moving or poignant story (unlikely at this early point but it sometimes happens) then it is OK to say something about what her story evokes in you and then ask the other group members for their reaction.

It is highly likely that the story Francine tells will involve some aspect of her life at some point in the past, outside the group room, that is, there and then. That's the verbal content. Your task as group leader is to bring the focus of the interactions into the here-and-now, and thus to look at the effect of her disclosure on the interpersonal context of the group.

When Francine has finished telling her story, there are two reactions that are most common. One is that another group member will say something, either beginning to tell his or her own story or responding to Francine, or some mixture of both. The other is that there will be silence. If the former, you need not intervene; if the latter, you can

1. Thank Francine for her disclosure and then turn to Alex, who made the second strongest bid for the group's attention, and ask him about his anxiety
2. Ask Francine what kind of response she would like from you or the group
3. Ask if anyone else has had a similar experience
4. Comment on the group's silence
5. Remain silent
6. None of the above.

Which of these options you choose will depend on a variety of factors.

At this stage in the life of the group, (5) is likely to result in an increase in the group's anxiety (and a sharp increase in Francine's because of the absence of response to her disclosure). Commenting on the group's silence is quite likely to be perceived as finding fault with each member for failing to respond to Francine, also an inauspicious start.

Asking if anyone else has had a similar experience is an invitation to other group members to tell their stories and is an intervention that novice group therapists commonly make during the early minutes of a new group (as well as later on). If no one jumps in, then you'd turn to Alex and ask him what he does to reduce his anxiety in situations like this. The only problem with (3) as an initial response to Francine's disclosure is that it doesn't provide any recognition to her for having broken the ice by talking about herself.

Unless Francine has been in group therapy before, she is not likely to know what kind of response she would like from you or the group, and the question is likely to evoke an "I don't know" response. But it does have the advantage of beginning to orient group members to the interpersonal effect or outcome of their disclosures and may open the way for you to invite feedback from the group. Usually the group is too anxious at this point and too unfamiliar with the situation to be able to offer meaningful feedback; and usually the first speaker (Francine) is too anxious to hear it. But early orientation to the interpersonal context is important and may outweigh these concerns.

Thanking Francine for her disclosure, waiting for a moment or two to see if anyone else is going to comment, and then turning to Alex gives the group a lot of information about how you are going to run the group, at least in that first, anxiety-laden session. For one thing, it indicates that you are going to try to get everyone involved, and that if they don't volunteer you will call on them. A second possible inference to be drawn from following up in this way is that you are in charge and will make things happen: the group won't be sitting around wondering what to do next.

The problem is that starting the group in this way sets up a question–answer, teacher–pupil kind of expectation, which does not allow, let alone facilitate, the development of interaction among the group members. But the calling on group members by the therapist is only an initial strategy. Its purpose is to reduce the initial anxiety by providing structure and leadership while encouraging self-disclosure. As anxiety decreases and group members become more familiar with each other and with the group, their willingness to initiate interactions will increase and it will become possible for the group leaders to be less active and directive. There are some research data (Dies 1983b) suggesting the desirability of a more structured and active leadership role early in the life of the group, gradually decreasing as cohesiveness increases.

Novice group therapists frequently go into sessions with the idea that group members are supposed to talk to each other, and that they are supposed to talk about having similar experiences. Hence the most frequent initial interventions by therapists untrained in group techniques involve urging or directing people to talk with each other and then asking the group if anyone else has had similar experiences. Group therapists untrained in individual therapy may then offer advice or solicit the offering of advice by group members.

Early in the life of a group, this urging people to talk with one another is frequently experienced as puzzling by the group members. Most people do not talk easily about important matters with strangers. Indeed, clients may be referred for group therapy precisely because they have difficulty engaging interpersonally with others, for whatever reason. In addition, most clients have no experience as therapy group members and are uncertain about what to do, what is expected of them, what the rules are, what is appropriate.

Group members indeed benefit from talking with one another, and from discovering that others have had similar experiences. Advice-giving may also be helpful. These factors, which are discussed in Chapter 7, have been shown to be associated with good outcome in group psychotherapy (Bloch and Crouch 1985, Yalom 1985). However, another factor, cohesiveness, takes precedence. Cohesiveness is a complex factor that includes the importance of group membership to the individual as well as the client's sense of being accepted by the other group members and the therapists. At this very early stage in the group's life, one thing that tends to make group membership important is the client's sense or hope that such membership, and attendance at the group sessions, will benefit him or her. The development of cohesiveness depends in part on group members' assessment of the situation in which they find themselves. Providing structure and reducing anxiety will facilitate the development of cohesiveness more rapidly than will sitting and waiting for the group members to figure out what they are supposed to do in this new and unfamiliar interpersonal situation. Directing them to talk with strangers is not recommended. The group members will have met you already, and each one has some contract with you and your co-therapist—but not with the other group members. Until some relationships develop among the group members, urging people to talk with each other is not likely to be helpful or to facilitate group development.

Beginning a group is in some ways like beginning a chess game. There is a finite number of first moves and responses, but by the third or fourth move the possibilities are astronomical. Groups usually start in silence. You can wait for a group member to break the silence. If you do, the silence is likely to be long, anxiety high, and the first interactions very cautious and frequently hostile. You can break the silence yourself, providing structure and direction, through the technique of the opening survey described above. By the time the second client has finished telling his or her story (in this case, Alex beginning to talk about what he typically does when he feels anxious in interpersonal contexts), the number of possibilities for what to do next is as astronomical as the possibilities after the third or fourth move in chess.

The chess player follows principles or utilizes strategies at that point in order to decide which of the practically limitless choices to make. For the group therapist, theory provides the principles that help reduce the limitless possibilities for intervention to a manageable few, and the interaction of theory and experience (or common sense or intuition, if you're inexperienced at this) helps you to select which intervention to choose.

The principle to follow here is to allow or request each group member to say something, one thing, about himself or herself to the group that he or she is willing for the group (still consisting of strangers) to know. The opening survey does some of that. Following up on the leads provided by that survey allows the group members to begin to test the interpersonal waters: initially with trivial self-disclosures and then gradually with more important ones. Hence in our example, after a discussion of how Alex reduces anxiety—and perhaps offering him an opportunity to do so—you might invite Charles to talk about his nervousness, if he did not engage during Alex's discussion, and then talk with Halsey about her expectations about group therapy. By the time you have done that, it will probably be time to begin closing the session.

Before discussing how to end the first session, I should note that all the recommended therapist interventions involve responding to the verbal content rather than to the process of what is going on in group. Most clients, unless they are highly experienced group members, don't have the foggiest notion of what group process is. Indeed, it is a difficult concept for therapists to grasp even when the learning task is made explicit. At some point it will be important to begin to talk about the group process, what is going on in group rather than what is being said. But at this very early point, process comments are likely to be as puzzling to the group members as are directives from the therapists to talk with other group members. You start with attention to the verbal content in part because that is the ground the group members are on; teaching them how to attend to process is a task for later on, as cohesiveness develops and the significance of self-disclosures increases.

ENDING THE FIRST SESSION

In his description of the initial psychiatric interview, Sullivan (1954) suggests that toward the end of the interview the patient should be given something intended to make him or her feel that the hour just spent has been worthwhile. Sometimes that is a summary, sometimes a report of the therapist's first impressions. It is poor technique to spend an hour asking the patient questions and then close with little more than a "Thank you, see you next time."

It is more difficult in group than in individual therapy to work toward enabling the patient to feel that the time he or she has just spent has been worthwhile. This is particularly true if not much has happened beyond the opening survey and some tentative interpersonal positioning. However, making the attempt may be more impor tant than in a dyadic session, where at least the patient has had your attention to himself or herself for the hour. Sometimes so little has happened in the opening session for some patients that the most you can do is hold out the hope that future sessions will be worthwhile even if this one was not.

The general rule is to tell the group what happened during the session as you saw it, and perhaps something of how you evaluate it. You might observe, for instance, that the group was anxious initially, that the purpose of the opening survey was to allow people to take an initial interpersonal stance, and invite the group members to consider what they learned about the other members and perhaps about themselves. Note that the anxiety decreased, if it did, as the session progressed. You might say something about your activity level being higher now than it will be later on; and then to ask if there are any questions before the session ends. The following is a typical summary statement:

> We'll be stopping in a few minutes, and I'd like to summarize what happened today. People were pretty anxious at first. That opening survey we did, how you're feeling right now, did several things to help get started. It gave you some information about each of the other members, and allowed you to say a little about yourself without, I hope, feeling too much on the spot. As people began to talk, I thought the group's anxiety decreased. Francine told the group some of what was on her mind, and Alex and Charles talked about what they do when they're feeling nervous like at the start of the session. So we found out something about them. In talking to the group the way they did, they also gave us some information about how to relate to them, and some beginning ideas of what they're like. In other words, one thing that happened today is that people began to form initial impressions of one another, which is what happens when you first meet. We'll be paying attention in here to the kinds of impressions that you make and how that matches up with the kind of impression you think you're making or trying to make. We did a little of that today and will be doing more of it as we get better acquainted.

So I thought we got off to a pretty good start today, with the anxiety going down and people beginning to talk about themselves. Are there any questions before we stop for today?

Usually there won't be questions. If there are, they will probably fall into one of three categories:

1. A question that should probably be taken up by the entire group at the next meeting. Questions about how patients should live their lives, or about the plans the leaders have for group, fall into this category.
2. A question indicating that the group member had a genuine misunderstanding of something that occurred during the session. The leaders should correct or clarify the misunderstanding if it pertains to them, or allow time for its clarification if it lies between group members. Unless such a misunderstanding is blatantly and undeniably related to the patient's psychopathology, don't interpret it. Not every interpretation that can be made should be made.
3. Requests for information that are legitimate and relatively easy to answer. If the requested information would be of interest to the entire group, give it right there. If (as is usually the case with this category of inquiry) the question relates idiosyncratically to the patient, take it up with him or her immediately after group.

Sometimes you may be surprised to find that although the group has apparently ended, everyone has stood up, and the door is open, the group members are clustered around you and/or your co-leader. It is as if the group has continued, but on a different plane. You are still on stage. You are still the group leader, and your words carry more weight than those of any of the group members. Yet at the same time you are now in a social situation. There need be no rule against chatting with group members if you are comfortable with doing so and have some interest in it. But there also isn't any rule against excusing yourself, politely but firmly, and maintaining some distance between your group leader role and any other potential roles you may have or that may develop with the group members. Maintaining some distance is safer than not, especially if you are working with clients whose own sense of role boundaries may not be as firm as one would like. In these troubled times, it is important to remember that in the presence of clients you are always on a professional stage, even in apparently casual social interactions. Your willingness to engage in some polite chatter either before or after the group session depends not only on your degree of comfort with such interactions but also on how good your liability insurance is.

5

The Role of Theory

It is possible to go through all of the work of starting a group—finding time and space, a co-therapist, a supervisor, doing pre-group screening interviews, and getting through the first session or two—without paying very much attention to theory. The mechanics of getting a group started are usually determined by the exigencies of particular clinical settings and are more closely related to budget, architecture, and tradition than to theory. Once the group has started, however, some theory is necessary. This chapter describes the role of theory in group psychotherapy.

Theory performs a road map function: it tells the clinician what to expect, what is likely to happen, what the destination or goal is, and how to determine when it has been reached. It offers guidelines indicating what to pay attention to, how to understand what is attended to, how to respond to it, how to evaluate the effect of that response, and what to do next. Theory also performs a validating function: if you can interpret what is happening in terms of the theory, you are likely to feel that you understand what is going on and that your ability to correctly assess the situation is sufficiently high. Such feelings tend to reduce therapist anxiety and enhance confidence.

VALIDITY, UTILITY, AND FANTASY

The function of theory is to elucidate relationships among phenomena. Theory organizes data into a pattern that accounts for relationships among observable phenomena and predicts relationships or phenomena not yet observed. There is, however, some difference between those theories that seek to understand and explain and those that seek to understand and to heal. The former are likely to meet the criteria of science for observability, replicability, and communicability. The latter tend to be more useful to the clinician despite their sometimes shaky empirical basis.

A theorist who attempts to offer an understanding of human behavior, reality, and psychopathology is rather like the proverbial blind man encountering an elephant. Every theorist, without exception, selects some part of human behavior for explanation and ignores the rest. A proto-theory is one that explicitly addresses only some part of the domain of interest (theories of motivation, for instance, or of appetite and its disturbances). Major theorists seem to assume more or less implicitly that their part of the elephant is the whole animal.

As a result there are some events not accounted for, not even mentioned, by a particular theory, and which are therefore difficult if not impossible to fit into the conceptual framework of that theory. The failure of any theory to account for most or all significant human behaviors has led Hall and Lindzey (1970) to liken theory to a set of blinders, directing our attention toward some behaviors and away from others.

The breadth and complexity of human behavior is probably beyond the scope of any one person's understanding. A truly comprehensive theory of behavior has not yet appeared. When it does, it is likely to be the work of many minds, a ponderously slow accretion of data and proto-theories over a very long period of time.

Clinicians choosing not to await this truly comprehensive theory of behavior before attempting to alleviate the suffering that stems from psychopathology are confronted with a plethora of theories. Some are structurally elegant, arising from and supported by research and empirical data. Others lack such elegance, have equivocal empirical support, or do not readily lend themselves to experimental scrutiny. Yet it is the less elegant, less confirmable theory that frequently appears to address itself cogently to the realities of emotional suffering and its alleviation, the more scientifically respectable theory defining more modest and less ambiguous behavioral events. As to theory, clinicians must sometimes choose between validity and utility. Most choose utility. The question is how to choose among competing theories which have little demonstrable validity and questionable utility.

The answer is that whenever possible, clinicians should choose the theory that makes the most sense to them. A theory is a set of propositions about some aspect of reality. The propositions are usually supported by data, ranging from anecdotal reports of personal experiences to carefully controlled experimental manipulation of variables. One purpose of theory is to persuade the relevant audience that viewing reality in the way proposed by the theory is fruitful. Scientific audiences are persuaded by data competently gathered; but clinicians evince more interest in clinical reports that are consistent with their own clinical experience.

The novice therapist may have little direct clinical experience upon which to begin formulating personal theories of psychopathology and psychotherapy. But the principle for choosing a theory is not different later in one's career than earlier: choose the theory you yourself find most persuasive.

Each theorist makes some assumptions about the basic nature of people, about how things really are. These assumptions guide the theorist toward addressing some aspects of reality while ignoring others. Freud, for example, assumed that people are at heart merciless and savage. Therefore, affiliative and cooperative behavior required more explanation than hostile aggressive behavior. In addition, Freud's emphasis on unconscious processes led him to develop an entire theory of behavior based on the assumption that *things are not what they seem*. Maslow is representative of a group of theorists who assume that people are basically good and who therefore must explain violence as an aberration. Psychodynamic and, to some extent, behavioral theories assume that growth results from the inevitable frustration of individual needs; in terms of group therapy the point is most eloquently made by Bion (1961). Maslow takes quite the opposite point of view: frustration of individual needs is not inevitable, and growth does not occur until those needs are met.

The theory that makes the most sense to you is probably one put forth by a person whose basic assumptions about reality are similar to your own. A theory that dwells on some aspect of behavior you consider unimportant or improbable may reflect implicit assumptions about reality that are different from yours. A theory that does not make sense to you, and is therefore not persuasive to you, is not necessarily a poor theory. But it is not meaningful to you. Bridging the gap between theory and practice is difficult enough when you find the theory credible; if it does not make intrinsic sense to you, the gap is unbridgeable and the theory not useful.

The position taken here is that theory need not be true to be useful. Fantasy is not true, in the scientific sense of that word, but it is useful. Some theories are mostly fantasy and, like fantasy, are useful in making sense out of highly complex phenomena—such as a therapy group. A theory of groups presented below is based on Freud. Whether his theory is more fantasy than fact is not at issue here. It is a useful theory to many clinicians whose implicit assumptions about reality and about people are similar to Freud's.

In graduate schools in the various mental health professions, and in practicum training centers, the trainee is seldom asked which of the various theoretical frameworks is most congruent with his or her own experience or inclinations. There is, of course, a great deal of pre-selection: a student enamored of Maslow as a result of undergraduate exposure is not likely to seek out a predominantly psychoanalytic training center for graduate work—or, if he or she should stumble into such a place, to be accepted by it. Nonetheless, it is not uncommon for a trainee to be confronted with a theory foreign to his or her own conception of interpersonal reality, and to be required to learn and to practice techniques based on assumptions that are essentially alien to him or her. Indeed, graduate or postgraduate training may be the only situation in which the trainee is reinforced or rewarded for doing something incongruent with his or her construction of reality.

If you find yourself in such a situation, you may find that

challenging the theory espoused by your supervisor generates rather more heat than might be expected in such a presumably rational setting as a mental health training facility. That is because you may be challenging in some sense his or her construction of reality, *and he or she, yours*. The most beneficent results of such a challenge may well be a recommendation from the supervisor that the trainee seek therapy, and a privately held opinion by the trainee that the supervisor is narrow, rigid, and a bit daft.

THE INFLUENCE OF THEORY UPON PRACTICE

The influence of theory upon practice is exerted primarily during the group session. As the group interaction unfolds, theory guides the therapists' attention toward some events and away from some, while remaining silent about others. The events the theory focuses upon are those it can explain. The events about which it is silent are those it does not explain—perhaps because these unexplained or undescribed events did not fit into the theorist's implicit assumptions about behavior and reality.

Most theories of group therapy draw the therapists' attention toward the same classes of events and types of behavior (Shaffer and Galinsky 1974). The events to which the therapists are led are (1) interpersonal, between patient and therapist; (2) interpersonal, between patients; and (3) intrapersonal, when the patient explores his or her own psyche, but in the presence of others. Theory may be regarded as drawing the therapists' attention to certain cue dimensions, such as verbal communications and the relationship between them; to the sequence of events in the group; and (within the dimension of verbal communication) to the content and function of verbal activity. Considerable overlap exists in the cue dimensions that various theories define as important in the practice of group psychotherapy.

Where theories differ is in the importance assigned to the various cue dimensions and, within a particular cue dimension, to the type of response regarded as theoretically correct. While not ignoring the nonverbal dimensions and group process issues (what the patient or the group is doing), many psychoanalytically oriented theories tend to place more importance on verbal communication. The more process- and affect-oriented theories (summarized in Shaffer and Galinsky 1974) and the more interpersonally oriented theory offered here (Chapter 8), while not ignoring the verbal dimension, place more emphasis on nonverbal and experiential dimensions (what the patient or the group is doing).

In sum, theory defines for the therapist (1) which cue dimensions to attend to and in what order of importance; (2) how to discriminate among cues (e.g., if verbal, then whether to attend to content, semantics, tone of voice, or the like); and (3) having discriminated appropriately, how to interpret or understand the cues which have been selected as most meaningful.

From this standpoint, the first task of the therapist is to teach the group the language of the theory he or she is using. To the extent that theory functions as a road map, sharing that road map with the group facilitates more active patient participation in the achievement of group goals. In order to teach the map to the group, the events most readily explained by the theory must first occur. Therapists may be regarded by their supervisors as skilled to the extent that the therapists facilitate the occurrence of such events.

The therapist's second task, from the standpoint of theory, is to convince the group that the types of interaction the theory deems important are in fact important. In order to do that, the therapist must first be persuaded of the importance of the event. For instance, theories (and therapists) that assume that hostility mediates interper- sonal interaction until libidinal ties are established must convince the group that intragroup conflict is inevitable, natural, and necessary, and that one task of the group leader is the resolution of such conflict. That is not a particularly difficult task, for it is relatively easy to generate conflict in a group, and interpersonal conflict is observable behavior.

A more difficult task for the group leader is to convince the group that *things are not what they seem* (the psychoanalytic formulation), that unconscious motivations are present, and that what may appear to be a trivial interaction in group is actually quite significant because it reveals or portends some unconscious mechanism. Even when you believe such a formulation, it is difficult to sell to naïve audiences. Analytic group therapists may wait six months or so before venturing an interpretation of that type.

If you don't believe the theoretical formulation and your supervisor does, the best thing to do is to change supervisors, if that is possible. It's difficult to sell someone else on something you yourself don't believe in. Patients will quickly pick up your lack of enthusiasm for a technique you don't like, and your inability to produce or facilitate the kinds of interaction that theory says are important may be taken by your supervisor as a reflection on your general competence.

If you approach group therapy with a clear theoretical bias, and therefore some notion of what ought to happen, you will be confronted with the discrepancy between what *is* happening and what *ought to* happen, with no clear idea of how to get from what is to what theory says ought to be. In these circumstances feelings of frustration, ineptness, and stupidity are not uncommon among novice group therapists.

The situation is somewhat similar to that of individual psychotherapy, when the patient seems to be dwelling on something that theory does not readily account for. You know that the patient should be talking about something else, you aren't clear on how to get him or her to do so, and you envy your colleagues whose patients are producing material that is easily handled by the theory you are learning to apply. For example, your patient may drone on and on about how to catch fish. Your theory says he ought to be talking about his feelings, and the path from fish to feelings is not immediately obvious to you, although you may expect that it will be obvious to your supervisor later on. An analogue in group might be a session where most of the members seem quite earnestly interested in discussing the local zoning ordinances.

The dilemma this kind of situation puts you in is that you'll have

to say something to get the patient back on the right track because if
you don't, if you remain silent, the entire remainder of the session will
have been spent on something peripheral or irrelevant. Yet the very
theory that propels you into verbal activity fails to tell you what you
ought to say: this situation seems to have been unanticipated by the
theorist.

The influence of theory upon practice seems then limited to
generalities, to general principles, to abstractions, while what you
have to deal with in the group session (or in individual therapy) is
concrete and specific. Novice therapists may be tempted to make
theoretical statements during the sessions, stretching logic a bit in
order to fit theory to events. If you try that approach, if you try to
restrict yourself to statements that derive from theory rather than
from what is going on during the session, you will find that you're
working very hard, that you are defending your theory to your
patients, and that the discussion gets farther away from where you
want it to go in spite of your efforts.

This problem arises from the assumption that theory and practice are closely allied, that there are a finite number of theoretical
statements and practical situations, and that the task of the therapist
is to memorize as many of the former and experience as many of the
latter as possible. It is true that one role of theory is to reduce the
complexity of group interaction to manageable proportions, but it is
incorrect to infer that complexity can be reduced to a finite number of
statements, each of which produces a specifiable result.

In addition to its reductionistic role, theory serves as a focal point
or framework for the development, in the therapist, of a *point of view*.
The application of theory is comprised not of technical interventions
but of statements and actions by the therapist stemming from the
point of view generated by the theory. If you can find, reconstruct,
discover, or deduce a point of view, an attitude, a *set of implicit
assumptions about behavior and reality* that is consistent with theory,
then it will be considerably easier to decide when and how to
intervene therapeutically—what to say and when to say it.

It can be assumed that theory represents the point of view and reflects the implicit assumptions of the theorist. In order for the theory to make sense to you, therefore, it is necessary that you hold some of those same assumptions. In addition, an intimate familiarity with the theory is necessary if that theory is to serve as a focal point for the development of a point of view that, while your own, is also consistent with that of the theorist.

The influence of theory on practice, then, is manifested in two functions. The first is an ordering or guiding function, defining what the therapists should look for and respond to in group, and approximately in what order. The second function is to serve as a nucleus and stimulus for the development of an attitude or point of view from which therapeutic interventions may be generated.

THE INFLUENCE OF PRACTICE UPON THEORY

Practice influences theory after the group session, during the supervisory interview. At that time, the tasks of the group leaders include accounting to the supervisor for what happened in group in terms of the theory espoused by the supervisor. If things went as the theory predicted, this is not a difficult task. The initial silence followed by hostility that results from passivity on the part of the therapists is easily described in terms of group members' dependency, hostility, and hostile dependency, for example.

What is more difficult to account for is an event or behavioral sequence in group that does not readily fit into the framework of the theory but that the group clearly spent a good deal of time and energy on. Theory tells what should have happened; the tape (or notes or memory) tells what did happen; the task of the supervisor is to reconcile the two. Although the number of options available is probably infinite, they fall most frequently into one of the following three classes:

1. The group members are said to have failed to come to grips with problems defined (by theory and supervisor) as important. They

are not yet ready for the insight or interpretation or experience that the group leaders have correctly visited upon them. This leaves both the group leaders and the supervisors in the right, and the group members to be blamed and regarded as somewhat more immature or pathological than one might have expected.

2. The group dwelt on a point that theory regards as irrelevant or unimportant because of a technical error by the therapist. This formulation needs no further comment.

3. The behavioral sequence may be redefined as unimportant. Theoretical concepts may have to be stretched to cover the event and accomplish such a redefinition; thus does practice influence theory. Discussion of a zoning ordinance, for instance, may be seen as resistance, avoidance, or a symbolic attempt to establish ego boundaries. The possibilities are limitless.

What makes them so is the nature of the data with which the therapists work. Most behavior is ambiguous and susceptible of many interpretations. The very theories that are useful to the clinician because they address the quality of experience are similarly susceptible of many interpretations precisely because they reflect the ambiguity of experience rather than an attempt to quantify it. The greater the ambiguity of theory, the more it can explain and the more susceptible it is to the influence of events. The ambiguity of theory, however, and the elasticity of its concepts, need not necessarily reflect loss of validity. In interpersonal relations, truth is a judgment, not a datum. It is because of the judgmental nature of truth in human behavior that the function of theory is to persuade rather than to prove.

CONCLUDING COMMENT

In the natural sciences, and to some extent in the social sciences, the interaction of theory and practice involves the design and performance of experiments. Theory generates hypotheses, that is, performs a road map function. Experiments test hypotheses, and empirical data determine whether or to what extent the hypotheses are supported. Theory is then modified to conform to empirical findings.

In the mental health professions, each therapeutic intervention is rather like an experiment, whether that intervention is the administration of medication, the application of a schedule of reinforcement, or the comment of a therapist during a group or individual psychotherapeutic session. That experiment tests an hypothesis stemming, ideally, from some theoretical point of view. The result tends either to support the hypothesis or not.

However, theory is not modified to conform to empirical findings. It may be *distorted*, that is, applied in an erroneous or deviant fashion, but it is not modified. Object relations theory represents development, not modification, of psychoanalysis as Freud left it. Some of the behavioral theories have undergone similar development as the barriers to exploration of thinking erected by Watson and Skinner have gradually crumbled. Research findings have also failed to influence practice, a fact that the first volume in the monograph series of the American Group Psychotherapy Association (Dies 1983a) was explicitly intended to address. The findings reported in that volume have not appreciably influenced clinical practice, while the work of Yalom on therapeutic factors in group psychotherapy has been more generally accepted despite the sometimes shaky empirical support (Block and Crouch 1985) and the methodological flaws described by Weiner (1974).

In personality and psychotherapy, theory behaves more like philosophy than like science. Philosophy is noncumulative. Science is a cumulative enterprise, and a theory that fails to undergo major modification over the course of several decades is either venerable or highly suspect. It is because we are closer to philosophy than to science that we find truth in judgments rather than empirics.

The judgmental truth that prevails is, therefore, that which is most convincing. Theory provides a conceptual context within which judgments are made, and the context lends credence to these judgments. The point of view advanced here is that behavioral episodes such as those that occur during therapy group sessions are inherently ambiguous and thus will support a number of interpretations of what really happened. To attempt to place any particular interpretation somewhere along a continuum of *correct* or *incorrect* is fallacious, except in the context of theory. The theory itself derives its power not from accuracy (i.e., from empirics) but from its ability to convince people and thus to form a pool or consensus of judgments about reality.[1]

If there is no ultimate truth in interpersonal relations, but only opinion, then the clinician must function in a situation that is inherently and unavoidably ambiguous, and in which certainty will be forever elusive. It is this inherent uncertainty and ambiguity of the therapy situation, combined with the awesome responsibilities of the helper role (as he or she perceives them) that so terrifies the novice therapist. The problem is compounded in group therapy. There, any consensus reached by the group about what really happened may be deviant or fruitless relative to the rest of society. But it is more powerfully convincing to the therapist in the group because such a consensus is, by definition, the pooled judgment of a number of people. Few novice therapists have the chutzpah to say to a room of six or eight people that things are not what they seem, in effect holding that their judgment of reality is better than that of the six or eight people put together.

The first task of the novice clinician faced with doing therapy is to confront his or her terror and to function effectively in spite of it. To the extent that the sources of that terror are the ambiguity and uncertainty of the therapy situation, whatever steps the clinician takes to reduce ambiguity will reduce anxiety. Theory provides a way of reducing ambiguity in the therapy situation. It also provides a set of judgments, preformed and readily available, about those aspects of reality that are reached through judgment and experience rather than through experiment and the accumulation of facts. If those judgments embodied in the theory do not make intuitive sense to the

---

[1]Thus, Sullivan's concept of consensual validation.

clinician, are not congruent with his or her own road map of reality, then theory cannot function as a road map (you have to trust a road map if you're going to use it); it contributes to rather than reduces ambiguity, and at best fails to help the clinician reduce the terror of the situation of uncertainty combined with responsibility that appears to be characteristic of psychotherapy.

If, on the other hand, the theory does make intuitive sense to the clinician, it may serve to reduce ambiguity and thus anxiety to tolerable levels, and to buttress the clinician's own sense of reality. Theory in psychotherapy is ultimately a set of judgments offering to the clinician consensual validation of his or her own experience. Theory cannot offer certainty, although some theories provide that illusion; but the validation of one's own experience is requisite to the maintenance of sanity. The role of theory, then, is to help the clinician to maintain his or her own sense of interpersonal reality, and to help him or her to make that sense of reality prevail when there is nothing else to buttress it and the edge of the abyss looms near.

6

The Application of Freud's Theory of Group Psychology to Group Psychotherapy

This chapter and the two that follow present a theoretical basis for the new clinician's practice of group therapy. The chapters provide a conceptual road map for the purpose of helping the novice group therapist make sense of the complex interactions and emotional interplays that occur during a group therapy session and during the life of a therapy group. Such a road map guides the clinician toward the events it is important to attend to and away from those that may be interesting but not relevant, provides a basis for the construction of therapeutic interventions, and helps the clinician to understand and overcome the initial uncertainty about what to do and the concomitant fear of doing the wrong thing.

This chapter applies Freud's theory of group psychology, as described in his *Group Psychology and the Analysis of the Ego* (1922), to group psychotherapy. The following chapter describes the therapeutic factors found by Yalom and others (Bloch and Crouch 1985, Yalom 1985) to be associated with successful outcome in group psychotherapy. The next chapter offers an interpersonal theory of psychopathology for group psychotherapy. The theoretical journey of these chapters proceeds from the intrapsychic to the interpersonal from the standpoint of group psychotherapy.

Freud's theory of group psychology represents one of his earliest forays into social psychology. Based on his study of and reasoning about the behavior of people in three types of group organization (a mob, the army, and the Catholic church), it differs from the psychoanalytic theories of group therapy, which stem from clinical work with patients and which apply the basic concepts of individual psychoanalytic therapy to the group setting with more or less transmutation. (The origins of group psychoanalysis are described in a slim volume edited by Kaplan and Sadock 1972). What follows is not a summary of Freud's theory of group psychology but its application to four group phenomena that, though not ubiquitous, occur with sufficient frequency as to require explanation. They are:

1. The source and nature of the interpersonal power accorded the group leaders by the group members
2. The development of an atmosphere of warmth and supportiveness facilitative of self-disclosure and cohesiveness
3. The willingness of the individual to allow the group to influence him or her, and
4. The willingness of the group members to help one another.

In our discussion, we will also take up other group phenomena, such as scapegoating, the factors underlying group cohesiveness, and the like. The purpose is to offer the group therapist some conceptual tools with which to make sense of quite complex sensory input in the group sessions.

The facets of group experience that concern us here are not limited to therapy groups, but occur in other types of groups as well (see, e.g., Lakin 1985, Lieberman, Yalom, and Miles 1973, Shaffer and Galinsky 1974). Our theoretical model is, therefore, not limited to groups explicitly designated as psychotherapeutic, but may also apply to others.

Freud's theory of group psychology is intricate but not complex, using only a few theoretical concepts to explain a number of group phenomena. Derived from that theory, the framework presented here does not lend itself readily to the development of specific therapist interventions—a point to which we will return at the end of this chapter—but is rather intended to facilitate the development of a point of view from which technical interventions can be formulated.

INTERPERSONAL POWER OF THE GROUP LEADER

Let us distinguish at once between the power of the group leader to influence the course of events occurring during the group session and the power he or she may have to influence events that happen outside it. We may call the former *leadership functions*, the latter *therapist functions*. Although the group leader has considerable power to influence events that occur during the group session, his or her ability to influence patients' behavior outside the sessions is much smaller, and at best is only one of many influences upon the patients.

The group leader is accorded some interpersonal power ex officio. In the group session he or she is an expert, using his or her expertise for the benefit of the patients. Initially the patients assume that the group leader is expert. Generally they hold this assumption unless (and until) they possess so much evidence to the contrary that it can no longer be denied. The group leader is generally given the benefit of doubt and must actively disprove his or her competence before the group member is willing to reassess it.[1]

Like the kind of interpersonal power accorded by a client to any expert practicing in his or her field—physician, attorney, television technician, forest ranger—so is the group leader's: his or her ability to influence events in the group is no more than the ability of a plumber

---

[1]An exception to this general rule is any situation where patients are assigned to therapy groups as a matter of course, as in many inpatient facilities, partial hospitalization programs, and substance abuse treatment centers.

to influence the activity of a family while he or she is repairing the kitchen sink and they are in the kitchen.

It is possible, then, to account for the interpersonal power of the group leader in terms of the structure of the situation, that structure being essentially a client–expert relationship. This formulation omits, however, the *intensity of emotion* that the group leader is capable of arousing within individuals or within the group. This ability of the group leader might be attributed to transference phenomena: the group leader is perceived as powerful in the same way that the group member's parents were perceived. Freud, however, does not take this route. He attributes this power of the leader not to transference but to identification. Let us look briefly at how Freud arrived at this conclusion.

Freud's starting point was the individual group member. Of particular interest to Freud were two characteristics of group membership: the intensification of emotion, and the impairment or reduction in the level of intellect. Freud (1922) wrote:

> We started from the fundamental fact that an individual in a group is subjected through its influence to what is often a profound alteration in his mental activity. His emotions become extraordinarily intensified, while his intellectual ability becomes markedly reduced. . . . We have heard that these often unwelcome consequences are to some extent at least prevented by a higher "organisation" of the group; but this does not contradict the fundamental fact of Group Psychology – the two theses as to the intensification of the emotions and the inhibition of the intellect in primitive groups. [p. 33]

Freud's "primitive groups" refer to the degree of the organization of a group, whether it has come together for one meeting or several. In the quoted passage, he is referring to a crowd or mob.[2] A therapy group of six or eight or ten patients similarly lacks organization: there

---

[2]The German title of his book, *Massenpsychologie und Ichanalyse*, could as easily have been translated as *The Psychology of Crowds and the Analysis of the Ego*.

are no subgroups, or at any rate shouldn't be,[3] and patients do not differ in rank or position. The "two theses" are at least potentially present in a therapy group and may, as Freud seems to be suggesting, be a function of its lack of structure. No other similarities between a therapy group and a mob are expressed or implied.

Having identified the phenomena he wishes to discuss, Freud then turns to a consideration of group cohesiveness. He suggests that the power holding the group together is that of the libido, that group ties are libidinal ties. As Freud was not a particularly careful theorist, defining the technical terms of psychoanalysis in somewhat different ways in different contexts, it is pertinent to quote the definition Freud used in this context:

> Libido is an expression taken from the theory of emotions. We call by that name the energy (regarded as a quantitative magnitude, though not at present actually mensurable) of those instincts which have to do with all that may be comprised under the word "love." The nucleus of what we mean by love naturally consists (and this is what is commonly called love, and what the poets sing of) of sexual love with sexual union as its aim. [1922, p. 37]

Freud applies the concept of the libidinal basis of group cohesiveness to the Catholic Church and to an army. He finds that the concept works (that is, explains certain phenomena) in both types of organization. Of particular interest for present purposes is his emphasis on the necessity of the leader of the organization to love each member of the group equally. The leader of the Catholic church is Christ, and of an army its commanding general.[4]

---

[3]Transitory subgroups may arise (based on sex, age, common experiences, etc.) and disappear within a single group meeting. If two close friends are inadvertently placed in the same group, what tends to get focused on is the relationship between them: seldom is that in their individual contracts, and seldom is it beneficial to the rest of the group.

[4]Strachey's translation has "commander-in-chief," which clearly has different connotations for American and British readers.

Freud speaks of this love by the leader as being an "illusion," but states that "everything depends upon this illusion; if it were to be dropped, then both Church and army would dissolve" (1922, p. 42).

Thus far, Freud has suggested that cohesiveness among group members is attributable to a libidinal tie, and that the love of the leader equally for all members is also in some sense libidinal. With these concepts it is already possible to account for a number of phenomena that are fairly characteristic of groups: the warmth and supportiveness that tend to occur, and the warm and loving glow typical of the last group session. Lieberman, Yalom, and Miles (1973) report this afterglow as having occurred in all of the fifteen encounter groups they studied, but as being absent in two leaderless groups that listened to encounter group tapes.

At this point in his exposition Freud takes what he himself calls a digression to consider a type of emotional bond between people that is not so directly (or blatantly) sexual. Libidinal cathexes are not the only bonds that bring people together. Freud introduces the concept of *identification* as a type of emotional tie; indeed, he suggests that it is the first or original form of an emotional relationship with another person.

The formation of this tie involves a complex process. The first step is *introjection* of the admired (or desired) object: the boy wishes to be like his father, and so introjects his conception of father: What would Father do or say in this situation that I am now in? The process is fairly devoid of nuances, since it occurs initially in children who are in transition between the anal and phallic stages of psychosexual development. The second step involves equating of the introject with the ego: I am like him, we are at one with each other. (The pathological form is, we *are* one: I am my father. It is the non-pathological form, the I-am-like-him formulation, that is pertinent to our understanding of group behavior.) The end point of Freud's disquisition is his suggestion that the members of a cohesive group have all performed the same mental work: they have introjected the group leader, and the introject is equated with, or takes the place of, not the ego but the ego-ideal.

Although Freud did not address this specific point, it may be helpful to remember that it is not the group leader who takes the place of the group member's ego-ideal, but rather the group member's concept of what the leader is like. Introjection is not veridical, either in the child or in the adult. The group member's perceptions of the leader will of necessity contain some gaps and some distortions, because it is not possible to know another human being completely and fully. If the group leader is bland, impassive, and unresponsive, opportunities for distortion and gap-filling by the group member are maximized. The ways in which the introject is distorted and the ways the gaps in information about the introjected object—the group leader—are filled are functions of the group member's personality. The process of distortion that occurs here may be regarded as projection. However, it is not the ego-defense mechanism of projection that stems directly from libidinal involvement with the cathected object. Rather, the projection here is that which accompanies the first step of the process of identification. The formulation is, "This is how I think you are, this is what my information about you leads me to infer," rather than "This is a characteristic that I need for you to possess" (e.g., strength, wisdom, forbearance, etc.). It is this type of projection, the projection attendant upon the introjection-identification process and associated with an information deficit about the introjected object, which psychoanalytically oriented group therapists have labelled *transference* and have sought to foster.

The introjection of the group leader by the group members and the equation of the introject with the ego-ideal is the first step of a two-stage process. The second step is the recognition by the group members that their ego-ideals are identical. Such recognition is the basis for the identification of group members as *we*, upon which group cohesiveness is built. Freud put the matter quite succinctly: "A . . . group . . . is a number of individuals who have substituted one and the same object for their ego-ideal and have consequently identified themselves with one another in their ego" (1922, p. 80). Freud goes on to account for the individual's willingness to become susceptible to the influence of the group by referring to his theory of the Primal Horde.

We need not follow him thence. Instead, we now return to the tasks we set ourselves at the beginning of this chapter: to account for some characteristic, if not ubiquitous, phenomena of groups.

Source and Limits of the Interpersonal Power Accorded the Group Leaders

The interpersonal power accorded the group leader can be understood in terms of the introjection by group members of the group leader, with the introject taking the place of the ego-ideal. The function of the ego-ideal, put simply, is to visit praise or reproach upon the ego for actions taken or contemplated. The ego-ideal is the source of many, if not all, of the injunctions against action that the ego seeks to take in order to satisfy strong instinctual drives. When the ego-ideal is supplanted by the introjection of an external object, this external object (in this case, the group leader) is able to exert considerable influence over the individual. Because the individual does not discriminate between the introjected leader and his or her own self, reproach or praise from the group leader is experienced in the same manner as reproach or praise from one's own ego-ideal. (In the latter case, as Freud notes, the result may be mania; in the former, melancholia or depression.) The group leader is also in a position to give or withhold consent for any number of activities that are prohibited to the individual by his or her own ego-ideal, and with this consent the group member can engage in actions he or she would not normally engage in without feeling guilt, remorse, or shame. But when the group member's survival is at stake, when he or she feels that his or her survival is threatened by a particular request from the group leader, he or she will simply refuse to obey. Nevertheless, the group member will feel bad as a result, and may magnify any hint of reproach from the therapist well out of proportion.

We now have also the theoretical tools to account for the phenomenon of *scapegoating*. Scapegoating is most likely to occur when the group members have introjected the group leader, substituting him or her for their ego-ideals, and have identified with one another. If the group leader is critical of a group member, and especially if the leader is critical and hostile, the other group members will frequently turn on the one who has been thus singled out. This is the clinical, observable phenomenon called scapegoating, and it can drive the victim out, out into the cold, out away from the we-ness of the group in much the same way as the biblical scapegoat was driven away from the tabernacle and into the cold and barren desert, there to perish.

The group leader, by attacking, sets an example. It is as though he or she grants permission to the others to attack. Perhaps the attack of the group serves both as a kind of ingratiation and as a distraction, turning the leader away from attacking other group members: I am with you, I am like you, I too attack your enemies; therefore don't attack me.

The group does not need to see an actual attack by the group leader. Rather, the group has what amounts to an uncanny sense of who is in favor, who is in disfavor. Some group members are as adept at picking up subtle cues as is the group leader; the difference between them is that the group leader has some obligation to report rather than to act on what he or she sees.

In effect, the group leader speaks with the loudest, most powerful voice in the group. Consequently, what the group leader may issue as a mild reproach or a faint disapproval may be heard by the group member (and the rest of the group) as though it were the severest of condemnations. This tendency of the group to amplify nuances places the group leader in something of a quandary: the group leader must be able to challenge, question, in some sense perhaps find fault with the patient's conception of reality, or with the patient's mechanisms for dealing with reality. Yet, if the leader does make the challenge, he or she runs the risk of making the patient a scapegoat who will be attacked by the other group members.

Thus the group leader must be aware that the group will tend to magnify and exaggerate his or her comments, and that any comment that has even a remotely negative tone may invite scapegoating. The leader must watch for any signs of attack from group members and must come to the rescue of the patient. Such rescue will not usually be perceived by the group as favoritism, but rather as an extension of the protection by the group leader of each member of the group unconditionally. The perceiving of this protection is likely to lead to a decrease in tension rather than to an increase in sibling rivalry. The latter might be expected if transference rather than introjection and identification factors mediated group cohesiveness and the interpersonal power accorded the group leader.

If the group leader does not come to the rescue, the group sooner or later will act on the leader's suppressed aggression and attack the group member who is the target of that aggression. But, as Freud said, when the group leader does not love all the group members equally, the group dissolves. If you allow the group to attack and don't protect the victim, you will in effect be showing the kind of negative favoritism that may impede or even dissolve group cohesiveness.

To summarize: the interpersonal power accorded the group leader during the initial few sessions of a therapy group may be attributed to the structure of the situation: the leader is the expert to whom patients will listen precisely because they are soliciting, and in many instances paying for, the leader's expertise. Soon, however, the process of introjection begins. Through this process, the group members' perception of the group leader gradually takes the place — in what Freud refers to as "the mental apparatus" — of the group member's ego-ideal, and thus the leader's power over the individual becomes similar, or perhaps analogous to, the power of the ego-ideal. Principally, that power is one of giving or withholding permission. When the individual follows the dicates of the introjected leader, approval is granted, and that approval is experienced by the ego as love or enhanced self-esteem. When disapproval is experienced, it is in the same manner as disapproval by one's own conscience, by feeling loss of love, lower self-esteem, and guilt.

Development of an Atmosphere of Warmth and Supportiveness

We turn now to a consideration of factors affecting group cohesiveness. As we shall see in the next chapter, the early interpersonal moves in the opening sessions of group are likely to involve efforts by the group members, facilitated by the leaders, to seek common ground and common experiences. This perception or awareness of shared experience is the forerunner of the later identification (which is based on the same perceptual mechanism) through which the group members come to realize in their egos that they share the same ego-ideal, that is, the introjected group leader. The theoretical formulation, "I identify with you because we share the same super-ego," is not an especially compelling one if it is conceptualized as pertaining to a dyad. In a larger group, however, the shared permission that constitutes the functional manifestation of the introjection of the ego-ideal can begin to intensify the phenomenon of identification through the kind of feedback loop which Freud described as he was accounting for the phenomenon of contagion in crowds, church, and the army.

This feedback loop is composed of the following links: (a) the perception or awareness by the group member of some internal affect; (b) the perception in others of the manifest signs of a similar emotion in the first group member, whose behavior (c) then reflects this intensification, which (d) intensifies the emotion and its behavioral manifestations in others, and so on.

For example, in an inpatient group, a group member begins to feel angry as she talks about the apparent indifference of the doctors on the ward to her plight and realizes that she is feeling that anger (a). As her voice takes on an angry tone and she begins to look angry, the other group members perceive these signs of her anger and begin to speak angrily themselves about the attention paid them by their own doctors (b), which makes the first woman feel even angrier and complain more forcefully (c), resulting in the other group members intensifying their complaints in an escalating spiral. A similar kind of escalation and intensification of affect can occur when the target of the anger is one of the other group members, or when the affect being expressed is more supportive and nurturing. The entire emotional experience is further intensified if it occurs in a context where the group leaders have given permission to each member of the group to allow his or her feelings into conscious awareness or focus and has approved of their visible manifestation. "Let your feelings show" is not an uncommon message from group leader to member, though the words of that message may vary.

We may now address quite directly one of the problems we set ourselves at the beginning of this chapter: namely, to account for the atmosphere of warmth and supportiveness in which intimate self-disclosure is most likely to occur. The establishment of group cohesiveness is a prerequisite. The psychodynamics of the group may be understood in terms of the introjection of the group leader and the substitution of the introject for the ego-ideal of the group members, followed by identification of the group members with one another. The group members have thus yielded a critical faculty to the group leader. In so doing, they also acquiesce in his or her leadership.

The identification of group members with one another, based on this acquiescence, is not sufficient to establish the desired conditions of warmth and supportiveness. In some types of groups, as for example classes in school or athletic teams, where the emphasis is on competition rather than cooperation (as in swimming or gymnastics), and of course (as Freud pointed out) in the military and the church, cohesiveness may be based on introjection and identification but the atmosphere may be hostile and suspicious. In such instances, the permissions given by the leader may involve hostility and aggression, while the shared identification may be based on such emotions as fear and hatred of a common enemy. Freud apparently felt that the cohesiveness of groups characterized by this type of emotion was not as strong as that of groups where the identification was associated with warmth and supportiveness. Our point here is merely that group cohesiveness is a necessary but not sufficient condition for such an atmosphere to become manifest.

In a group, if the permissions given by the leader involve hostility and aggression, the prevalent atmosphere will reflect those permissions. In order to establish and maintain the desired warm and supportive atmosphere, the group leader must "love" all the group members equally. To some extent, permission for the group members to be friendly may stem from a general attitude on the part of the group leader of warmth, empathy, and positive regard for all the group members. However, the manifestation of such an attitude toward the group as a whole is not sufficient: the group leader will have to demonstrate his "loving" attitude—patience, empathy, and warm regard—toward one or two specific group members. Which group members in particular receive this "love" is in one sense not important. What is important is that the other group members feel that they have an equal chance of receiving it from the group leader, an expectation that they will in fact receive it if they so desire, and that the other group members identify with those who have directly and specifically received the loving attention of the group leader. This identification with one who is loved has some observable behavioral concomitants: in posture, facial expressions, body movements, tone of voice, and the like, and thus is susceptible of intensification through the feedback loop mechanism of contagion described above.

This theorizing has clear implications for leader technique in the early stages of a therapy group, and later on as well. While the group leader may be opaque about personal matters, at least some transparency about what is going on in the room at the moment, in the here-and-now, is commonly advocated in the literature (see, e.g., Bion 1961, Kadis et al. 1974, Rutan and Stone 1984, Wolf and Schwartz 1972). The display of these qualities of interest, warmth, and regard are not technical errors in group therapy. On the contrary, they facilitate the development of group cohesiveness and set the emotional tone of the group. The point is made here because of the tendency of psychoanalytically trained therapists to adopt an impassive and non-reactive stance—what Alonso[5] has referred to as "the therapist as

---

[5]Personal communication (1992).

cadaver" when they first begin to do group therapy. Even Foulkes and his associates, not noted for their activity level, caution against such an approach (Kadis et al. 1974). The importance of active engagement of the group by the leaders in order to begin the processes leading to cohesiveness and other components of a therapeutic group cannot be overemphasized.

Thus, the penultimate step in the development of the atmosphere of warmth and supportiveness involves approval of the respective egos of the group members by the introjected group leader functioning in place of the group members' ego-ideals. The ego feels loved, esteemed, worthy, and perhaps at times elated—provided that the leader permits, if not facilitates, the development of these feelings through some manifestation of warmth, emphathy, and positive regard for the group members.

The final step involves the identification of loved egos with one another: we are worthy, we share together esteem and love; and if the formulation is that we love and *identify* with one another, then to love another is also to love oneself. It is the latter permission (ultimately, the permission to love oneself) that, in a therapy group, the leaders may be able to give so powerfully that group members' egos are strengthened to the point where change becomes possible.

The kind of intimate self-disclosure that precedes change may occur only when the individual group member has enough self-love to display himself or herself, enough to feel confident of the love of others, and when the group member loves others enough to share the gift of intimacy with them. The task of the group leaders in this regard is to help the individual reach a point of self-love, and to help the group reach the point where it can tolerate the intensity of intimate self-disclosure. When the group member has some considerable investment in self-hate (as in schizophrenic patterns of adaptation), considerable skill may be required of the therapists in order to bring a group to this point.

We have taken Freud's concepts of introjection and identification considerably farther than he took them in his book on group psychology. We have, however, but followed a path Freud might have taken if his interests had led him thence. Freud, incidentally, did not feel that serious therapeutic work could be undertaken in group.

Willingness of the Individual to be Influenced by the Group

What remains in this analysis is to account for two phenomena that frequently (but not invariably) occur in group: the willingness of the individual to allow the group to influence him or her, and the willingness of the individual to attempt to help others. Freud was so inner-directed that he could apparently conceptualize one person allowing himself or herself to be influenced by others as some kind of pathological state. Yet Freud's concepts of introjection and identification lend themselves readily to accounting for these phenomena. The individual accedes or succumbs to the influence of group because of the introjection of the group leader and the identification of group members with one another on the basis of the shared introject. The formulation is, We are in this together, we have a common goal, common interests, a common ego-ideal. It is as though one part of the individual's mental apparatus (the ego-ideal) becomes equated not only with the group leader but also with the other group members. Thus, when permissions are given, some of those permissions come from the group functioning as an agent of the group leader. *We* is a powerful concept when identification is involved: consider the intense emotional reaction of crowds at sporting events who identify with the teams of professional athletes: we are winning, they say, and that "we" is available for the price of a ticket.

Willingness of the Individual to Attempt to Help Others

Somewhat difficult to account for theoretically, this phenomenon is nonetheless quite common in groups. The extent to which one individual is willing to help another, in the rather special ways that help can be given in a therapy group, is related to group cohesiveness and group ambience. When the group has reached the atmosphere of warmth and supportiveness in which intimate self-disclosure can occur, the help that is given through the interaction of helper and helpee may be considerably more intense emotionally than at earlier — or later — stages of group. Sometimes that help may consist of a willingness to be uncomfortably honest about one's own reaction to another group member; sometimes it consists of working with, rather than rejecting, behavioral patterns about other people that are outrageously unworkable. The problem for theory is why an individual who comes for help and who is (at least in some settings) paying for it should be willing to subsume his or her own interests to those of another — should take time, effort, thought, and emotional energy away from himself or herself and bestow them on another.

Here, too, the concept of identification, which has thus far stood us in such good stead, must again be called upon. The identification of group members with one another is never complete; that would be as pathological as the formulation noted previously, *I am* my father. The pathological formulation is, We are one person. To the extent that group members identify with one another, love for one another is also self-love, and thus the willingness to exert oneself for another becomes also exertion for oneself.

To the extent that identification is incomplete, the helper may be projecting his own needs, problems, and solutions onto the other group member: in other words, may infer a greater similarity than actually exists, basing the inference on perceived similarity. Thus role playing, for example, becomes a powerful tool for the group. The group member who volunteers to role-play another's parent may at first say figuratively, "I am playing at being your mother," but this frequently changes to "I am playing our mother," and then to "I am playing my mother, who is like yours." Freud, who was a basic pessimist about human nature, tended to attribute helping behavior to self-interest, and we see here that he gave us the conceptual tools — which he himself did not use in this particular way — to understand patients' willingness to help each other in group as a manifestation of self-interest.[6] A concomitant of the above is that the individual must

---

[6]Hence, the effectiveness of the therapeutic factor of altruism, described in the following chapter.

feel sufficient self-love, must possess enough sense of self-worth, to offer to help another. Patients with schizophrenic adaptations may feel unable to be of help to others, and this perceived inability may allow, or enable, them to deepen their self-hate. Patients who are depressed may also find helping others quite difficult until their depression begins to lift.

However, just as with self-disclosure, there is a range of behaviors that are helpful. The steps taken along this range may be small early in the life of the group, and for some individuals the steps may remain small throughout. They still count.

FREUD'S THEORY OF GROUP PSYCHOLOGY: CONCLUDING COMMENT

In Chapter 3 I suggested that one function of theory was to reduce the complexity of a group therapy experience to manageable proportions. Freud's theory of groups is not simple, but like all of his theories it is reductionistic. Given Freud's assumptions about the structure of the mental apparatus, a few additional concepts—introjection and identification in particular—suffice to account for a considerable number of group phenomena.

Nonetheless, Freud's theory of groups, as applied here to therapy groups, is a proto-theory, for it is not an exhaustive and encompassing accounting. In particular, the theory does not readily lend itself to the construction of therapist comments; it does not make it easier for the group therapist to decide what to say about what is going on. It also does not attempt to offer a theoretical language that the therapist can attempt to teach the group. And that is why it is a proto-theory: it lacks direct clinical applicability and is a language of therapist and supervisor but not of therapist and patient.

The theory does, however, offer some guidelines for types of intervention, for what kinds of things to do and to avoid doing, as in its emphasis on treating group members equally, and in its alerting the therapists to the dangers and mechanisms of scapegoating.

The theory presented in this chapter can serve as a kind of framework, a skeletal structure, which can be translated into whatever theoretical language therapist and supervisor share. Clinical theory—which is another way of saying a therapeutic point of view—is best learned in interaction; competence in therapy comes from supervised experience, not from books. What has been presented here is a foundation. What is built on that foundation must depend on the interaction between the supervisor and the therapist seeking to understand and to heal.

7

Therapeutic Factors in Group Psychotherapy

The following three interventions comprise a large proportion of the interventions typically used by theoretically naïve and untrained group therapists. They are:

> Is there anyone else here who has had a similar experience?
> Tell us (or tell the group) more about what you have just said.
> How do you *feel* about that?

These questions appear to stem from therapists' belief or intuition that the discovery that others have had similar experiences is itself therapeutic; that self-disclosure is beneficial; and that the frequent use of words connoting affect brings a desirable decrease in the intensity of that affect. Research has shown that the therapists' belief in the efficacy of the first question is usually justified, the second less frequently so, and the third gets mixed reviews. The underlying question is, What works in group psychotherapy or what makes group psychotherapy effective?

Several lists of factors have been shown more or less empirically to be associated with good outcome in group psychotherapy somewhat independent of therapist theoretical orientation. The best known of these lists was compiled by Yalom (1985). His work was extended and its empirical base strengthened by Bloch and Crouch (1985), whose list differs slightly from Yalom's. Because of its stronger empirical support, clearer conceptual formulations, and more extensive discussions, it is the Bloch and Crouch list that is discussed here.

The first of the interventions listed before, the move to encourage group members to discover that they have similar problems or experiences, is a manifestation of the therapeutic factor called *universality*. Bloch and Crouch suggest that it is probably a multidimensional factor: perceiving that he or she is in some way similar to others may permit the group member to feel less odd, which may in turn be linked to some relief from a negative self-image. In addition they refer (p. 190) to Foulkes's suggestion that the sharing of the knowledge of suffering makes that knowledge more tolerable.

Freud's theory of group psychology offers a clear and relatively straightforward explanation of the potency of universality. The sharing of experiences and the concomitant perceived similarity among group members facilitates identification and thus cohesiveness. It is from there but a short step to the perception, conscious or otherwise, of the shared introject of the leader as ego-ideal.

The second of the interventions listed previously, the request for the group member to talk further about some topic, is related to the therapeutic factor of *self-disclosure*. Bloch and Crouch (1985) define this factor as

> the act of revealing personal information to the group. We suggest that the factor operates when the patient: reveals information about his life outside the group; or his past; or his feared, embarassing, or worrisome problems; or his fantasies, which he regards as private and personal—even though such revealing and sharing may be difficult and painful. [p. 128, emphasis in original]

Bloch and Crouch carefully differentiate between verbal activity and self-disclosure. The latter "entails a shift in attitude, which allows the patient to share much of his private self with others in a new constructive fashion, and to generally act more openly and honestly with himself and others" (p. 128).

In the early stages of group, therapists (especially those who are relatively inexperienced) will encourage verbal activity, partly in the belief that they are invoking the therapeutic factor of self-disclosure and in part as a maneuver born of desperation or anxiety, in order to get group members to talk with one another. Significant self-disclosures are unlikely to occur early in the life of the group. When they do, the patient is at higher risk for premature unilateral termination. Therapist prompting for significant early self-disclosure is therefore contraindicated. In addition, there is some evidence that self-disclosure in group therapy is associated with negative outcome for schizophrenic patients (Strassberg, Roback, and Anchor 1975). In my own experience, requests for self-disclosure from borderline patients result in negative outcome also, for the group if not for the patient.

Consider the following examples. The first is from an inpatient group on a psychiatric ward in a general medical hospital. Because of the very short length of stay and the very high turnover, each group session is regarded by the group leaders as a group that meets only once. The excerpt is therefore, in effect, taken from the initial meeting of a new group.

Patient: I'm here because my family tricked me into coming. They told me we were just going for a ride and they brought me here. (*Begins to cry*) I just want to be with my husband and my daughters and their children. I love them and want to be home with them. I stopped taking my medicine. They wouldn't let me go into town so I started walking. They tricked me into coming here.

Therapist: Tell us more about your family.

The therapist's request for additional information about the patient's family is not actually a request for self-disclosure but for disclosure about the patient's family. The therapist's rationale for the intervention was that she was attempting to get the patient to talk about what was troubling her, and clearly it was her family that was troubling her. As a rationale it seems reasonable enough, but it is not what is meant by self-disclosure. There are some notable gaps in the patient's story (why she stopped taking her medicine, whatever was going on when she decided to "go into town," for instance) but a more fruitful domain for intervention might have been her presentation to the group that she had been tricked by those she loved and victimized by being brought to the hospital.

The second example is an interchange between a patient and therapist in an outpatient group that had been meeting for some months. The patient is the newest group member; this is his fourth session.

Patient: It takes a while to feel comfortable enough in here to talk about things that are really important. I'm starting to feel comfortable in here and to have some trust. Getting here tonight was really important to me; I'm starting to look forward to the group sessions. I think my family is more dysfunctional than Connie's [another group member] and there are some things I want to tell the group about, soon.

Therapist: Now is your chance.

In this example, the patient indicated that he was approaching readiness to make some disclosures that were clearly significant to him, that he would make only when he trusted and valued the group sufficiently. The therapist's invitation for him to proceed carpe diem was therefore technically correct in terms of the therapeutic factor of self-disclosure.

In Freud's theory of group psychology, interactions among group members are explained in terms of imitation (contagion) and identification (perception of sharing the same introject). The power of self-disclosure as a therapeutic factor may be understood in terms of its facilitation of both imitation and identification. The imitative factor involves the perception by the group of the affect with which the self-discloser speaks. In addition, self-disclosing behavior itself seems to establish some pressure on other group members to engage in similar behavior. In terms of identification, it is necessary to know something about another individual, to have some impression of him or her, in order for the process to begin. Otherwise what is going on is *projection*, which is not a concept Freud uses to explain the group phenomena he addresses (the interpersonal power of the leader, the warmth and supportiveness of the group, and the willingness of the individual to be influenced by the group). Self-disclosure facilitates identification by providing the other group members with information about the discloser (how he or she relates, the affect with which the message is conveyed), as well as the information contained in the disclosure (the content of the verbal message itself.) Both the verbal message itself and the way it is delivered thus facilitate the growing perception by the group members that they share the same introject. An increase in group cohesiveness and supportiveness results.

The therapist question, "How do you feel about that?" is a request to talk about rather than to experience affect. *Talking about* feelings is not the same as *experiencing and expressing* them. The question is, in my experience, asked so frequently by novice group therapists and so seldom with positive results that an explanation of its persistence in the repertoire of therapist interventions may be more salient than a discussion of its utility.

The question "How do you feel about that?" seems to be triggered in therapists' minds when one or more of the following conditions are present during a therapy group session:

1. The patient focuses exclusively on what he or she thinks about something while giving no clue as to its affective impact, The therapist believes that there is some affective component of which the patient may be unaware, and asks the question in an effort to make the patient more consciously aware of the emotional concomitant of what is being discussed.

2. There is a discrepancy between what is being said and the way it is

being expressed, as when a patient speaks unemotionally or smiles while describing the death of her child.

3. An interaction occurs in the group which the therapist believes may evoke some unexpressed reaction in the other group members and asks them to disclose their affective reaction primarily for the benefit of the speaker.

4. The therapist poses the question in an effort to avoid an uncomfortable or awkward group silence.

Let us consider each of these in turn as they relate to the therapeutic factors described by Bloch and Crouch.

In the first instance, the expected expression of emotion is missing from the patient's interpersonal communication. The therapists and perhaps the other group members frequently have the impression that the patient is "not in touch" with his or her feelings. Consider the following comment made by a 35-year-old man during the second meeting of a therapy group:

> I am very depressed. I need to find a reason to want to go on living. My partner and I lived together for fifteen years. When AIDS started we knew we were OK because we did not have symptoms and we had already been faithful to each other for a long time. I was always faithful to him. He died of AIDS four months ago and I am HIV positive. He did not tell me he had it until he got very sick.

These words were spoken earnestly, sincerely, and energetically. The patient leaned forward as he spoke, making eye contact with the other group members and the therapists. The second sentence was uttered with somewhat more emphasis than the others, and the last sentence was almost an afterthought. Although there was some discrepancy between the patient's words and his affect (he did not appear depressed, as he reported he was), the therapists suspected that he harbored considerable anger at his partner, both for the latter's unfaithfulness and for infecting him with the lethal virus. There was no sign of this anger in either the patient's speech or his manner. The therapists, convinced that such anger must be present, sought to elicit its expression by asking the patient how he felt about what had happened. Both that and a later, more direct question about his anger resulted in the patient's denial of any feeling other than sorrow.

What is the benefit the therapists were seeking to make available to the patient by asking him about his feelings and about his anger? It is not self-disclosure, which refers to events, problems, and fantasies (see above) rather than to affect. It is not catharsis, which involves the expression of intense emotion followed by feelings of relief (Bloch and Crouch 1985). It is almost certainly not universality (see above).

In this example, as in many instances when therapists ask group members to say something about their feelings, the therapeutic factor is most likely what Bloch and Crouch would call *insight*. They describe insight as having four components: the patient (1) learns something important about himself or herself, (2) learns how he or she comes across to the group, (3) learns more clearly about the nature of his or her problem, (4) learns why he or she behaves the way he or she does and how he or she got to be the way he or she is.

In the above example, the first two of these components seem clearly relevant, depending on what followed the therapists' questions and the patient's response. Presumably they were seeking to facilitate his learning something about the magnitude of his anger (1), not all (or any) of which may have been conscious. In addition, it may have been both surprising and helpful to him to learn that the group perceived him as angry even though he did not manifest visible signs of anger (2). It might then have been possible to lead the patient (and the group) toward an enhanced awareness of the relationship between depression and suppressed anger (3), which in turn could potentiate the patient's learning at some future time about how and perhaps why he learned to suppress or deny anger but found depression more tolerable (4).

The problem with this formulation is that it involves a series of conjectures anchored in contingencies. The question "How do you feel about that?" is not itself therapeutic in the context of group therapy but may lead to or facilitate the employment of therapeutic factors, provided that there is appropriate follow-up to the question.

In the previous example, the therapists should have followed up their questions by telling the patient of their assumption that anger was present and their surprise or incredulity at his continued denial.

Consider the following interchange between George, an unmarried young man in his early twenties living with his parents, and Donna, a married mother of two in her late thirties.

George: My parents are still trying to run my life. They're always telling me to get a job, clean my room, don't leave my stuff laying around the house. It's my house too, and my life.

Donna: (Quite sharply) You mean you're not working? Who's supporting you?

George: Nobody's supporting me.

Donna: (Even louder) You're living with your parents, eating their food, and not working? Your parents are supporting you! Why can't you get a job?

Therapist: Donna, how are you feeling right now?

Donna: Amused.

In this example there is a discrepancy between the patient's manner, which is angry, and her verbal report of her subjective emotional state. Upon further questioning by the therapists, Donna continued to insist that she was amused by George's disclosures and by his situation. When one of the therapists finally asked if she had felt some anger, she denied it. At that point the therapists felt stymied and dropped the matter.

When the patient responds to or answers the question "How do you feel about that?" it is important to follow up by placing the response in the interpersonal context here-and-now in the group. Otherwise both the intrapsychic and interpersonal learning implicit in the Bloch and Crouch definition may be less likely to occur. This interpersonal component of insight is a point to which we will return later.

When there is a discrepancy between what is being said and the way it is being said, many therapists tend to respond by asking the "How do you feel about that?" question rather than by pointing out the discrepancy itself. The tendency is somewhat stronger in inexperienced therapists who are still learning how to formulate therapeutic interventions. In my experience the question in this context is almost always ineffective in making the patient aware of the discrepancy between words and affect.

> During the ninth session of a therapy group, a woman described in graphic detail an incident in which she had been sexually abused and tortured by her brother while both were in their early teens. She told the story in an offhand manner, almost in passing, and with a little smile. When asked by the therapist how she felt about it, the patient replied only that that was not the worst thing that had ever happened to her. She had made other allegations of abuse in previous group sessions, always following similar but less graphic disclosures by other group members. Her offhand, casual manner was in marked contrast to the upset and tearful way the others told of their childhood sexual abuse, and raised questions in the minds of the therapists, at least, about the credibility of her stories. The therapists never commented on *how the story was told* but continued to ask how the patient felt about her disclosures. She continued to be evasive and terminated therapy unilaterally two weeks later.

A third type of situation that seems to generate the therapist question "How do you feel about that?" follows an interaction in the group that the therapist believes may evoke some unexpressed reaction in the other group members, and asks them to disclose their affective reaction primarily for the benefit of the speaker. The question may take the form "How did you feel when . . ." or "When that happened, how did it make you feel?" An example is, "Lynette, how did you feel when Garland called you a stupid asshole just now?"

The therapeutic factor involved here is a component of insight as defined by Bloch and Crouch in terms of learning how one comes across to other group members. In asking one group member to disclose his or her subjective reaction to another, the therapist is encouraging and perhaps teaching the group to engage in *interpersonal feedback*, a term attributed to Lewin (1947), which is afforded a somewhat more central role in the group dynamics literature than in the theoretical literature on group psychotherapy. Clinicians coming to group therapy from a group dynamics background, especially those who have had sensitivity-group or T-group training, may tend to place more emphasis on such feedback than do clinicians whose group therapy training follows or accompanies training in individual therapy in psychiatric clinical settings.

Feedback by itself is not necessarily therapeutic. In the context of a therapy group, it *may* be helpful to the individual in that it provides him or her with a kind of information about his or her effect on other people that is relatively unbiased, at least potentially relatively frequent, and which is difficult to obtain in ordinary social contexts.

The role of interpersonal feedback as a component of insight suggests a strong interpersonal component in the definition of insight from the standpoint of group therapy. For our purposes, insight may be defined as *the patient's awareness or realization of the relationships among felt emotion, manifest behavior, and the reactions of others to that behavior.* This is a somewhat formal way of saying that emotions drive actions, and actions lead to and influence the responses of other people. It is difficult for most people to hide their feelings entirely. A facial expression, a tone of voice, a choice of wording, offer clues to observant others as to what emotion is being suppressed. The awareness by others of the presence of the suppressed emotion modifies their response. On the other hand, there are many instances where people make no particular effort to hide what they are feeling; at such times (in lovemaking, for instance) emotion drives the behavior, which evokes reciprocal behavior from the interested observer. In a group setting the phenomenon may be similar to what Freud (1922) defined as contagion. Insight as we are defining it here may therefore be understood as the individual's conscious awareness of the process of contagion.

OTHER THERAPEUTIC FACTORS

The three therapeutic factors described before (Universality, Self-disclosure, and Insight) are the ones with which novice group therapists are usually concerned at the outset. Bloch and Crouch (1985) describe seven others: Learning from Interpersonal Action, Acceptance, Catharsis, Guidance, Altruism, Vicarious Learning, and Instillation of Hope. They are discussed here not in terms of their relative potency in producing desirable interpersonal change, but rather in terms of their relevance to the new group therapist who is trying to figure out what to do and is typically concerned both about doing the right thing and not doing the wrong thing.

Learning from Interpersonal Action

We have defined the purpose of group therapy as the facilitation of change in interpersonal behavior. Implicit in such a definition is the concept that the development of insight is not itself a goal of group therapy, but rather a way station en route to behavior change. Whether or not insight is always prerequisite to behavior change is an argument (usually, between the psychodynamically oriented and the behaviorist schools) in which we need not engage here. At the least, it seems probable that interpersonal insight as defined above facilitates change in behavior.

Once insight has been attained, the task of the therapist is to orient the patient and the group toward behavior change, unless such orientation occurs spontaneously. Learning from Interpersonal Action (LIA) is the relevant therapeutic factor. It involves the development of new and more adaptive behavioral strategies in the group. The emphasis here is not on trying something out to see if it will work, a kind of trial-and-error approach. Rather, LIA involves *manifesting a desirable change in behavior as a result of earlier group interactions.*

George flirted playfully with the women in the group, including the co-therapists. He seemed not to take anything they said seriously, making their comments and observations into little jokes. Consequently the women, uncertain about how seriously to take him, responded very little even when he was saying something important to him. When confronted with his behavior and its interpersonal effects, George said that he was uncomfortable around women. The therapist suggested that it was not women who made George uncomfortable, but his own feelings about them, as for example his feelings about the women in the group. He said nothing for the remainder of that session but in the following session expressed his admiration for the therapists and, a bit awkwardly, the warm feelings he had toward one of the women in the group who, he said, reminded him of his daughter. The women responded *respectfully* and with some warmth.

Catharsis

Another therapeutic factor, catharsis, is defined as *the expression of intense emotion followed by feelings of relief*. Not unique to group therapy, catharsis may occur in individual therapy and in other settings as well. There is general agreement in the literature, though not always among clinicians, that catharsis for its own sake is not necessarily therapeutic and may even lead to serious emotional injury. Such an effect has been well documented by Lieberman and his associates (1973). The later literature reviewed by Bloch and Crouch (1985) leads to a similar conclusion.

What makes catharsis therapeutic is what happens afterward. After catharsis, patients feel better. There are many ways for people to feel better without engaging in catharsis—lovemaking, for instance, ideally involves the experiencing of intense emotion followed by feeling considerably better—which are not particularly therapeutic. What makes catharsis therapeutic is the subsequent orientation, usually provided by the therapist, toward change in interpersonal behavior. Such an orientation provides a context in which the meaning of the cathartic event can be placed, imbuing that event itself with meaning. In the absence of such a context, research suggests that the cathartic event has little value.

Novice therapists are usually reluctant to encourage the expression of intense affect. They are not likely to see a cathartic experience in group unless co-leading with a more experienced therapist knowledgeable in its facilitation. The factor is mentioned here because, like insight, it requires therapist intervention and orientation toward change in order to meet the goals of group therapy.

Guidance

At some point, usually early in the life of a therapy group, the patients begin to tell the stories of how they came to be in the group: the precipitating circumstances or problems that led them into therapy and into the group, problems that seem intolerable and intractable to them and that appear impossible to solve. On inpatient units with short-term lengths of stay, such disclosures may occur the first or second time the patient attends a group therapy session.[1] When the novice therapist joins an already ongoing group, the presenting problems will probably have long since been discussed and the stories the patients tell are more likely to be about current interpersonal problems.

Usually the problems are presented in such a way that no solution or relief is readily apparent. The patient may solicit advice from the group and/or from the therapists. If the therapist perceives a solution, he or she may be tempted to offer advice in addition to or instead of whatever is offered by the group. The following story was told by a 30-year-old married office clerk in an ongoing group she had been attending for about a year, but which was the fourth session for one of the co-therapists.

---

[1]The typical presentation of the recidivist substance abuser, "Hi, my name is Kimmie and I'm an alcoholic," is a different issue requiring a different kind of therapist response.

I'm getting really mad at my husband. He just comes in and eats and watches television and goes to bed. He won't talk to me. When I try to tell him about what's going on with my boss, he says he doesn't want to hear it. We never talk any more. I don't know what to do to try to get his attention.

This kind of statement tends to elicit responses beginning "Have you tried . . ." or "Why don't you . . . ," that is, to elicit advice. The offering of advice is one component of a therapeutic factor labelled *guidance* by Bloch and Crouch (1985); the other component consists of offering information. As Bloch and Crouch note, most clinicians are trained to not offer advice despite the fact that many patients consult mental health clinicians in the hope, and frequently with the expectation, of obtaining it. Given the general prejudice among clinicians (and, presumably, clinical supervisors) against proffering advice, the novice group therapist should probably avoid doing so unless there is some clear theoretical rationale for doing so and clear sanction from the clinical supervisor. In terms of the above example, making suggestions to this young woman as to how she might get her husband's attention would therefore be inadvisable.

The distinction made by Bloch and Crouch between advice giving (which is quite acceptable when done by patients, though not by therapists) and imparting information is especially helpful to the novice therapist because it enables the new clinician to make pertinent information available on request while avoiding the putative pitfalls of offering advice.

It is necessary to impart information about how the group works and the role or function of the therapists. Such information includes things like meeting times and payment policies for missed sessions, the need for confidentiality, and the like. Perhaps because such information pertains to the group itself, it is not particularly controversial. Indeed, there is some evidence that the more information a patient has about how the group functions prior to entering, the higher the probability that benefit will be obtained (Dies 1983b, Heitler 1973, Yalom 1985).

The problem for the novice group therapist arises when a patient seeks information held by the therapist about something outside the group—anything from a bus schedule to the side effects of medication. The principle to follow in resolving the problem is one of simple common sense.

> *Carol:* What time does the last bus leave?
> *Eric:* Five-thirty.
> *Therapist:* No, on Tuesdays the last bus is at 5:45.

> *Terry:* Can lithium affect your sex drive?
> *Therapist:* Not necessarily your sex drive, but sometimes it can affect your ability to perform.

> *Brad:* My doctor prescribed both Haldol and Prozac. Isn't that unusual?
> *Therapist:* You should ask your doctor about that. Sounds like you have some concerns.
> *Brad:* Yes, I do.
> *Therapist:* Your doctor would be the person to talk with about them.

Acceptance

Acceptance is a complex therapeutic factor. At its simplest, it involves an individual's expectation or awareness that he or she will be listened to respectfully, heard accurately, and responded to gently by other group members and the therapists, independent of the social acceptability of the individual's disclosures. In order to make such disclosures, the individual has to value the group sufficiently to be willing to feel vulnerable to it, to feel that the group is similarly valued by the other members, and to believe that the outcome of the disclosures will be positive. Bloch and Crouch differentiate between Acceptance and *cohesiveness*, which they define, following Cartwright (1968) as "'the resultant of all forces acting on members to remain in the group"

(Bloch and Crouch 1985, p. 100). For the novice group therapist, the importance of differentiating between Acceptance and Cohesiveness may not seem very great. Feelings of belonging and of being accepted seem related, and it is difficult to imagine changes in one without concomitant change in the other. Present to some extent at the outset (depending on the tone set and modeling offered by the therapists), feelings of belonging and being accepted usually intensify as the intrapsychic and interpersonal bonds among the group members gradually strengthen with time and the increasing amount of shared experience.

Early in the life of a group, the therapist may facilitate the development of Acceptance and Cohesiveness by acting as though the group is important to him or her and by manifesting interpersonal warmth and interest in each of the group members. Freud's (1922) idea that the leader should show "love" to every group member equally is relevant here.

For the novice group therapist, two problems frequently make the task of showing such warmth and interest difficult. One is the new therapist's anxieties and uncertainties about being a group therapist. It is difficult to show warmth, empathy, and genuineness when one is highly anxious. Hence the importance of taking steps to reduce one's own anxiety before attending to reducing the group's anxiety during the opening sessions.

The second obstacle to displaying one's own warmth is more of a systems issue. Group therapy tends to be added on to the responsibilities of busy clinicians in both inpatient and outpatient settings, with little or no reduction in case load requirements or other responsibilities. In addition, most groups meet in the late afternoons or evenings after the clinicians (and the group members) have had a full day of other activities. The double burden of fatigue and concern about other responsibilities can make it difficult for therapists to focus on the task at hand. Fatigue and preoccupation can easily be mistaken by group members for indifference and boredom, and such perceptions impair the development of acceptance and cohesiveness.

Vicarious Learning

Some patients come faithfully to group, listen and watch, and speak only when spoken to but volunteer nothing. Novice therapists, noticing the minimal verbal activity of these group members, seek to draw them into ongoing interactions or encourage them to volunteer, usually with minimal effect. When half or more of a group consists of such patients, the groups are usually regarded as highly problematic by the therapists.

Bloch and Crouch describe two forms of vicarious learning. One involves imitation. The vicarious learner watches how other group members develop more effective interpersonal strategies and adapts those strategies for his or her own use outside the group. The other involves "learning that stems from the observer's identification with a fellow-patient's specific experience in therapy" (1985, p. 194). Bloch and Crouch suggest that identification is the central process involved in vicarious learning. They do not refer to Freud but define vicarious learning in terms of perceived similarity and conscious or unconscious modeling. They argue for, and cite some research in support of, the value of vicarious learning as a therapeutic factor. The importance of the factor for the novice group therapist (and the more experienced therapist finding himself or herself with a group of silent patients) is that low *verbal* participation is not necessarily an indication of the absence of benefit, any more than high verbal activity is invariably an indicator of its presence.

Altruism

Attending a group therapy session is seldom convenient. Attendance involves coming to the clinic or office, usually after a full day's work, finding a parking place, going through the clinic's procedures to register attendance, and in many settings going through a maze of corridors to a marginally comfortable room. Once there, the group member may spend the entire session focusing on other group members, being more frank and open about his or her own personal reactions to the others than would be customary or appropriate in most social settings, and experiencing some discomfort in the process. For this the group member pays a fee.

The willingness of group members to focus on and help others for entire sessions at a time is understood as altruism. Bloch and Crouch (1985) offer no empirical support for the therapeutic benefit of such behaviors, but are persuaded by their own clinical observations. They offer some speculations as to the origin of altruistic behavior, which indeed seems pervasive if somewhat inconstant in human behavior. Freud's theory of group psychology, discussed in the preceding chapter, easily accounts for altruism in groups in terms of the identification of group members based on the shared introject of the group leader. To be of help to others is then also to be of help to oneself.

The novice group therapist, and also those clinicians not familiar with group therapy, frequently overestimate the resistance of patients in individual therapy to referral for group therapy. Specifically, therapists are frequently concerned because they are asking patients to go from having the therapist to themselves for a session to sharing the therapist with five or more other patients. It is the patient's reaction to this sharing that is so frequently overestimated. Patients are more concerned about issues of disclosure and privacy than about sharing the therapist.[2] Indeed, the opportunity to be of help to others seems to act as an inducement in many instances. Hence, especially for the novice therapist learning the skills involved in making a referral to group therapy, altruism as a therapeutic factor is an important component of the process of educating the patient about group therapy, and a factor that should probably be mentioned in the screening interview as well.

---

[2]In public clinics, the trade-off is a half-hour individual session monthly or bimonthly versus a 75- or 90-minute group session weekly. Most patients given the choice prefer the latter if the privacy and disclosure issues are resolved.

Instillation of Hope

Both Yalom (1985) and Bloch and Crouch (1985) define this factor in terms of the group member's perception of the improvement of other group members. Such a perception takes time, since it is not possible to gauge lasting improvement in a single session or two. As with altruism, there are no empirical data to support the effectiveness of hope as a therapeutic factor, though its power seems indisputable to clinicians and others.

It is possible for hope to be instilled at once, in the initial or early sessions of group, by the therapist. The opportunity arises when the patient first tells his or her story: the story of how he or she came to be a patient, came to the group. Such stories, as already noted, tend to be told (and experienced by the patient) in such a way that the problems described are not susceptible of resolution or amelioration; that is, they end in defeat or stalemate. The therapist's task is to reject that particular kind of ending to the story, and to persuade the patient that other endings are possible in the future. That is the instillation of hope. Early in the course of therapy, whether individual or group, such hope—essentially, borrowed on faith from the therapist—may keep the patient in therapy. The intervention of the general form *We can help you* or the more impersonal *There is hope for you*, is important for hospitalized patients to hear as early in group therapy as practicable. It can be assumed that they will have heard those words from other hospital or ward personnel, but that does not diminish the importance of their hearing them from the group therapists as well.

Combining this factor with the message *And you can be of help to others* puts the concepts of both help and hope into an interpersonal context, the context of both giving and receiving help, support, succor, and optimism, which comprises the most important and healing work of group therapy.

Having discussed the intrapsychic factors related to the power of group therapy in the preceding chapter, and the specific therapeutic factors here, we turn next to the interpersonal realm. The following chapter offers an interpersonal theory of psychopathology which, together with these chapters, provides the clinician with a conceptual and theoretical basis for the formulation of effective interventions during group therapy sessions.

8

An Interpersonal Theory of Psychopathology for Group Therapy

Group therapy is an interpersonal context the purpose of which is facilitation of change in interpersonal behavior. There is some disagreement among theorists as to how that change might best be accomplished, and there is considerable variability in the language used by different theories to describe what goes on during a group session and what the purposes and goals of group therapy are. (Shaffer and Galinsky [1974] have surveyed the most commonly encountered theories and models of group therapy.) Those languages, in turn, may reflect the theorists' conceptions of the nature and remediation of psychopathology.

An implicit premise of most psychotherapies is that intraindividual, intrapsychic factors are responsible for the patient's suffering. Therefore, the healing process involves change in intrapsychic factors. This strong emphasis on intrapsychic psychology has clearly proven fruitful for individual psychotherapy, and its validity is not at issue here. Group, however, is above all an interpersonal context. Therefore, for the group therapist the most fruitful way of conceptualizing psychopathology is in interpersonal rather than intrapsychic terms.

In interpersonal terms, psychopathology may be broadly defined as maladaptive behavioral patterns and strategies of relating to others. Such patterns and strategies may be associated with difficulties in assessing the accuracy of one's attributions of characteristics to other people and to oneself, in assessing the interpersonal and intrapsychic outcomes of one's own behavioral patterns as well as the possible goals and outcomes of others, and in devising strategies and modifying behavioral patterns to produce more satisfying and adaptive interpersonal outcomes. Following is a discussion of each of the terms comprising this definition.

Maladaptive is a very tricky word. How it is defined depends greatly on who is doing the defining. In the present context it may be defined as behavior leading to or associated with unintended and/or undesirable outcomes of interpersonal interactions. The problem remains of who decides what is undesirable; *unintended* is a little easier to define since it rests solely on the verbal report of the individual doing the interacting. The terms *maladaptive* and *undesirable* both have a judgmental component that is unavoidable, as does any definition of psychopathology, and perhaps the concept of psychopathology itself.

People make evaluative judgments all the time about the efficacy and hedonic value (Carson 1969) of their interpersonal relationships. These judgments may be regarded, for present purposes at least, as contributing to the evaluation of behavioral patterns or strategies as maladaptive and/or undesirable. In terms of group therapy, such judgments are made by the therapists, the patient, the other group members, and by people outside the group with whom the group member (patient) interacts or who have some knowledge of the patient. Such judgments by the therapists are not in terms of good or bad (except, perhaps, very privately) but rather in terms of efficacy and of desirability both in the immediate context of the group and of the larger society within which the individual functions. It is the sum of these judgments about the individual that contributes to the evaluation of his or her behavior as maladaptive and therefore undesirable. The therapists may be the only people involved in the process who do not contribute a moral component (good or bad) to the judgment. The interpersonal reality faced by the patient nearly always has such a component. The sum of judgments made by others, as well as the patient's own self-judgments, comprise the interpersonal context in which the patient leads his or her life.

From this point of view, both psychopathology and its manifestations in maladaptive behaviors and affect are defined as judgments about an individual, made by other individuals and preferably but not necessarily including the patient himself or herself. The fruitfulness of such a definition outside of group therapy is not at issue here: one need not abandon one's concepts of mental illness or psychopathology as based on intrapsychic conflict, biochemical or genetic factors, or learned deficit in order to adopt this view of psychopathology from the standpoint of group therapy.

Patients or clients do not always share therapists' concepts of what is maladaptive. Self-mutilating behavior is a dramatic example. Patients who engage in this behavior frequently report that, for them, it serves a highly adaptive function, which differs from case to case. Withdrawal and social isolation is another example. Individuals who become depressed or psychotic as a result of extreme social isolation may report that interpersonal interactions are so distasteful to them that such interactions are generally to be avoided. There are numerous other examples, all of which involve (from the therapists' point of view) the patient's reluctance or refusal to abandon symptomatic behaviors in favor of behaviors regarded (by the therapist, but not necessarily by the patient) as healthier or more satisfying.

When patient and therapist concepts of maladaptive or undesirable behavior differ, it is likely that their concepts of what needs changing, and the consequences of such changing, will differ also. Therapists, especially early in their careers, tend to assume that patients want to get well, or at least better. In some sense that is true, especially for voluntary patients. However, it is prudent that therapists and patients reach explicit agreement on what *getting better* or *improvement* or even *relief* comprises, and on the most probable consequences of achieving such goals.

A behavioral pattern is defined as a characteristic, habitual, or typical way of relating. A strategy is an individual's plan for attaining a desired or anticipated interpersonal outcome. Behavioral patterns are observable. Strategies are intrapsychic and must therefore be inferred unless they are reported by the individual doing the strategizing. Both behavioral patterns and strategies depend for their efficacy upon the individual's assessment of intrapsychic factors and his or her environment; that is, upon what might be called ego functions. When ego functions are impaired, so are the resulting behavioral strategies.

In the interpersonal definition of psychopathology offered above, the phrase *attributions of characteristics to other people and to oneself* refers to one's own ideas of what other people are like, what their motivations might be, and what behaviors they are likely to exhibit in general and in response to specific situational contingencies (e.g., a person who characteristically responds angrily vs. one who is expected to become angry in some situations but not in others). The phrase also refers to one's understandings and explanations about one's own subjective experiences, motivations, and characteristic ways of responding. *Difficulties in assessing the accuracy* of these attributions suggests that the individual does not or cannot evaluate the accuracy of his or her perceptions of others and consequently does not modify those perceptions and expectations on the basis of experience, that is, of reality. Suppose, for example, that your own experiences in your family of origin lead you to conclude that most people are motivated by rage, lust, and an insatiable desire to control others. However, your observations of and experiences with most people are inconsistent with the behaviors you expect based on these assumptions. Realizing that your attributions are inaccurate, you would begin to modify them. (Coming to that realization might be one result of being in therapy.)

Ordinarily, the evaluation of accuracy of attributions (also known as reality testing) is carried out on a much less global, more mundane, and considerably more easily modifiable scale. Attributions of characteristics, not only of people but of events, is carried out constantly; your own attributions of characteristics about yourself, what you are doing, and about the immediate world surrounding you are present as you read this book (though, I hope, somewhat in the background). These attributions may be regarded as hypotheses, subject to empirical verification. Is there another person in the room with you? That is easily tested. If so, is he or she bored, indifferent, sleeping, studying—or consumed with rage, lust, and an insatiable desire to control you? These things are less easily tested, particularly the latter three, especially if your companion is sitting quietly reading a book. However, you can have confidence in your judgment that they are improbable. If your companion's possible boredom, indifference, or lust is of concern to you, you can ask him or her about their presence, and, in most situations, believe what he or she says. If your companion looks bored to you but says that he or she is impatient or angry or not bored but only mildly interested in his or her task, you make some slight modifications both in your attribution of what is going on here and now in the room and perhaps also in your attribution of characteristics of your companion (e.g., sometimes reports feeling OK when looking bored to me).

These are mundane transactions indeed, comprising the minutiae of experiencing. Yet it is difficulty in assessing the accuracy of one's attributes in such situations, in the mundane minutiae of life, that impair the individual's ability to function in a manner that he or she, and mental health professionals and others in that individual's interpersonal world, would agree is satisfying and healthy.

The difficulty may be regarded, for present purposes, as manifesting itself in two domains. One, by far the more common, is the failure to make any attributions at all to other people. Patients are characteristically self-absorbed, and the more self-absorbed they are, the greater the magnitude of psychopathology attributed to them by mental health professionals.[1] In such instances, therapy consists of

---

[1]Hence the therapist question "What kind of reaction do you expect from the group now that you've told us that?" is frequently met with "I have no idea," more so in inpatient than outpatient groups.

first enabling the patient to formulate, or to become aware of, attributions and outcomes, and then to evaluate the accuracy of his or her formulations.

The second domain, less common but by no means rare, includes the above discussion and involves both the making of unrealistic or faulty attributions and the evaluation of those attributions as valid. Some schizophrenic behaviors can be understood in terms of difficulties in the attribution of causality in both the physical and the interpersonal world; the evaluation of such faulty attributions as accurate; and the rejection of evidence to the contrary. The behaviors of some patients diagnosed as having borderline personality disorder can be understood in terms of difficulties in the attribution of affect and failure in the process of evaluation of the accuracy of attribution. Other disorders can be understood in similar terms.

A more extensive discussion of this theorizing and the testable hypotheses it can generate would take us too far afield. The point that I am making here is that whatever we call psychopathological or maladaptive can be understood in terms of the assessment of accuracy of one's attributions of characteristics to other people and to oneself.

Assessing the interpersonal outcomes of one's own behavioral patterns means, simply, looking at the effect that one's words and actions have on others and determining the extent to which that effect is desired or intended. As noted above, some people are so self-absorbed that they do not attend to interpersonal effects at all; their failure to do so is seen by mental health professionals as manifesting psychopathology, though others involved with such self-absorbed people may respond to them with anger, rejection, or withdrawal. Other individuals seem persistently puzzled by the effects of their actions on others; such puzzlement is one characteristic of patients diagnosed with borderline personality disorder (Grinker 1977).

Group therapy offers a forum in which the interpersonal outcomes of one's behaviors and behavioral patterns can be studied and discussed in some detail. Such study and discussion can influence the individual's assessments of interpersonal outcomes and his or her evaluation of the accuracy of such assessments. The mechanism through which this is accomplished involves feedback from the other group members about their reactions to the individual. A patient may discover, for instance, that behaviors intended to elicit nurturance in fact consistently provoke anger and that his or her own personal history and other factors have led to some confusion about nurturance and anger, so that the patient has characteristically assessed the angry response of others as being nurturing. The therapists and the other group members can sometimes lead the patient to evaluate his or her assessment of this interpersonal outcome (anger in response to nurturant-eliciting moves) as unfruitful or undesired, and can sometimes offer the patient the opportunity to develop new and more successful ways of eliciting the desired nurturance when it is appropriate to do so. The effective therapeutic factors in this situation involve *interpersonal learning* and perhaps *insight* on the part of the recipient, and *altruism* on the part of the other group members. These factors have been shown to be associated with positive outcome in group therapy (Bloch and Crouch 1985, Yalom 1985).

Assessing the possible goals and outcomes of others pertains to the accuracy of attribution of motivation and intent of other individuals primarily in relation to oneself but also in relation to others. As noted above, patients who are self-absorbed tend not to make such assessments at all. People who are narcissistic may have some tendency to assume that the goals and desired outcomes of others pertain largely to meeting narcissistic needs, while those who are paranoid may assume that the goals of others are malevolent, or will be unless something is done to avoid malevolent outcomes.

For most people most of the time, the assessment of possible goals and outcomes of others occurs in mundane interactions, even with significant others. A spouse's need for attention may be perceived as an insatiable desire to control; the outcome of the resulting interactions is likely to be negative for both partners. People misread each others' intentions all the time. Usually the misreading is of small consequence and corrected so readily that neither the misreading nor its correction are notable—like two people walking in opposite directions but headed for the same spot on the sidewalk, perceiving the collision course, and then both veering in the same direction; when this is perceived, each moves to his or her right (or left) and the collision is avoided. It is when such mundane intentions are misread (*he or she intends to collide with me or force me to give way*) that interpersonal difficulties arise. A similar kind of difficulty arises if person C consistently misreads the goals and outcomes of persons A and B in interaction with each other.

Group therapy is an interpersonal forum in which the validity or accuracy of the patient's assessment of the possible goals and desired outcomes of others can be checked out with those others. Group members will generally report, spontaneously or on request, their motivations and desired outcomes in mundane interactions with other group members. The question "Why did you do that?" or "What kind of response were you trying to get by saying that?" can yield information that is both credible and useful to the group, and can lead to exploration of how such assessments are made and how their accuracy might be enhanced. The therapeutic factor involved here has been described as *learning from interpersonal action* (Bloch and Crouch 1985).

Devising strategies and modifying behavioral patterns to produce more satisfying and adaptive interpersonal outcomes refers to the change in the patient's interpersonal behaviors resulting from improvement in his or her ability to assess the accuracy of attributions of characteristics to others and to his or her self and in assessing the most probable outcomes of his or her behavioral patterns as well as those of others. (Such change may also involve re-evaluation of the hedonic value of probable and alternative outcomes [Carson 1969], a point to be discussed later, but that is a technique common to both individual and group therapy.) Difficulties in devising effective strategies, and in adopting them, are frequently perceived by mental health professionals as manifesting psychopathology: the more difficult it seems for a patient to figure out what needs to change and how to change it, the more pathological he or she may be viewed by therapists and diagnosticians. The amount of help a patient may need in learning how to devise and implement effective strategies can then be understood in terms of the magnitude of pathology: the greater the disturbance, the more help the patient will need. Thus, hospitalized schizophrenic patients, for instance, may need considerable help in devising effective interpersonal strategies. Group therapy can provide opportunities for role-play and for behavior rehearsal, where the patient follows a script provided in considerable detail by the therapists ("Now tell Johnny that you are glad to see him"). Patients whose psychological distress and impairment in functioning are minimal and largely resulting from transient situational stress may also benefit from role-play and instruction, but are probably better able to devise effective strategies and modify existing ones on their own.

Whatever the level of distress or impairment, people come to mental health facilities at least in part because they are having some difficulty devising effective interpersonal strategies and implementing them. The exploration of interpersonal outcomes, so readily accomplished in group therapy, facilitates both change in interpersonal behavior within the group and the development of strategies for change in such behavior outside the group, with people who are not group members.

It is the facilitation of change in interpersonal behavior, and the establishment of strategies for maintaining such change, that is the most important purpose of group therapy. To accomplish this purpose, the therapists help the patients focus on the mundane interactions occurring here-and-now during the group sessions, helping them to identify those interpersonal components that are effective as well as those that need modification in order to produce desired outcomes. Thus, detailed exploration of a patient's personal history in the group is neither necessary nor particularly desirable. Nor is extended discussion of events and relationships outside of the group (reporting what happened there-and-then to others important to the patient but not to the group). The development of insight into the historical roots and underlying motivations influencing one's here-and-now perceptions and interactions has been shown to be of benefit to group members, as has the expression of intense affect; the therapeutic factors of *insight* and *catharsis* have been described by Bloch and Crouch (1985) and, in somewhat different language, by Yalom (1985). However, the benefits derived from the operation of these factors should not be regarded as ends in themselves, but rather as preceding and facilitating change in interpersonal behavior.

The facilitation of change involves an assessment of discrepancies. There may be discrepancies in the way the group member has organized his or her understanding of what happened in the past; discrepancies between his or her experience of himself or herself and the way others perceive his or her actions in the present, and he or she theirs; discrepancies between where he or she is now, in relation to needs, wants, and expectations, and where he or she would like to be. These discrepancies may be more visible or obvious to others than to the individual who experiences and maintains them; and they tend to be highlighted in emotionally intense interactions during the group sessions.

The assessment of discrepancies by the group cannot occur until the group has sufficient data about the individual. These data come from the individual's self-disclosure and from the group's own experience. Self-disclosure that is of particular importance to the individual has been shown to be associated with good outcome (patient improvement and satisfaction) in group therapy (Bloch and Crouch 1985, Yalom 1985). The importance to the individual of subsequent change in behavior may be related to the intensity of the interactions during which the disclosure occurred, and to the extent to which the disclosure is linked to self-esteem, self-evaluation, and to the individual's assessment of his or her ability to survive in the prevailing interpersonal atmosphere.

Once the individual has given the group the information it needs, either through discussion or through interaction, the group can help him or her to identify and reassess discrepancies. The group may then help the individual to develop new coping mechanisms (ways of relating) or to accomplish a reformulation of the psychological environment in such a way that the individual feels (and thus becomes) able to derive satisfaction and perhaps fulfillment with the coping mechanisms already in his or her response repertoire.

The task of the therapists is to guide the group toward facilitation of change. Thus the therapists' orientation should always be toward change in behavior. The probability of change is enhanced if the therapists direct the focus of the group toward that end. Without such change in behavior, the benefits derived by the patient from self-disclosure or catharsis are likely to be transient and quite difficult to maintain.

One final note: The emphasis this book places on behavioral disturbance and behavioral change should not be misunderstood as representing advocacy of a behavior therapy technology. Rather, behavior is emphasized because it is manifest, directly observable by all members of the group, and provides explicit rather than inferential information about other people. Intrapsychic disturbances, such as disturbances in affect, perception, and formal thought processes, are not emphasized here because, being intrapsychic, they are not amenable to close examination or assessment by the group. Behavior is *public*, while intrapsychic events remain private, hidden, unobservable. The group's own observations of the individual constitute the data it assesses as it helps the individual explore the discrepancies in life that brought him or her into therapy. Intrapsychic events, however compelling, are firsthand knowledge only to the individual experiencing them. The relationship between such events and external reality remains inaccessible to the group except through inference from observable behavior and from the individual's verbal report. Focusing on intrapsychic events may be fruitful in groups; a number of technical approaches to group therapy favor such an emphasis (Shaffer and Galinsky 1974). However, this focus does not provide the common experience readily and directly shared by the group that an emphasis on observable behavior offers. The present emphasis on behavior, then, stems from the fact that observable behavior constitutes the directly available experience of the interpersonal context of group. In that context, it is easier to deal with what can be seen than with what can only be inferred.

9

What to Focus on during a Group Therapy Session

In this chapter we return to the practical situation of the new group therapist, seated in a room with a co-therapist and optimally with four to eight patients. Even when people are sitting silently, there is considerably more going on in the room than is the case in individual therapy, and when group members are talking, there is so much happening in so many dimensions that it is difficult to determine what to focus on. This chapter addresses that concern.

There are three dimensions of interest that pose some quandaries for the novice therapist—and sometimes for the expert as well. These are (1) a focus on here-and-now versus there-and then, (2) a focus on the interpersonal versus a focus on the intrapsychic, (3) a focus on what is happening in the group (process) versus a focus on what is being said (content).

FOCUS ON HERE-AND-NOW VERSUS THERE-AND-THEN

The problem for the group therapist attempting to focus on what is going on here-and-now in the room is that not much is happening in the early sessions, which are likely to be characterized by long silences punctuated by therapist efforts to get some interactions going between people. You cannot very well ask people to focus on the silence, and if you comment that no one is talking, the response is most likely to be more silence.

The opening survey technique described in Chapter 4 is one way of handling the initial silence of group. Each member in effect makes a bid for the group's attention, and as this happens, you can rank order the bids in terms of their urgency or the patient's readiness to respond. Usually by the time you have invited the third group member to talk further about what he or she said during the opening survey, people are relaxed enough to initiate interaction without your prompting. Starting a group this way is a bit like starting an outboard motor or lawnmower: after a couple of vigorous pulls on the cord the engine coughs, and on the third or fourth pull it starts humming.

As patients begin to tell their stories, or the events that led them to the clinic or the group, or simply to report on what has happened to them during the past week, there is at least verbal activity, but it is focused on events outside the group. The following is an example of an announcement made by a patient just after the completion of the opening survey during the second session of a therapy group.

> My problem is that nobody likes me in the dormitory that I live in. They are all very cliquish there and they all know each other from high school. I try to be friendly with them but they just ignore me. I don't know why.

What follows, in such a group of college students, is a discussion of dormitory life. The group agrees that dorm life is difficult, that people are unfriendly, and that roommates, in particular, are hard to get along with. The conversation might then go on to other familiar gripes about college life: the food, the unfairness of the professors, difficulties in relationships with parents.

Usually when a group takes off like this in the second session (and sometimes in the first as well), nothing much comes of it in terms of behavioral change. The conversation is not different from the superficial, polite, and conventional talk that strangers or acquaintances engage in to while away the time. This kind of talk in a therapy group allows the group members to become better acquainted and less fearful of each other and of the group as a whole. Focusing on there-and-then may be interpreted as allowing group members to avoid talking about what is going on here-and-now between the group members, and as enabling them to avoid looking at the group as a microcosm of the interpersonal strategies and relationships characteristic of their lives outside the group. Such an interpretation is premature in the early sessions of group. The initial focus on there-and-then should be regarded as simply the ordinary and mundane social discourse that occurs among strangers in our society when they are attempting to broaden their relationships. (However, when the group has been meeting for some time, has progressed past the initial stages of group development, and when some significant disclosures have been made, the focus on a there-and-then topic may have a different kind of function and a different meaning.)

The therapist need not, and indeed should not, follow the verbal content of the group into there-and-then. The best way to avoid getting into there-and-then is to ask yourself the question, *What is the group doing at this moment* or *What is happening in the group right now* or simply, *What is going on?* The answers to these questions will be found by attending to what you can see going on in the group. What you will see, usually, is people sitting around talking. The talking has a purpose. In the early sessions of group, the there-and-then talking most likely serves the purpose of broadening the members' acquaintance with each other. That is (usually) what the group is doing. A comment to that effect by the group therapist would not be out of place.

In many clinical settings, the new clinician is introduced to group therapy as a junior co-therapist with a more senior clinician and in a group which has been meeting for some time. That is, the trainee rotating through the clinic does a rotation as a co-therapist. Starting a new group with an experienced co-therapist is considerably easier than coming into an ongoing one, which is very much like being the new kid on the block. You're walking into a web of ongoing relationships and gradually discovering what those relationship are and how the web is anchored.

In terms of here-and-now versus there-and-then, you can expect, as a new therapist in an ongoing group, that the first several sessions you attend will have a lot of there-and-then, if not about the patients' lives, then almost certainly about events that occurred in group prior to your entry and about which you therefore can say little or nothing. One function of the there-and-then in this situation is to maintain the group boundaries and to exclude the newcomer. A similar phenomenon is likely to occur when new patients are added to the group. The other group members will talk about events that occured in the past. Even though the events they discuss happened during the group sessions, the verbal content is nonetheless there-and-then since it does not pertain to what is going on between people in the room at the present moment. If the discussion persists for very long, therapist intervention may be needed.

FOCUS ON THE INTERPERSONAL RATHER THAN THE INTRAPSYCHIC

The shift from intrapsychic to interpersonal is the key to good technique and perhaps also to good outcome in group psychotherapy. Most clinicians come to group therapy after training in individual therapy. In individual therapy it is frequently appropriate to make inferences about and to discuss what is going on inside the patient's head: thoughts, feelings, fantasies, free associations, and the like, the specific focus depending on one's theories of personality, psychotherapy, and psychopathology. In group therapy it is essential to avoid making inferences about what is going on inside the patient's head and to focus instead on what is going on between people in the group. The theory described in Chapter 8 is intended to facilitate such an interpersonal focus.

The following example is taken from the second session of an outpatient group. The patient, Letty, is a 33-year-old unmarried library assistant with a very long history of psychiatric treatment (which is known to the therapists but not to the group) but no prior hospitalizations. In the opening survey, she was the last person to speak, and this is what she said:

> I feel awful. I feel like I'm falling apart. I'm having trouble sleeping. I can't get anything done at work. I'm in really bad shape and I don't know how I can go on—how things can go on like this.

The therapists, both of whom were relatively inexperienced, invited Letty to talk more about her distress, which she did. The more she talked, the more agitated she became, until she burst into tears and ran from the room. The rest of the group sat in stunned silence until she returned about five minutes later.

The therapists focused on Letty's intrapsychic distress and encouraged her to describe it further. From the interpersonal point of view, what the therapists should have done is acknowledge Letty's distress and then look at the interpersonal context created by her report of it. Because this occurred very early in the group's life, some modeling would probably have been appropriate. Hence, a therapist response might have been:

> You sound very distressed to me and I'm really concerned about what kind of shape you're in. What you're saying makes me want to help and to comfort you. I wonder how the other people in the group are reacting to what you're telling us. Is it OK with you if I ask them?

Such a comment focuses on the interpersonal effect of the disclosure. What is this patient trying to accomplish by telling the group of such a high level of distress at this point in the group's life? What kind of response is she trying to evoke? In a group of psychologically sophisticated patients, these questions could perhaps be asked directly. However in most groups these questions would result in puzzlement because it would not have occurred to Letty to consider either the effect her disclosures might have on the group or the kind of response she might hope for or might expect. The therapist intervention begins to orient her and the group toward the interpersonal context. (In this particular example, it would also be prudent for the therapists to evaluate the potential suicidality implied in Letty's statement that she does not know how she, or things, can go on as they have. Depending on how alarmed the therapists are, such evaluation might occur at once, during the group session, or immediately afterward, after the other group members have left. In addition, Letty's individual therapist should be notified.)

Interpersonal interactions have outcomes. The interpersonal context is changed by the interaction. People are not always aware of the probable or actual outcomes of their interactions. For the group therapist, it is important to attend to such outcomes. The outcome of Letty's disclosure in the above example was that people felt sorry for her and alarm at the magnitude of her distress. They wanted to comfort her but had no clue as to how to do so. At the same time, the group members were concerned at being placed in a group with someone who was so highly distressed, and at least a little puzzled about how to respond. The net effect of Letty's disclosure and subsequent behavior (running out of the room) was that the other group members were reluctant to engage with her or to interact with her. While this patient's report of distress could be understood as a plea for help, support, and attention, the outcome was an increase in interpersonal distance between her and the other group members. Letty had efficiently reproduced, in the group, a salient characteristic of her life outside the group, namely interpersonal isolation associated with urgent pleas for help.

People are generally skilled at producing the interpersonal outcomes that they desire or intend. Approval-dependent people know what to do to obtain approval; people with high dominance needs place themselves in positions where a high proportion of their interpersonal interactions involve dominance in one of its many manifestations. However, it is obviously true that one cannot always predict or control outcomes, that usually reliable interpersonal strategies do not always work, and that outcomes are sometimes surprising, unintended, and undesirable. When people realize that they regularly obtain undesirable interpersonal outcomes, or become aware of the emotional concomitants of those outcomes, they may seek the help of mental health professionals to modify the situation. The self-esteem of the patient in the above example was quite low, in part because of her interpersonal isolation and in part because her attempts to reduce that isolation were continually unsuccessful. The origins of both her low level of interpersonal skill and her low self-esteem could be traced back to her family and to her relationships with her parents and siblings as a young girl – relationships characterized by sexual abuse and horrifying physical violence. These events were being explored in her individual psychotherapy. In such a family, interpersonal strategies leading to increased interpersonal distance – to other family members leaving her alone or ignoring her – were probably highly adaptive. Once Letty left the family these same skills prevented her from forming relationships that might have offered sources of esteem-building, among other things.

Relationships among group members can be regarded as a microcosm of the pattern of interpersonal relationships of the members outside of group. Letty had begun, in the second session, to reproduce the interpersonal outcomes she had probably learned to obtain while still living with her family of origin. (She pursued this strategy with considerable tenacity in subsequent sessions.) Her interpersonal strategies could be understood in terms of early childhood trauma and as a manifestation of her psychopathology. Thinking of her interpersonal strategies in this way might be fruitful for the individual therapist but is not particularly helpful for the group therapist in maintaining a focus on what is going on between people. In the group, Letty's behavior could be understood as self-defeating: she asks for (and wants) help, sympathy, support, and the like, but is frequently unsuccessful in eliciting it. The task of the group therapist is to help Letty develop more successful strategies for obtaining the support she seeks.

The group therapist seeking to maintain his or her own interpersonal focus will find it helpful to attend carefully to the outcome of interpersonal interactions, both the moment-to-moment transactions between group members and the patterns of interacting that become more perceptible over some period of time. In evaluating such outcomes, two assumptions are particularly fruitful. One, as in the example of Letty, is that the patient does not know how *not* to produce undesired outcomes. Her repertoire of interpersonal strategies is quite small. She does what she knows how to do because she lacks alternative strategies and because what she does know how to do had, at some point in the past, adaptive value for her. In these circumstances, the therapists (after determining that the patient indeed does not desire the outcome) might seek to help her develop strategies more likely to produce a desired outcome.[1]

The second assumption is that the negative interpersonal outcomes are in fact desired by the patient but that they do not produce the desired result or meet the need the patient is attempting to meet. One example of this kind of interpersonal move is the patient who seeks angry interchanges in the belief or hope that hostile interactions can somehow meet nurturant needs. Such patients are skilled at generating anger. They may reciprocate enthusiastically or they may assume the role of the self-righteous victim. While their characteristically angry and anger-generating interactions can be understood in terms of the eruption of an internal seething cauldron of anger, it will be more fruitful for the group therapist to view the hostility-provoking behaviors as interpersonal maneuvers that produce unsatisfying outcomes, and thus to retain an interpersonal focus.

To sum up: focusing on the outcome of interpersonal interactions allows you to discern the intent and sometimes the motivation of the patient, when those are not clear from the interaction itself.

---

[1]In this example, if Letty were to be successful in eliciting support and nurturance, it is unlikely that she would know what to do with it. Lacking that knowledge, it would be difficult for her to develop strategies for maintaining supportive and nurturing relationships; but that is another chapter in the story of her journey toward interpersonal effectiveness and better mental health.

Negative outcomes may occur either because the patient does not know how to produce more positive ones or because the negative outcome itself is in some way reinforcing to the patient, however temporarily. In any event, focusing on interpersonal outcomes and strategies helps maintain therapist orientation toward interpersonal rather than intrapsychic events, and thus to retain focus on what is happening here and now in the group between people.

FOCUS ON GROUP PROCESS
RATHER THAN VERBAL CONTENT

Group process refers to what is going on in the group, as distinct (to some extent) from what is being said. It is the non-verbal envelope within which the verbal meanings of the group are contained. Thus, it is what the group is doing rather than what the group is saying.

A group is an abstraction. It consists of an aggregation of individuals. These individuals influence one another; each person influences all the others. Some group members are more influential than others across group sessions. Within sessions, patterns and levels of influence change as the experience unfolds. Group process refers to the patterns of interpersonal influence exerted simultaneously by each group member on all the others. Group process interventions by the therapist generally address what is occurring between or among individuals rather than what may be going on inside people's heads or what they are telling each other.

If group is an abstraction, then so also is group process. The concept, group process, refers to a conceptual tool to help group members describe what is going on as the pattern of mutual influences unfolds over time. Because the term *group process* refers to a concept rather than an entity (it is a name for some components of experiencing), the definition of the concept varies as a function of the conceptualizer's theory of group therapy or of group development. I think most theorists would agree that process refers to what is going on in the room, as distinct from what is being said. Theory provides the group leader with a descriptive language to use in describing group process. Theory also guides the group leader toward some particular aspects of what is happening in the room—for instance, the relationship between the group and the leader, or what is going on in the group as a whole, or what kinds of interactional patterns are occuring among the group members. Descriptions of group process (defined as what is going on in the room) are theory-bound, not theory-free. The theory presented in this book is interpersonal and the process interventions discussed here reflect that orientation.

The most common technical error of the novice therapist, and sometimes of the more experienced therapist as well, is to become focused on and interact with the group on the basis of what is being said rather than what is going on in the group: to become involved with content rather than process. It is the ability to articulate process that constitutes the exercise of technical skill in psychotherapy, whether individual or group.

If process is defined as what is going on, as distinct from what is being said, then a whole host of new problems and quandaries can potentially present themselves to the group therapist. How do you know what is going on? Experience is multidimensional. Which dimension is process? Which dimension best describes what is going on? What is the right answer? How can you tell? What if you pick the wrong dimension? What if you don't know what is really going on?

These are questions that the new group therapist typically asks, inwardly if not aloud. Fortunately, answers are at hand. In the first place, when you start to lead a therapy group, you may as well plan on being quite confused initially: there is more going on than you can keep track of, you're likely to get totally focused on content rather than process, and as you begin to focus on process you are not likely to be able to keep track of all that is going on at that level. This period of initial confusion can last for two or three months, no matter how well read you are. Doing your first group with a more experienced co-therapist is usually highly advantageous because your more experienced colleague can help you to minimize and shorten the time of total confusion. Observing a group for a while before you start leading one is also helpful but is no substitute for co-leading with a more experienced group therapist. Good supervision provides both support and further reduction of utter confusion.

The initial confusion is gradually replaced by a growing sense of what is going on. Most new therapists have little confidence in their first few perceptions or conceptualizations of what is happening in the room and in the group. They tend to watch the more experienced therapist, whose actions generally confirm their own hypotheses about process. The result of these confirmations, over time, is usually an increase in therapist confidence. The next task is to begin to formulate interventions and to do so in a timely manner. How does one articulate process without getting into verbal content, there-and-then, or speculations about what is going on inside someone's head? The answer to this question is presented in the next chapter.

10

How to Formulate Therapeutic Interventions in the Second and Subsequent Sessions

The second session will probably begin like the first: in silence. The group members assemble silently in the waiting room. They barely acknowledge each other's presence. They walk wordlessly into the group room. There they sit immobile, as before the first session, not looking at anyone in particular, waiting for the group to begin.

This silence is best understood as a reaction of the group members to the newness of the situation, a manifestation of their uncertainty as to how to proceed and of their reluctance to interact with people who are still strangers. Outgoing, extraverted individuals with good interpersonal skills are seldom referred for group therapy. If left unattended by the therapists, the initial silence of the second session may continue for a needlessly long time, fostering anxiety, uncertainty, and dissatisfaction among the group members. Most people are unwilling or reluctant to come to an event that involves their sitting silently for an indefinite time in a room full of strangers about whom they know little or nothing. It is therefore prudent to break the silence and, as with the first session, to provide structure and seek to reduce the group's anxiety.

One way of breaking the silence is to introduce new group members, if there are any. If there are one or two new members, the group leader should do the introduction. Introduction of the new patient(s) does not involve revelation of the patient's case history. The concern of the group is likely to be about how the new patient will relate to each of the group members. Why the new patient might relate in one way rather than another is probably of greater concern to the therapist than to the group.

With three or more new members, however, you have in effect another initial session of the group. You may wish to follow the procedure for starting that is described in Chapter 4, including a brief reminder about the procedural guidelines. Each newcomer is likely to assume that he or she is the only one and that everyone else in the room already knows all the others and knows what to do. Therefore you should indicate that there are several new members and who they are, and then ask each person, including those who were present last week, to introduce himself or herself.

An example of what the group leader might say in order to start the session is:

> I think we should start. We have two new members today, Pat [*indicates with gesture*] and Dave. I'd like for each person to say your first name, and to say a word or two about how you're feeling right now.

The specific wording is not very important and should suit your own style. Asking each person to say his or her name is part of the introduction of the new members. It also serves to remind the other group members of names that may have been forgotten or never learned because of the high anxiety that characterizes the first session.

If there are no new group members, the opening survey technique described in Chapter 4, without the review of procedural guidelines, gives each person an opportunity to bid for the group's attention and perhaps for its solace; and it allows patients in acute discomfort some opportunity to let that be known. In addition it gives you some clues as to what to do next, in terms of inviting the person who has made the clearest bid for the group's attention to proceed.

This is the point at which all the work of referral, screening, and selection of group members begins to pay off. If you have assembled a group with an eye toward how these patients will interact with each other, there will be at least one patient who is likely to seek the group's attention, to begin engaging the other members, and to begin the therapeutic work of the group. The problem is that if you haven't done a group before, you may find it difficult to predict, from a series of individual screening interviews, how people will interact once they are all together.

Groups that are easiest to get started, and which will frequently start by themselves with little therapist intervention, are those comprised of intelligent and highly functional people whose need for therapy is minimal, stemming from transient situational or developmental stress. Such groups are most likely to be found in student mental health or psychological service clinics on university campuses. The higher the level of interpersonal pathology and the lower the level of psychological sophistication, the more difficult groups are to get started and the more active the intervention required of the group leaders. Thus, the most difficult groups to start and to lead are those consisting of chronically hospitalized state hospital patients. Chronicity serves as a good indicator both of prognosis and of the magnitude of difficulty you are likely to experience in attempting to get group members to relate to one another.

Regardless of the level of patient pathology and the clinical setting in which the group meets, your concern as a therapist is likely to be, What if I complete the opening survey and there are no clues as to what to do next? What if no one has made a bid for the group's attention and the group again has fallen silent?

How do you get the silent group moving? What on earth are you supposed to say now? *What does the book say?* The book, or at least this one, says that at this point your own anxiety is likely to be at least as high as that of the patients. The difference between you and them is that you are generally somewhat better at doing something to reduce anxiety than they are, and that this is what you should do before you go on.

Ideally, you begin with some topic that has been left over from the first session. Leftover topics are those which someone—either patient or therapist—has indicated during the first session would be taken up again at this time. Sometimes there aren't any such topics, and if there are, they seldom occupy much of the group's time. Once again, silence.

It will be difficult for you to avoid feeling that you should be doing *something*, even if your supervisor has counseled explicitly against breaking the silence. The position taken here is that most silences, particularly those during the first few meetings, are not likely to be therapeutic and that it is incumbent upon the therapist to break the silence if the group does not.

As you look around the room, you are likely to see what you saw at the beginning of the first session: there is not much eye contact, people look at the walls or off into the indeterminate distance, or at the floor or at their hands. The room is still, except perhaps for the small movement of hand or foot that is like the twitching of a waiting cat's tail. Yet there are differences in patients' readiness to engage with you. How to find them, how to find the right door to knock on when all the doors look alike?

The answer to that question is most likely to be found in the very small, almost imperceptible cues that people emit more or less inadvertently through posture, gesture, facial expression, and movement. When the group interaction is verbal, changes in characteristic speech rhythms and syntax, as well as in tone of voice, may provide you with hints about the affective state of the individual or the group. In the silent group, look now at the way people are sitting. It is reasonable to assume that the person who looks poised for action probably is, and you should knock first on that door. The patient who sits curled up into herself, legs crossed, arms folded, hands grasping her own arms, may be more prepared to defend than to interact. Sometimes a very slight movement of the shoulder – as though some motion was started and then inhibited before the patient was irretrievably committed to it – is all the indication you will get.

What interpersonally sensitive therapists sometimes experience at times like these involves a rather complex and swift intermixture of perception, intuition, and cognition. The perceptions are most likely to be visual, involving your concentrating on the smallest details of observable behavior. Intuition, which is subjective and potentially idiosyncratic, is difficult to describe. It generally includes perception and interpretation of one's own internal processes, an awareness of minute changes in the magnitude or location of tension or fear or arousal. It may include perception of a particular affective state and is usually not verbal. Cognition is the verbal rational component of subjective experience. Talent in psychotherapy involves integration of all of this into a verbal formulation or a behavioral interaction.

FORMULATING THERAPEUTIC INTERVENTIONS

In general, the group therapist faces three major procedural problems. These are (1) what to pay attention to, (2) what to do about what is paid attention to, and (3) when to do it. The theories discussed in the preceding chapters provide some general guidelines about these procedural problems. During the group session itself, a much more detailed road map is needed because the therapist must resolve the three procedural problems on a moment-to-moment basis as the experience or *process* of the group unfolds.

Under these conditions it is fruitless to try to remember the ten therapeutic factors (Chapter 7) or the nine stages of group development (Beck 1983), or to attempt to evaluate the extent to which the group members are introjecting the group leader (Chapter 6). A simpler cognitive task is required if the therapist is to be able to accurately monitor what is going on moment to moment, decide quickly how to understand it, and formulate a response to it, all in the blink of an eye. Experienced group therapists do this sort of quite rapid work all the time, and novice group therapists are frequently astounded at both the perspicacity of the more experienced therapists and the speed with which therapeutic interventions are formulated. What follows is a description of how this apparently magical therapeutic facility is accomplished. Like any complex technical skill, it takes some time to master, and the new clinician should not expect to do it with either the speed or the elegance typical of the more experienced therapist. If you are doing one group meeting weekly, and if you have adequate supervision, it would be fair to allow yourself a year to come up to speed.

What to Pay Attention to

When you are first learning how to do groups, pay attention to what you see and hear going on in the room, nothing more. As your skill in attending to these sensory dimensions grows, add a third one: pay attention to your own internal reactions to what you see and hear.

Attending to what you see going on, and describing it, turns out to be surprisingly difficult. The process of attending to what is going on may be regarded as having four components: observation, inference, conclusion, and interpretation. *Observation* refers to the sensory input. *Inference* transcends the immediate sensory input and is a guess or hypothesis about what underlies what you are seeing. Generally inference refers to something you think may be going on inside someone's head. *Conclusion* refers to the sense you make of what you see, given the inferences drawn from the sensory data. *Interpretation* includes the trans-situational aspects of what is going on, including its historical context and possible implications for future interactions. These four elements are also the components of therapist interventions, a point discussed more fully below.

Most of the time what you see, especially in the early sessions of a group, is people sitting around; ideally they are talking. If you were to report what you see, you could say, "I see people sitting around talking." That would be true, but not helpful. Let's be more specific. You might say, "Ed is being angry with Linda." But you don't *see* Ed's anger. What you see is Ed speaking loudly and rapidly, eyes flashing, informing Linda in some detail of what he regards as her deficits. From these *observations* you *infer* that Ed is angry with Linda. Although this kind of interaction is not likely to occur in the early sessions of a new group (except perhaps in couples therapy), the first group experience of many therapists is coming into a group that has already been meeting for some time. Emotionally intense interactions between group members may occur at once or within a week or two after a new therapist enters.

Perhaps a more typical observation for the early sessions of group has to do with people looking anxious or sad. Again, you can't *see* anxiety or sorrow. Those are, or may be, things going on inside someone. All you can see is the behavior of the client, and from that behavior you *infer* the presence of anxiety or sadness. If you are going to say anything about it, the intervention would be to report your observation and inference: *You look sad to me.*

An intervention that begins with therapist observation and inference is a good deal easier to understand and respond to than an intervention that begins with conclusion or interpretation or something else. You might say to a patient, "Why are you sad?" only to find that the patient does not feel particularly sad, was not aware that he or she looks sad, and has no way in the world to answer your question. But "You look sad to me" is an invitation to the patient to talk about how he or she feels, to deny that he or she is sad, or even to ask you why you think so.

A conclusion is the sense or meaning you make of what you see. As you look around the group at the beginning of the second session, you may see one patient leaning forward, eyeing you intently, poised on the edge of her chair. That's your observation. You might infer that the patient wants to say something. (You can never *see* what a patient wants; wants are always inferred.) You might conclude that the patient is trying to catch your eye in order to be called upon; a conclusion is an hypothesis about what is going on in the present situation.

Based on that conclusion, you might interpret the patient's apparent readiness to respond as an intolerance of silence, as a tendency to be an initiator or to take the lead, or as an eagerness to take control of situations. Like inferences and conclusions, these are hypotheses. Interpretations are trans-situational generalizations. They involve making some generalization from the present situation to other situations, usually in the future but sometimes in the past, if your theory is historically oriented.

What to pay attention to, then, is what you see and hear, and your own internal reactions (both thoughts and feelings) to what you see and hear. It is difficult but most helpful to keep in mind the distinction between what you observe and what you infer.

What to Do about What You've Paid Attention to

The answer to the question of what to do with what you see going on in the group is answered differently by different theorists and depends on such things as the stage of group development. Most theorists advocate some level of therapist activity initially, but vary in terms of how rapidly to become less active. In the present discussion, we are concerned with the first few sessions of a therapy group, when the therapist is necessarily concerned with establishing group boundaries, structure, norms, and atmosphere, and is therefore quite active.

Your decision about what to do with what you have paid attention to will be influenced by your concept of your role as a therapist, as a *group* therapist. The concept of therapist role in group therapy from several psychoanalytic viewpoints is discussed in Klein, Bernard, and Singer (1992). Your concept of that role should come from your theory. If you have not done much therapy before, you may find it difficult to adopt the kind of role that your theory would suggest and then to generate interventions from that point of view.

The role that the group is most likely to perceive you as filling is that of *mental health expert*. The group members expect you to know how to do groups. Patient conceptions of therapist roles differ at least as much as therapist conceptions of their own roles differ. What the various patient concepts of therapist role are likely to have in common, at least initially, is an assumption of therapist competence and expertise.

At least in the initial sessions of the group (coming into an ongoing group as a new therapist is somewhat different), it will be most fruitful if you will assume that role. The patients come to the group session with differing problems and varying levels of motivation and enthusiasm for the therapeutic enterprise. Nonetheless, they are there, seeking to benefit from your expertise.

What your expertise consists of, at this early point, is your ability to say what you see going on in the room here and now between people. That is, to report your observations of what people are *doing* in the room at the moment. The task is conceptually simple but requires some practice to accomplish consistently. Consider the following example:

> Barbara was describing to the group her troubled relationship with her mother, which is what had led her to seek therapy. As she talked, Mike began to fidget and squirm, his brow furrowed, his lips pursed. He crossed his legs and drew them up, arms crossed in front of him, and as Barbara finished her story, he began intently studying the nearest wall. At that point the therapist said, "Mike, I see that you're uncomfortable about what Barbara is saying. Would you like to tell us about it?"

What the therapist saw was Mike squirming around, looking grimly away from the group. She inferred that he was uncomfortable about something and concluded that it was what Barbara was talking about that was making him uncomfortable. Her intervention was based on her conclusion. An intervention based on observation and inference would have been preferable: "Mike, you're moving around as though you're uncomfortable," or "You look uncomfortable to me" makes it clear that the concept of discomfort is the therapist's and that she is checking it out with the patient.

The answer to the problem of what to do with what you have paid attention to, then, is simply *to report your observations and inferences from the standpoint of your role as mental health expert.* Early in the life of a group, or early in your career as a group therapist, that is all you need do; and it will be difficult enough. As the group matures, as your skill grows, it will be possible (and easier) to formulate conclusions and then interpretations. But early on, as in the second session, conclusions and interpretations are difficult because you don't have enough information about or experience with this particular aggregation of individuals.

When to Do It

The timing of interventions is part of the art of therapy. Offering an intervention too soon frequently puzzles the group; too late may result in a perfectly sound intervention being ignored or dismissed. Sometimes the window of opportunity for an intervention is quite wide; sometimes it is narrow. However, the interval during which an intervention would be at its most potent is seldom as narrow as you might fear.

In my experience, novice group therapists seem to go through five stages in formulating what to say and when to say it. The first stage is one of confusion, because of the complexity of the stimulus flux. More is going on in group than is possible to keep track of, think about, and draw some conclusions from. The second stage is the process described above in terms of making observations, drawing inferences, and perhaps formulating conclusions. The third stage is putting those observations and inferences into words but not saying them aloud. During this stage, your (more experienced) co-therapist is likely to say something quite similar to what you are thinking, and to say it before you can get the words out. Hearing your co-therapist say it tends to be validating and reassuring for you, whatever pressure you may be feeling to carry more of the load by becoming more verbally active. The fourth stage involves having the intervention on the tip of your tongue but waiting for just the right moment to say it. The fifth and final stage is reached when you say what you have in mind, in a timely fashion.

For the inexperienced group therapist, the largest obstacles to making timely interventions appear to be (1) fear of saying the wrong thing, and (2) looking for just the right moment to say something.

Fear of Saying the Wrong Thing

This fear is associated with lack of self-confidence. The magnitude of the fear may be related to personal factors, the therapist's anticipation of possible consequences of saying the wrong thing, the level of perceived support or punitiveness from one's co-therapist and/or supervisor, and other situational factors. As to personal factors, some people seem naturally more self-confident than others. For most, self-confidence grows with increasing knowledge and experience in new tasks and situations. If you are leading a group that meets weekly, allow about three months to begin feeling some self-confidence. In leading groups that meet more frequently, the time of maximum discomfort may be shorter.

The consequences of saying the wrong thing are usually overestimated by inexperienced group therapists. Such consequences may include feeling bad (foolish, stupid, incompetent, boorish, weird) and the fear of being thought foolish, incompetent, boorish, weird, unfeeling, by one's co-therapist, supervisor, and the group members. In addition, fear of saying the wrong thing may be experienced as fear of saying something that would be damaging to the group or to an individual group member.

The most probable consequence of saying the wrong thing (whatever that means) is indeed that you will feel bad, foolish, and so on, for a time. Everyone has said the wrong thing (however you define it) at some time, and the world did not come to an end. How bad you feel and for how long will depend on personal factors and also on such situational factors as the skill of your co-therapist (to repair or smooth over, if you have really made a gaffe) and the supportiveness or punitiveness of your supervisor. It's likely that you have already survived a number of instances where you have felt bad about saying the wrong thing; you'll survive this one too.

The fear of looking bad to others seems to be based on the untenable assumption that others' opinions of you are quite labile. Thus, saying the wrong thing one time may result in a permanent or persisting loss of esteem, respect, good opinion, support, liking or affection, and so on. Concomitant with this assumption is another, that people (co-therapists, supervisors) are predisposed to think poorly of you and will do so unless your performance is estimable. These twin assumptions almost never hold up under scrutiny. Technical errors early in your career as a group therapist are more likely to be interpreted by others (even patients if they are aware of your newness) as stemming from inexperience, not stupidity, and the lability of others' opinions of you is unlikely to be greater than the lability of your opinions about them.

Fear of saying the wrong thing is magnified by the misconception sometimes held by new therapists—those with little experience in either individual or group therapy—that there are only one or two right things to say, but many things that are wrong. Actually, the reverse is true: There are very few things you might say that would really be wrong to say, the number of technical errors you might commit is not only finite but small, and the range of things that are both technically correct and "right" is virtually unlimited.

The fear of saying something that would be damaging to the group, or to a group member, appears to be rooted in the misconception that negative (wrong) interventions are quite powerful, while positive (correct) interventions are weak. This assumption vastly overrates the power of the therapist and underestimates the power of the group member to evaluate and to handle therapist interventions. On closer examination, the fear of saying something damaging has an element of inadvertence: it is the fear of saying something that then turns out to be damaging, and you are not sure what that might be, so you don't say anything, or you wait until you are sure it won't do damage, at which point it's too late.

One way of combatting this fear is to stay with the construction of interventions described above: say what you see going on in the room between people at this time, and whatever you may infer from what you see. It is hard to say something that's likely to be damaging if you follow that procedure. Another way of dealing with this fear is to consider the possible outcomes. One of the worst possible outcomes would be that a patient would become upset. Groups are usually supportive, and if you say something that upsets a patient, he or she is likely to get considerable support from the group at the time. In addition you are likely to get some support afterward, if needed, from your co-therapist or supervisor.

So, if you look at it, the probability of saying the wrong thing is minimal, and if you do it, the outcomes are not likely to be as negative as you would fear. Thinking through the possible consequences of really goofing allows you to see those consequences more realistically and perhaps helps make it easier for you to offer interventions in a timely fashion before you're absolutely certain that you're saying just exactly the right thing. If you wait for that certainty you'll be forever silent.

Looking for Just the Right Moment to Say Something.

In the early sessions of a new group, there are likely to be a lot of silences. These silences are like stepping-stones in the verbal stream. In the first few sessions of a group, the stones are usually large and close together. As the group members become more familiar with each other, with you, and with their roles, the stepping-stones become smaller and farther apart. Consequently, it is easier to say something, to break into the verbal stream, earlier in the group's life. Unfortunately, there's usually less going on at such times, so it's harder to think of something to say. Later on it is not as easy to say something because there are fewer openings, breaks in the verbal stream, pauses where you might begin to talk without interrupting a group member. And when such breaks do occur, you may find that your co-therapist will get there first. In addition, there are some theories of group therapy that discourage therapist intervention, regarding therapist silence as a virtue. It seems that there are more reasons for remaining silent than for speaking. From this point of view, the right moment to say something almost never appears.

That might be true, in one sense: The exactly right moment to say something seldom announces itself. If you wait for it to appear, you are likely to be less verbally active than is optimal. Remember that the group members come to the group sessions at least in part to avail themselves of your expertise. One aspect of your expertise, even early in your career as a group therapist, is your ability to say what you see going on in group, in a non-judgmental manner, as described above. Although it could be argued that expertise consists in knowing when to remain silent, new group therapists have not usually developed that level of expertise. For them, the opposite problem is much more salient: figuring out when to say something.

If the exactly right time to say something is not obvious, then what you are left with is the necessity of speaking at a time that may not be optimal. To do that, you have to be willing to risk saying something at the wrong time: too early or too late. The less clinical experience you have, the more likely you are to say it too late. When you say something too late, the response to your intervention may be minimal or even ignored. When you say something too early, the group members may be puzzled or distracted. In either case, if your timing is off you are not likely to do much damage, just as the amount of damage stemming from saying the wrong thing is likely to be considerably less than you fear. Given the propensity of new group therapists for tardy rather than premature interventions, the answer to the question of when to say it is, *as soon as you can*. And that frequently means, as soon as you have enough self-confidence to say it at a less than optimal moment.

Timing is an important variable in therapy, difficult to teach and difficult to learn. Poor timing can rob a potent intervention of its impact. Good timing helps to make a group session an experience of artistry. A sense of timing in group therapy is learned by trial and error, more so than in individual therapy. The task of the supervisor is to help the student to see that errors in timing are not fatal and that the course of events may be slowed but is seldom stopped by poor timing. The art of therapy is knowing when to work hardest at helping patients to find what is true. If you are new to the art, allow yourself a year to get comfortable with the task of saying what you know to be true, and doing it at a moment that may be less than optimal.

11

The Co-therapist Relationship

In Chapter 1, I discussed briefly some factors relating to the choice of a co-therapist. In this chapter I will examine some aspects of the relationship between co-therapists that are likely to be of particular concern to the novice.

It has been assumed more or less implicitly throughout this book that groups are, and should be, led by two therapists rather than one. There is general agreement in the group therapy literature that novice group therapists should co-lead. In the clinic settings in which most group therapy is done, both empirical and clinical-anecdotal studies are concerned with maximizing the advantages and minimizing the disadvantages of co-therapy, while the question of whether or not to do co-therapy at all, after training, has faded into the past (Berne 1966, Davis and Lohr 1971).

The advantages and disadvantages of co-therapy have been nicely summarized by the Russells (Russell and Russell 1980). Their list covers virtually all the topics covered in the co-therapy literature.

Advantages include (1) a good teaching method; (2) a useful device for role modelling; (3) a source of support in the face of powerful psychopathology; (4) it dilutes the drain caused by very pathological groups;

(5) it affords continuity of care; (6) it clarifies transference and counter-transference problems; and (7) a co-therapist acts as a mirror, foil, and sonar screen.

Disadvantages include (1) diluted or confused transference; (2) an expensive use of scarce therapeutic time; (3) it increases the possibility of forming counterproductive alliances; (4) the choice of co-therapist is frequently involuntary; and (5) erotic issues in cotherapy arise and need to be handled. [p. 401]

Common sense would suggest that a new group therapist begin to co-lead with a more experienced therapist. There are advantages and disadvantages to such a model, and outside of clinics with a primary training mission it may be difficult to adhere to. In primarily service settings, co-therapy with an equally inexperienced therapist may be the only choice available. Rice and colleagues (1972) studied the relationships between experienced and inexperienced co-therapists in couples co-therapy. They found that inexperienced and experienced therapists had different personal therapeutic styles and different preferences for the therapeutic styles of their co-therapists. The more experience the therapists had, the less satisfied they tended to be with having a co-therapist—though it should be emphasized that this finding pertains to couples therapy and may have limited generalizability to a group therapy situation. In addition, Rice and colleagues found a relationship between therapist comfort and acceptance in the co-therapy relationship and subjectively rated effectiveness of co-therapy.

THE SUPERVISOR AS CO-THERAPIST

The advantage of doing a first group with your supervisor is that you get to see at first-hand how group is done, without having to shoulder the responsibility for doing it right. On the other hand, performance anxiety may inhibit you: if you make an error, it will be under the very eyes of your supervisor, and you may fear that the consequences of such errors may be career-threatening as well as embarrassing. Some authors caution against the supervisor or staff member pairing with a trainee (Bowers and Gauron 1981, Poey 1985) while others feel that the disadvantages can be overcome (Van Atta 1969). Alpher and Kobos (1988) see the training relationship as gradually evolving into an egalitarian, collegial relationship. One view of the developmental stages of co-therapy relationships has been described by Dick, Lessler, and Whiteside (1980).

While the literature is somewhat mixed on the issue of supervisor–trainee co-therapist pairing, reports of equal-status cotherapist pairs are generally favorable (Friedman 1973, Hellwig and Memmot 1974). The problem of two co-therapists of equal status, both doing their first group, can be compared to a surgical procedure in which both the surgeon and assistant surgeon are performing their first operation. Even if they have watched many other operations first, the difference between watching and doing is considerable. In addition, new and unforeseen problems are likely to crop up—problems the more experienced clinician can deal with easily, but which tend to pose formidable quandaries for the novice.

The problem of two novice therapists doing their first group together is further compounded by the difficulty in many clinics of arranging for new therapists to observe existing therapy groups before starting their own group. That is less of a problem in clinics with a primary training mission, as in college campus or medical center settings. But in clinics with a primary service mission, as in many community mental health clinics, administrators may be quite reluctant to permit staff therapists to observe other therapists doing group for any length of time. Under these conditions the pairing of a trainee or novice group therapist with one who is more experienced is essential.

The ideal, then, is a short group with your supervisor as co-therapist, followed by a longer group with a friend of equal status and experience as co-leader. Thus your first experience as a group leader should be in the position of assistant therapist.

Usually, as an assistant, you will go through four distinct stages.

In the first stage, you will feel in awe of your co-therapist, who appears confident, relaxed, knowledgeable, and infinitely resourceful, while you yourself feel quite puzzled as to what to do or say, are nervous or anxious, and utterly unable to come up with any comment worth uttering.

In the second stage of such an assistantship, you begin to have some idea of what cues your co-therapist is paying attention to, begin to see what he or she does with them, and, toward the end of this stage, may be able to predict approximately what he or she will say or do. Post-group discussion facilitates this process. Videotape, if it is available, allows you to focus in some detail on the relationship between what your co-therapist perceives as happening in group and what he or she does about it. As you begin to feel that you have some idea of what is going on, you may find that you are talking more, and if you are an especially bold person you may even initiate some interaction. If you tend toward being intropunitive, however, you may still upbraid yourself for not carrying your share of the load.

Implicit in these first two stages is the notion that everything that your supervisor-co-leader does is *right*, and is done with a skill and flair and ingenuity you cannot ever hope to match. If your supervisor has had a great deal of group experience, the perceived unattainability of his or her level of competence is likely to be greater than if he has only two or three years of experience. The tendency of novice therapists is to forget that it takes time, effort, and a great deal of supervised experience to develop skill and smoothness in group therapy. It can be painful and frustrating to have to learn to walk when your supervisor is loping along, graceful as an antelope, and apparently without effort.

In the third stage you see what needs doing, formulate how to do it—what you want to say, and to whom—and then hesitate until your co-therapist goes ahead and does it. At first, your co-therapist goes ahead because he or she is faster at seeing what to do—or, rather, because it takes you longer to get there than it does your co-therapist. Or you find that you are getting there at about the same time, but it is as though the words stick in your throat: what if you said the wrong thing? With your supervisor as co-therapist, the consequences of saying the wrong thing, or of sounding *dumb*, might be serious, since he or she is also evaluating you and his or her evaluation may have considerable bearing on your life. Low self-confidence, uncertainty, and cautious weighing of words before speaking may become magnified, with the result that you become even more hesitant than usual (or, if you're not usually hesitant, you find yourself being so now) and you have another opportunity to upbraid yourself for lacking all of those qualities your supervisor possesses in abundance.

Here again the post-group discussion is an essential component of learning how to do groups. A lot of paragraphs in treatises on technique begin with *The therapist should.* . . . Here, there is a *The supervisor should.* . . . The supervisor should be supportive of the "assistant therapist" and should encourage the development of self-confidence. In the post-group discussion, the supervisor should encourage the student to take risks, and perhaps should explore with him or her some of the consequences of saying the wrong thing. Students frequently anticipate catastrophic consequences of errors in timing, in conceptualization of what is going on, and in the application of technique. Errors are seldom catastrophic when you work on a short-term basis with outpatients. If your propensity for making catastrophic errors were as high as you fear, you probably would not have been admitted to the program of clinical training you are in. Your supervisor knows these things, and these he or she should communicate to you as frequently as necessary during the post-group discussion sessions.

The fourth stage is one in which you are initiating interactions, are guiding the group at least some of the time, and find yourself working with, rather than passively assisting, your co-therapist. You are perceiving what is going on and what to do about it quickly enough that your co-therapist can now afford to wait for you to formulate and take appropriate actions. And then there comes the time in the post-group discussion when your supervisor says something like, "I'm really glad you did what you did with Joan. I hadn't seen that, hadn't thought of that, and you did really well." You are adding your voice and your skills to those of your supervisor at least some of the time, and you may begin to feel that you are carrying your weight. You may still feel utterly lost at times, but you will more and more frequently retain the sense of being able to at least know what is going on and what your supervisor-co-therapist is likely to do next.

How long it takes you to get through these stages depends in part on the group, in part on your supervisor, and in part on you. If the group is a good one, verbally active, not too hostile, not too intense, and without a great deal of psychopathology, it will be easier than if these characteristics do not obtain. If your supervisor facilitates learning as well as healing, he or she will gradually relinquish the senior position and will not only allow you, but also help you, to grow. Alpher and Kobos (1988) have described a similar progression toward a collegial working relationship. McMahon and Links (1984) describe six stages of co-therapy development and relate them to stages of group process.

If you have talent and your self-esteem is not pathologically low, you will find it possible to take risks and thus build self-confidence earlier than if you had little talent and risk taking were therefore associated with failure. To get from stage 1 to stage 4, from silent awe to participatory co-therapy, frequently takes about a school year. It may take you less time, or more. In any event, the pace is not solely dependent on you. Doing two or three different groups during the same time does not seem to speed up the process of growth. Time is important; it takes time to integrate the complexities of a therapy group in such a way that they become manageable and manipulable.

When the group is not a good one, or the supervisor does not facilitate learning (worst is a supervisor who is competitive), or you are convinced that you have been admitted to the training program through some quirk of fate or clerical error and that your best hope of getting through lies in your remaining as silent as possible, you will learn less, and you will go through these four stages more slowly. Particularly if your supervisor is competitive, or too narcissistic to allow you your own space in group, you are unlikely to get to the point of doing co-therapy, of being truly a co-therapist. And that's a shame. However, these four stages are not a necessary part of learning how to do groups. If your first experience is with an equally virginal co-therapist, you won't go through them at all; you'll have a different set of problems. The issues of growth in technical skill and in self-confidence will be experienced differently and perhaps more slowly. But sooner or later you are likely to end up at the same place, having survived one group and ready to do another.

Choosing a Co-therapist

When you have no (or little) experience in doing groups, it is difficult to know how to choose a co-therapist because you don't know what will work: you don't have much information on which to base a decision. The general principles discussed in Chapter 1 are reviewed here briefly: (1) If at all possible, don't ask strangers to lead groups with you. Choose a friend or colleague whom you know and like. (2) Choose a therapist whose theoretical orientation is similar to your own (Paulson et al. 1976). (3) In general, look for an opposite-sex therapist who handles emotions in the same way you do, or a same-sex therapist who handles emotions differently. (4) It is not necessary to seek a co-therapist of opposite sex (Alfred 1992, Friedman 1973).

In addition to the above, there is some evidence suggesting that trainees and perhaps more experienced therapists prefer to work with co-therapists of equal status (Anderson et al. 1972, Friedman 1973, Rice et al. 1972). In addition, Friedman found that for the small sample of psychiatric residents in his study ($N = 11$), success in group therapy depended in part on choosing one's co-therapist and starting a new group rather than picking up an ongoing group that came with a co-therapist. Convenience and opportunity seldom make for good relationships when people must work as closely and intensely together as co-therapists do.

Consider the co-therapist pairings where one therapist is also the other's administrative superior, with line management responsibilities not defined by clinical competence. This kind of pairing may occasionally be tempting in longer-term inpatient settings or in outpatient clinics where there is some mandate to increase the number of therapy groups and where the number of experienced group therapists is quite small.

This pairing is not necessarily dysfunctional if the administrative superior is also the senior or more competent member of the dyad. The problem appears if the subordinate is, or is perceived to be, more competent than the co-therapist/administrative superior. Then the administrative superior may feel threatened, and the subordinate therapist may feel frustrated and contemptuous. These are difficult feelings for co-therapists to discuss openly, particulary for the subordinate member. Because of the power differential, the superior may be able to influence promotions, salary increases, or course grades.

One implication of the above is that a young therapist with little or no previous group experience can come into a therapy group and function more effectively, more competently, than a therapist-administrator with considerable previous group experience. Competence is difficult to define and to measure. The fact is that people enter training for the mental health professions with quite different aptitudes. Success in an institutional setting is not necessarily related to clinical aptitude, or ability, or success. It may indeed come to pass that a novice student with considerable aptitude for group therapy may be paired with an administrative supervisor (instructor, charge nurse, field placement director) with significantly less clinical talent. It may take several months for the differences in aptitude to become apparent. If the student is exceptionally talented, the differences may not become apparent at all.

The first question for the student is, What do you do if you perceive yourself to be more competent than your co-therapist, to whom you are otherwise subordinate? If your co-therapist is also your supervisor, it may be best to follow the First Rule, which is survival, and remain silent. Some supervisors in this situation will recognize and applaud your talent. But it is difficult for supervisors, or for other teachers, to avoid feeling threatened by students whose aptitude is higher than their own. When people feel threatened, they frequently attack. The most vulnerable point, in this instance, is your own competence, of which there is as yet little evidence because you are a beginner at group therapy. Therefore, the co-therapist/administrator who feels threatened by your competence may assault it. You will need to do all you can to retain your faith in yourself, in your perceptions of what is happening in group, and in your ability to draw rational and realistic conclusions based on those perceptions. In this kind of situation, what you will need is some social support — from your spouse or colleagues or even from your own therapist. Clinical training may produce transient situational stress sufficiently severe as to warrant entering therapy, and the support available from this source may be especially meaningful if your competence is under assault by supervisors who are threatened by it.

There may also be situations where the shoe is on the other foot, so to speak, when the person with administrative responsibility and power is the less experienced co-therapist. Such a situation might arise on psychiatric wards in teaching hospitals, where the senior co-leader might be a nurse or nurse's aide and the junior co-leader a first-year psychiatric resident having his or her first major encounter with psychopathology and psychotherapy. The resident will be junior in experience and perhaps in age. If he or she takes a subordinate role in the group, the result may be considerable confusion on the part of the patients. If the resident does not take the subordinate role but plunges ahead, exhibiting behaviors that are appropriate on the ward but discrepant for group, the senior therapist may seethe silently because of the potentially harmful consequences of confrontation. Generally, in mental health settings, both inpatient and outpatient, the pairing of doctoral level therapists with those who have master's degrees or no graduate training can be problematic because of the power and status differential between the two therapists.

Nurturant Versus Cold

Another way that co-therapists differ, and are perceived by the group to differ, is along the dimension of a nurturant supportive stance versus one that is cold and interpersonally distancing. There are three possible pairings here: both therapists are nurturant, both are cold, and one is nurturant and the other cold. When both therapists are cold and aloof, there may not be much dysfunction between them, but the potential for a dysfunctional, noncohesive, hostile group is high. When both therapists are warm, nurturant, and interpersonally approaching, there may be some potential for competitiveness, especially if both are strongly approval dependent, but this is probably the easiest pairing once the therapists have learned how to work together.

When one therapist is nurturant and the other cold, the potential for dysfunction in the co-therapy relationship is greatest. To the nurturant therapist, the cool aloof therapist is likely to look inept, uncaring, hostile, and judgmental. To the cool therapist, nurturant behavior may look sentimentally gushing, inappropriately rescuing, and dependency fostering. These are epithets that people occasionally hurl at each other, or comments they make to their friends or spouses, when there are such major differences. Such epithets may be more or less accurate. What happens in a co-therapy relationship, as in a marital relationship, is that small differences in the way that people relate are perceived by the co-therapists as major after they have been working together for some time. These perceptions are then generalized, usually in an unfavorable way, so that it seems that your co-therapist is cold and indifferent not only to you but also to the group.

In discussing the potential problems associated with status and power differences between therapists, and differences along a dimension of warmth and aloofness, we are really talking about the two major interpersonal dimensions described by Leary (1957) and his associates. The interpersonal circle has not, to my knowledge, been systematically applied to group therapy, but it does have some predictive value in terms of potentially workable versus potentially dysfunctional relationships. Therapists who would score high on any of the four poles (love, hate, dominance, submission) would probably be more difficult to work with in co-therapy than therapists whose positions on these dimensions are more moderate. The empirical data suggesting that therapists who are similar to each other function better as a team than those who are dissimilar (Piper et al. 1979) implies that therapists who are in the same or adjacent positions on the interpersonal circle will work more smoothly and perhaps more effectively than those whose positions are opposite or complementary. It does not, therefore, seem prudent to seek a co-therapist who possesses interpersonal skills or other characteristics that you yourself lack but admire. Opposites may attract, but they neither work well nor live happily together.

INTERACTION OF LEADERSHIP STYLES

Style is defined as the manner in which a given task is performed. Leadership style refers to the manner in which the group leaders carry out the tasks that theory tells them are important to carry out. Here we will consider three main leadership dimensions: active–passive, authoritarian–collegial, and cue emitting–cue suppressive. In this context, *active* means verbal activity, *passive* means verbal reticence.

Authoritarian–collegial refers to an interpersonal stance that the therapist takes toward patients. At one extreme is the group leader who chooses to regard himself or herself as just another group member, a colleague in the human experience that is held in common with his or her patients. At the other extreme is the leader who plays doctor, claiming implicitly or explicitly the wisdom of an oracle, the omnipotence of a mythical hero, and the warmth and empathy of a fairy godmother.

Cue emission refers to the non-verbal cues (facial expression, body language, tone of voice, and the like) people emit that reveal information about their interest in and emotional response to what is going on. An individual who utilizes facial expression, posture, and (when speaking) tone and volume of voice in an ongoing communicative process is defined here as a *cue emitter*. A glance or two at such a person gives you a lot of information about what's going on with him or her. At the other end of this dimension are *cue suppressors*. Their facial features are less mobile, their body language harder to read. They do not typically engage in verbal self-disclosure. Cue suppressors give no indication, verbal or nonverbal, about *how they are feeling* about what you're saying: whether they are bored, listening politely, think you're dull or brilliant, or wholeheartedly agree with your position and empathically understand it. Cue suppressors offer very little information (metacommunication) about their responses, except verbally.

Now, consider these three dimensions with respect to the co-therapy relationship. In terms of the activity dimension, the three co-therapist pairings are: active–active, active–passive, and passive–passive. It is possible for two verbally active therapists to dominate the group, particularly if the group is composed of quiet or non-verbal or impassive patients. These co-therapists can become (or appear) more interested in their relationship with each other than with what is happening in the group. This seems to happen without the therapists' being aware of it, and it is not difficult to handle if supervision is adequate and competent—that is, both frequent enough and pertinent.

When one therapist is verbally active and the other more quiet, the situation is potentially dysfunctional unless the therapists' expectations of each other are clear. If both are expecting to share the verbal load about equally, both will be unhappy with the unequal verbal output. If both accept that one is quiet and the other more prolix, and that this is all right, problems are less likely to occur.

The more talkative therapist is not necessarily the more influential or dominant. A relatively quiet co-therapist can have a powerful influence on what occurs during group sessions. The group tends to listen carefully to the few words uttered by the more quiet therapist, to respond more readily to suggestions, and to challenge him or her less. For groups to respond in this way to less verbally active co-therapists, two conditions must generally be present. One is that the more quiet co-therapist is not unresponsive but is simply parsimonious with words; a nonresponsive therapist paired with a verbally active therapist will simply be ignored by the group. The other is that what the more saturnine therapist says has to be on target or directly germane to what is going on in the group. Consider the following examples, the first from a more, the second from a less, prolix therapist:

Well, I see that our time is drawing to a close for today. I think this has been a very good session, with a lot of good work being done. The time seemed to go very quickly for me, and I hope that it did for you too. It just got to be late, poof, before you know it. Like, all of a sudden. Now I just want to remind you about confidentiality, don't talk about the group outside the group, and remember that we'll meet again next week right here, same time, same place. Have a good week, and we'll see you all next Tuesday.

It's time to stop for today. Things happened today which bear thinking about. Please remember to respect each other's privacy. See you next week.

If the two co-therapists are approximately equal in warmth (nurturance), the group may well tend to listen more closely to the therapist who speaks more briefly. The situation is potentially dysfunctional since the more verbal therapist may perceive himself or herself as doing most of the work while his or her more quiet partner gets most of the credit. Issues of competence and support may come to the fore: the more verbal partner tends to feel that the quieter one should express verbal agreement more frequently, and that silence indicates non-support.

When one co-therapist is active and the other passive or impassive, passivity may nevertheless be interpreted (by the group as well as by the co-therapist) as warm acceptance and acquiescence: passivity and aloofness are not necessarily synonymous. However, if both therapists are passive or impassive, they are both likely to seem to the group to be cool and aloof rather than acquiescent and accepting. There has to be something to accept before acceptance can occur, and if neither of the co-therapists offers anything, then neither of them can readily demonstrate warm acquiescent behavior. The converse, two active therapists, is not the same as two nurturant, interpersonally approaching therapists, since verbal activity can cover a number of spectra, only one of which involves interpersonal warmth.

If co-therapists differ greatly, such as in the *authoritarian–collegial* pairing, the result is likely to be disaster. The extreme would be a situation where one therapist wears his white coat into the group room, announces, "I'm Dr. Butterfield," and sits in a chair, while his (male) co-therapist comes in wearing a ponytail, blue jeans, and a T-shirt, sits on the floor, and says, "I'm Fred, and I'm here to help." Of course, this great a discrepancy in behavior is quite unlikely, and manifest differences in approach of this magnitude will have been resolved before the group begins. However, conceptual differences that are more difficult to identify and resolve may not be greater than those underlying this caricature.

If the level of competence of co-therapists differing along the authoritarian–collegial dimension is roughly similar, the pairing is not necessarily dysfunctional. The more collegial therapist will probably be better liked by the group, the more authoritarian therapist more respected. This dyad is workable as long as the more authoritarian therapist prefers respect to affection from group members, and the collegial therapist prefers the converse. If there is much difference in level of competence, the more collegial therapist may look indecisive, the more authoritarian one arrogant, and the prevalent affect between them is most likely to be contempt.

Since a great deal of the communication which goes on during a group session is behavioral rather than verbal, co-therapist pairs that are *cue emitting* are likely to have an easier time communicating during group than those pairs that are *cue suppressing*. A therapist who is impassive, authoritarian, and cue suppressing is likely to have a difficult time in co-therapy relationships unless the technique espoused by both, and by their supervisor, calls for this leadership style. A verbally active cue-suppressing therapist is one who lets other people know how he or she feels about what is being said through verbal responses and not through facial expression, tone of voice, or body movement. Since the message rather than the medium is critical in co-therapy teamwork, the verbally active cue suppressor is a workable co-leadership style.

Leadership Style, Co-leadership, and Activity Level: Concluding Comment

People discover their leadership styles, rather than choose them. You may discover that your style lends itself readily to co-therapy, or that it doesn't, or even that it does not lend itself easily to group work. Group therapists' attitudes toward co-therapy and intimacy were explored by Silverstein (1981). She found that therapists who co-led groups tended to reflect attitudes of closeness and intimacy and those who worked alone were more inclined toward attitudes suggesting a desire for control and resistance to intimacy. If the latter seems to describe you better than the former, you may want to consider doing solo group work after an initial stint as junior co-therapist with a more experienced colleague. You may also discover that group therapy work is not for you. Just as there are some patients who are not likely to benefit from group therapy, there are some therapists who are not likely to be effective in this modality, whatever their level of effectiveness in individual therapy. Lieberman and colleagues (1973) have described leadership styles associated with negative outcome (casualties) in very short term (encounter) groups, which may be regarded as somewhat of a therapy analogue. In my experience, therapists who go beyond impassivity into nonresponsiveness in their own interpersonal style, at least in groups, fare poorly as group leaders—as do their groups. This model of therapy has sometimes been described as *the therapist as cadaver*, a model that has received no empirical support. Put more simply, people who tend to be silent observers of others do not make good group therapists. Fortunately, such people seldom want to try group therapy. If your own style is reticent but observant and you tend to feel quite uncomfortable in groups but feel that you *should* learn how to do them, consider the possibility that this is one instance where instinct should prevail over superego, and leave the field to your more outgoing colleagues. There is much to be said for focusing on what you like to do and do best and avoiding techniques for which you know in your heart you are not really suited.

CO-THERAPY TEAMWORK

In this section I will describe three ways that co-therapists may function as a team: (1) attending to the same person or the same stimuli; (2) attending to opposite, or very dissimilar, aspects of the group experience—as when one therapist focuses on intrapsychic and the other on interpersonal events in group; and (3) functioning at different levels of abstraction, with one therapist taking a more concrete, the other a more theoretical stance. In the course of any group session, both therapists are likely to find themselves in all three positions, regardless of their personal preferences and of whatever they have agreed to as a team. These three styles of collaboration, which I call *similarity*, *complementarity*, and *parallelism* are characteristics rather than inviolate contractual arrangements.

Similarity

In order for both therapists to attend to the same person or the same stimulus dimension at the same time, there must be considerable overlap in their assessment of the situation and in their awareness of the possibilities of what to do next. Reaching the point where you are both working on the same thing is probably the most difficult part of the process. Once there, it is possible to proceed effectively even though you may not be in agreement. Reaching that point where you are both working on the same thing involves a decision, usually without verbal communication, based on where you think your co-therapist is going, on your assessment of whether or not he or she wants you to join in, and on the subjective evaluation of your own ability to join in effectively at this time, with this patient. The situation is less critical if the focus of attention is broad, involving several group members rather than one or two. In that case, your participation is from the standpoint of one who shares leadership responsibilities with another individual somewhat different from you rather than from the standpoint of one member of a team, a quite similar pair, working toward the same goal.

There are at least three ways that co-therapists can readily function as a team in focusing on the same individual or topic. The first is for both to take virtually identical interpersonal positions; the second is for one therapist to function as a moderator of the interaction between the other therapist and the patient or the group; and the third is to function as a modifier or alleviator of the interaction, a buffer rather than a facilitator.

An example of two therapists taking identical interpersonal stands is:

     Dr. T.: Betsy, you looked like you were going to say something a moment ago.

     Betsy: No, I was just thinking about something.

     Dr. M.: Would you like to tell us about it?

     Betsy: I don't want to take the group's time.

     Dr. M.: Why not?

     Betsy: It's not important enough.

     Dr. T.: You feel that you're not important enough for us to pay attention to?

     Dr. M.: Or be concerned about?

     Betsy: No, It's not that. It's just that, ah, I'm afraid I'll bore you.

     Dr. M.: Are you afraid that we'll be bored or that you'll be embarrassed?

     Betsy: Oh, I hadn't thought of it that way. Both, I guess.

Here, both therapists are working to engage Betsy. Dr. M.'s addendum to Dr. T's comment—"Or be concerned about?"—is the critical phrase, requiring rather deft timing in order to add to rather than intrude on Dr. T.'s question or on Betsy's answer. It is this addendum which indicates to the group and to Dr. T. that Dr. M. is right there with him, at the same point and working toward the same goal.

This example is not particularly dramatic or intense. It is characteristic of the earlier sessions of a group. Later on, the interactions can become considerably more intense, and the comments of a co-therapy team working in tandem like this can function like hammer blows landing in rapid succession on a patient's reluctance to engage—or on a patient's privacy, or on a patient's defenses. Teamwork is a powerful tool. Your eagerness to reach a particular point, to get somewhere with a patient or with the group, can divert your attention away from how you are getting there, away from your impact on the patient. This sometimes happens because when you and your co-therapist are in tandem, functioning as a team and engaging synergistically with the patient, it feels good—the teamwork, working in harmony, the timing going well, as though you and your co-therapist were playing a duet or performing a complex dance together. The first time that this feeling of teamwork occurs, that you are *together*, that you both know what's happening and what to do, is such a feeling of relief and of pleasure that things are happening as they should that it is easy to lose sight of the impact of your statements on the patient. Such an outcome is by no means an inevitable result of two therapists working in tandem and taking identical interpersonal stands. Because of the potency of teamwork of this sort to influence interpersonal interactions in group, it is important to attend carefully to the apparent impact of your interventions whenever it feels like things have really started to flow with your co-therapist.

One of the most useful functions of a co-therapist is to serve as a moderator when one therapist is involved in intense emotional interaction with a patient or with the group. Anger and sexual desire are the emotional states that are most easily handled by the co-therapist when one therapist is the target. The moderator can help the patient explore his or her angry feelings without sounding defensive. The patient can usually hear the moderator more accurately and is less irrationally fearful of retaliation, since the moderator is not the target of hostility. What the moderator does, in effect, is give the patient permission to be angry and to talk about his or her anger. If the therapist who is the target of the anger tries to give this permission, what tends to come through to the patient is that the target therapist does not take the patient's anger seriously: "Oh, it's all right for you to be angry with me. Let's talk about it." If you take someone's anger seriously, then you are not usually going to sanction it. One way of defusing anger aimed at you is to interpret it as a transference phenomenon. The therapist working alone might say, "I understand that you *feel* as though you're angry with me. In similar situations in the past, who did you feel angry with? Who does this remind you of?" The co-therapist acting as moderator can more easily move toward resolution of the interpersonal situation in the present before going on to generalize. In the following example, the co-therapists are Doug and Anne. Both are rather quiet; Doug tends to be more outspoken than Anne, who has a very soft, gentle manner. The patient is an aggressive graduate student named Paul. The example is fictitious but based on an actual group interaction.

Paul (to Anne) You don't like many people, do you?

Anne: What do you mean?

Paul: I mean, you don't get very involved here. As far as I'm concerned, we're just like bugs under a microscope. You sit there and observe us and you really don't give a damn.

Doug: You're angry with Anne.

Paul: Damn right I am.

Doug: What's that about?

Paul: She just sits there, never smiles, never gets rattled, always says "And how are you feeling about that?" and never says anything about how she's feeling.

Doug: You feel that she doesn't really care, that she's just an aloof observer.

Paul: Damn right. And I resent it.

Doug: If Anne were to get upset, would you feel that she was more involved with the group?

Paul: Yeah. I'd like to see her show some of *her* feelings.

Doug: If she showed some of her feelings, would you feel that she cared?

Paul: Yeah.

Doug: So a woman has to show her feelings—maybe show that she's upset—before you know that she cares, or is concerned about you?

Paul: Well, now, I don't, uh, I don't know about that. If she laughed once in a while that would be all right, too.

Anne: Paul, I haven't found anything in here to laugh about. I *am* concerned, or I wouldn't be here. I wonder what I can do to make clear to you that I am concerned and involved, besides getting upset or laughing with you.

Paul: Well, you could pay attention when people talk, and at least look interested—I guess you already do that—you could tell us something about yourself.

Doug: What would you like to know about Anne in relation to you?

Paul: In relation to me?

Doug: Yes—what's really most important for you to know about Anne right here, right now?

Paul: (*to Anne*) Do you like me?

Anne: Yes. There isn't anyone here I dislike.

Doug: It was because Anne is kind of quiet that you thought she disliked you?

Paul: Yeah.

Doug: I wonder who else in your life, in this room right now or in your past, was quiet and you thought didn't like you?

This example shows how a co-therapist coming in as moderator can say things that would be more awkward, less effective, and have quite different connotative meanings if they were said by the target of the patient's anger. There is some resolution of the immediate interpersonal situation, in that Paul finds out directly that Anne is not angry with him as he had assumed. Once that point is reached, Doug can begin the exploration of factors that will, it is hoped, lead to the development of insight on Paul's part.

The interpersonal situation is somewhat similar when sexual feelings, rather than anger, are being explored. The moderator can facilitate discussion without seeming either offended or seductive. It is more difficult for the target therapist to avoid one of those positions, particularly if there is some countertransference. The permission function of the moderator is somewhat different than when anger is involved. Anger is less easily concealed than sexual desire. The moderator's disclaimer of anger in an angry interchange between co-therapist and patient is therefore more credible than a disclaimer of sexual feelings. The main difference, however, has to do not so much with credibility—that won't be a problem if the trust level in the group is high enough to discuss sexual feelings toward the therapists anyway—as with the inclusion of the moderator as recipient of desirable feelings. The moderator's feelings aren't likely to be hurt if he or she isn't included in the patient's anger; but what about desire? With co-therapists of the same sex, there may be an implicit issue of jealousy or rivalry. At any rate, the patients may be watching for some signs of these feelings between the therapists. When co-therapists are of opposite sex, the implicit issue may be one of possessiveness, and the moderator's willingness to help explore feelings may be viewed as a kind of permission for the patient to have sexual feelings toward inappropriate sex objects. Since most of us have such feelings at times, discussion of these issues may be particularly helpful to the group.

A co-therapist functioning as a buffer rather than a moderator is working to blunt or lower the potential intensity of the interaction. This type of team function differs from that of the moderator in that the buffering therapist makes explanatory statements, while the moderator invites further interaction. A co-therapist taking a buffering stance makes statements of the general form, "What George [the co-therapist] meant by that is. . . ." This buffering role may be regarded as one in which co-therapists are functioning in a similar style, because it requires both therapists to be attending to the same person, to be in agreement about what should be done next, and to be confident enough in the co-therapy relationship to handle what is in effect some corrective action. When it is done well, buffering helps keep the group on track and on the work it is doing. When it is done poorly, buffering saps intensity rather than helping redirect it.

Complementarity

Therapists may agree before group starts that one will attend primarily to group and the other primarily to the individual. If you don't have much experience, you may not yet know which you prefer, or even if you prefer this kind of teamwork (as opposed to similarity or parallelism). In the absence of decision, what tends to happen is that you are more likely to focus on what is going on within individuals while your more experienced co-therapist focuses on what is going on between them. As your own experience grows and you begin to focus on the interpersonal as well as the intrapsychic, you may find your co-therapist shifting at times to a more intrapsychic complementary stance.

The biggest advantage of this type of co-therapist teamwork is that it allows for the range of group experience to be covered while each therapist covers only a part of that range. It is analogous to a zone defense in team sports. If you know that your co-therapist is going to be attending to the rest of the group, you can devote your full attention to working with one patient or one subset of patients.

In this situation, the therapist who is attending to the group probably has the more difficult task. The focus is broader, there are more people to attend to, and there is little or no verbal interchange so you don't know what they are feeling or thinking. The verbal activity in the group is generally limited to the dyadic patient–therapist interaction where the intensity or energy is. This is not to imply or assume that group is or should be a succession of such dyadic interactions, except during the early sessions.

There are several factors leading the novice group therapist to attend to verbal content (what people are saying), to intrapsychic events (what people are feeling), and to events that occurred outside the group room, in the recent or remote past. The result of this attention is the formulation of interventions such as "Tell us more about that," "What are you feeling?" and "When your father said that to you, how did you feel and what did you decide to do?" While these are not necessarily inappropriate interventions in a group therapy session, they do indicate that the therapist is focusing on the individual rather than the group. If you are doing your first group, and especially if you have had much training in individual psychotherapy, you may well find yourself formulating such interventions, if not actually saying them aloud. Your (more experienced) co-therapist, seeing and expecting this kind of focus from you, may then retain focus on the group as a whole.

But what if you realize that your co-therapist is functioning in this way? What should you do? There are three types of answers: (1) do what your supervisor or your theory tells you; (2) do what you have agreed with your co-therapist to do; (3) trust your instincts.

If you are doing a first or second group with your supervisor as senior co-therapist, you are not likely to get into intense one-to-one interactions with patients unless a patient really takes out after you. If that happens, your supervisor/co-therapist can, and probably will, move in as moderator or buffer. If you're doing a group with a colleague and see him or her getting drawn into an intense one-to-one interaction with a patient, you will ideally have discussed beforehand what to do in this situation. However, more typically you will not have done so and you are left in a quandary. This is the time to follow your instinct. If it is to move to a similar mode of functioning, go ahead; if it is to attend to the group, trust your instinct. If your relationship with your co-therapist is not dysfunctional, and you head off in the wrong direction, he or she will tell you so, right then and there in the group, and you can adjust accordingly.[1]

---

[1]Less experienced co-therapy pairs tend to talk to everyone in the group room except each other. It is as though the co-therapists were invisible to each other and as though they communicate in some extrasensory mode. While extensive dialogue between co-therapists is seldom appropriate during a group session, there are times when some brief discussion is quite helpful. Especially in the earlier phases of group, a verbal exchange with your co-therapist at least once during each session may facilitate group cohesiveness.

So your co-therapist engages intensely with one or two patients, and you think, OK, there he or she goes, and you look around at the rest of the group. The problems you face generally start with what to attend to, what to do about what you have attended to, and when to do it (see Chapter 10). The problems are compounded by the presence of an actively engaged co-therapist. Then the things to look for that are most likely to be fruitful involve the response – or nonresponse – of the other patients. Boredom, empathic responses, and efforts or readiness to break into the ongoing interaction are probably the most salient things to look for. If one group member looks bored by what is going on, but the others are attentive, then that should be noted. Boredom almost always involves closing off some aspect of experience. It is seldom that *nothing interesting is going on* (the most frequent rationale for boredom) but rather *I wish to block out what is going on, or my response to it*. This formulation of boredom, which is consistent with the Gestalt conceptualization, is not likely to be verbalized or agreed to by the group member who appears to be bored. When one group member appears bored and the rest are attentive, it may be worthwhile, after your co-therapist has finished his or her intensive one-to-one, to check with the apparently bored member to determine what he or she was blocking out.

On the other hand, you may find that most or all of the group looks bored except for your co-leader and the group member with whom he or she is working. Indeed, this is far more common than the situation where only one group member looks bored and the others interested. The problem, then, is whether to interrupt your co-therapist and disrupt the interaction between him or her and the patient, or to wait silently until that work is finished and then review the reactions of the group to what had been going on.

This is another of those situations where you have to trust your instincts, and if you are new at group therapy you don't have a lot of instinctive feelings about what is going on or what to do. In that case, it is generally better to wait and not to interrupt. As you gain experience and get to know your co-therapist better in the context of a working group session, you'll have a better idea of whether to refocus on the group or to permit your co-therapist to continue to focus exclusively on one individual.

Instead of reacting with apparent boredom, the group may respond empathically to the work being done by your co-therapist with one group member. Empathic responses on the part of patients who are not in the spotlight will take various forms. These responses are non-verbal and may involve very small interpersonal cues: shifts in posture, in skin tone (blanching or reddening or turning blotchy, with the patient showing no other signs of emotion at all), or in facial expression. Sometimes tears will well up in the eyes of one or more onlookers, and then disappear or be wiped away very quickly. The group member who sits silently on the sidelines and allows a tear to trickle down his or her cheek, making no effort to wipe it, is not offering a subtle cue; for all that it may be genuine, it is a very strong bid for attention. Think of what a tear feels like on your face, trickling down your cheek, and you will realize how much energy is needed to keep from wiping it away.

Whether or not to break in on the spotlight, or to allow or encourage the empathic patient to do so, depends on a variety of factors, including your assessment of the possible consequences of breaking in, or of waiting until there is some closure and the spotlight is ready to shift. Here the most cautious course is not to break in the first time the situation arises, and then to talk with your co-therapist afterward about what to do if it should arise again.

Parallelism

This term refers to a mode of co-therapist functioning in which the therapists attend to the same stimulus configurations but make very different types of comments. The difference between this mode and the similarity of functioning described above is that one of the therapists offers interpretations and then links them explicitly to some theoretical model, while the other therapist offers interventions based on what is going on here-and-now between people in the group room.

The therapist functioning on the more abstract plane relates what is happening or has just happened in group to the body of theory within which the co-therapists are working or (less commonly) to broader issues of society outside the group.

CONCLUDING COMMENT

Co-therapy is not for everybody, just as there are some quite good individual therapists who seem to have little talent for or interest in group therapy. Therapists who feel it important to maintain a high degree of control over what is going on, and who maintain more rather than less interpersonal distance from co-workers and clients alike, generally have a more difficult time with the co-therapist relationship than those who prefer a more collaborative stance and are not uncomfortable with high degrees of ambiguity. For the former, going solo *after the first group or two with a more experienced co-therapist* may be the best way to optimize therapeutic skill and energy. A therapy group skillfully led by one therapist is preferable to one that withers away because of the tension between two co-leaders, each of whom may in fact possess a high level of competence. There is some empirical support for these observations (Piper et al. 1979, Silverstein 1981).

The empirical literature on co-therapy appears in general to favor similarity between co-therapists in terms of experience level, theoretical orientation, and therapist characteristics such as warmth, acceptance, and interpersonal closeness. Taken as a whole, the literature offers some indications that when therapists are similar along these dimensions, the group functions better than when they are not; group members report benefit or satisfaction; and the co-therapists rate their own co-therapy experience as satisfactory and themselves as willing to do another group with the same person.

The problem is that you cannot always pick your own co-therapist, and even in those settings where choice is possible and encouraged, it is limited by the range of available and interested co-therapists. Consequently, you may find yourself doing a group, either your first one or subsequently, with a co-therapist who differs from you along one or more of the significant dimensions. Although such differences do not necessarily indicate probable failure in the relationship, they do suggest that you will have a more difficult or stressful or less satisfying time than if your co-therapist is similar to you in the relevant ways. If your co-therapist is also your supervisor, you may have a challenging time indeed and come away from the group therapy experience convinced that this treatment modality is not for you. However, forewarned is forearmed. If you are aware of the potential for difficulties, they are less likely to occur, and more likely to be readily handled if they do arise. In any event, when you do have a choice, it is important to *not* seek a co-therapist who exhibits qualities or characteristics that you admire but perceive yourself as lacking. Opposites may attract, but it turns out to be difficult for them to work together, at least in this context.

It is possible to negotiate with your co-therapist on only a very small part of what will happen in group. If you are both inexperienced, then what you will be able to anticipate is of course less than if either or both of you had been there before, and there will be less that you can agree on beforehand. In some groups, the structure of the group or of the co-therapy relationship will more or less dictate which co-therapist teamwork style you will follow most frequently. In other groups, particularly those that you do with an equally inexperienced colleague, learning how to function as a team is like learning how to do a dance that neither of you have done before and for which you get instruction only between performances. There is no reason why the interpersonal skill with which you seek to understand and influence patients should not be applied also to the co-therapy relationship, so that you come to sense intuitively where your co-therapist is heading, and how best to join your efforts so that the team functions with ease, grace, and elegance.

12

Problems

In this chapter I will describe some of the problems the novice might reasonably expect to encounter during the process of learning how to do groups. The chapter is organized around each of the necessary components for doing a group: a room, a co-therapist, a supervisor, and patients. It is of course possible to omit the co-therapist and even the supervisor. Omission of the co-therapist deprives you, and the group, of the potential benefits of a second therapist's presence. That may be a mixed blessing, as discussed in the preceding chapter. Omission of the supervisor, however, raises serious ethical and, in some instances, legal issues and, for the novice therapist, is wrong.

ROOMS

Unless you are in an unusual setting, you are not likely to have a great deal of choice about rooms. Some rooms will be available for group. They will be more or less desirable. A good room is one that is large enough, comfortable, carpeted, and quiet. A poor room is one that is too small or too large. In a room that's too small, people get uncomfortable because they are too close to each other. In a room that's too large, such as a day room large enough for twenty or more people, the group is apt to feel boundaryless, and self-disclosures of a very private nature may be inhibited. In rooms opening off busy corridors, distracting noise is sometimes a problem. In rooms that are cold, institutional, and uncomfortable, people are slower to become at ease with one another and with the group.

A good room facilitates the establishment of the atmosphere of warmth and supportiveness in which the group can do its therapeutic work. A poor room slows the process. If you have a choice of rooms, you will have less of a problem than if you have no choice and must either use a room that is marginally suitable or else not do group at all. If the room is poor, you will have to allow for the fact that the room will indeed make a difference. But it is usually better to do group in a poor room than to not do one at all.

CO-THERAPIST PROBLEMS

In Chapter 11, the co-therapist relationship was discussed. Here I will consider dysfunctional co-therapist relationships and some things it might be possible to do about them. The hazards of co-therapy have also been discussed by Bowers and Guaron (1981).

A dysfunctional relationship is, first of all, a poor relationship between two people. People define "poor relationship" in different ways. If you feel that the relationship is poor, then it is. It is not necessary to *justify* the feeling. It may be necessary to do something about it. A poor relationship between co-therapists inevitably affects the group, as does a good relationship between them (McMahon and Links 1984). When the relationship is experienced as poor by either co-therapist, it will usually be experienced as poor by both, though if the problem is severe it may not be acknowledged. The first action to take is to attempt to define the problem in such a way that it can be resolved.

For purposes of this discussion, I will define co-therapist problems as falling predominantly into either an affective or a cognitive domain. The affective domain centers on feelings of like–dislike, approve–disapprove, and similar feelings. The cognitive domain centers on assessment of competence: the assessment you make of your co-therapist's competence and your hunches about the assessment he or she is making of yours. Most problems contain both affective and cognitive components.

Problems in the Affective Domain: Negative Feelings

Perhaps the most difficult problem to resolve is the one in which you have no specific complaints but have come simply to dislike your co-therapist. The co-therapy relationship is in many respects analogous to a marital relationship, even when both therapists are of the same sex. The analogue stems from the necessity of spending many hours of intensely emotional experience with your co-therapist and (to a lesser extent) from the tendency of groups to assign sex-role stereotypes to the co-therapists. Coming to dislike your co-therapist, then, is somewhat similar to coming to dislike your spouse.

The analogue can, however, be carried too far. The co-therapy relationship is not a marriage. The personal commitment to one's co-therapist is different from, and less than, the personal commitment to one's spouse. Within some limits, it is possible to work effectively with a co-therapist whom you dislike. For some people, like or dislike is irrelevant to working well with others. For most, however, dislike precludes effective co-therapeutic teamwork.

In co-therapy, as in marriage, difficulties occur when affective variables are more important to one member of the pair than to the other. Co-therapists who share a cognitive, task-oriented approach may not even consider whether they like each other. If they are dissimilar, however, they encounter difficulties similar to those of a married couple where one spouse seeks verbal reassurance while the other prefers behavioral indicators. "George, do you love me?" asks Agnes after twenty years of marriage. "Hell, I married you, didn't I?" replies George. The analogue in co-therapy is, "George, do you like me?" and his task-oriented reply, "Well, you're a good therapist."

One element that makes this problem so difficult to resolve is the reluctance of co-therapists and supervisor to discuss or, at times, even to recognize the problem as a valid interpersonal one. If affective components of professional relationships are important to you, you are not likely to be very willing to confront your co-therapist, much less your supervisor, with the statement that you dislike him or her. Such statements will also seem out of place in a business relationship, as will any attempt you might make to justify your feelings.

But even unjustifiable feelings should be taken seriously. If you need to like and be liked by your co-therapist in order to function as an effective team, that need should be respected by both co-therapist and supervisor even if neither have that particular need. Ad hominem solutions, attacking the legitimacy of the need, serve only to deepen the problem.

Therefore, if you need to like your co-therapist and you don't, it will generally work out better to dissolve the relationship—or, if necessary, the group—unless the group will be ending within a tolerably brief period. Limping along indefinitely with a co-therapist you dislike may help you to learn how to tolerate frustration, impatience, and many other negative feelings. That learning does not take long. The benefits of adversity are small, however, and are frequently overrated. There is no virtue in suffering.

The most common problem between co-therapists is disagreement strong enough to cause anger. The question is whether to resolve the disagreement and the anger in the group's presence or in private. One rationale for resolving it in group is that seeing the therapists resolve their differences and their anger provides a role model for the patients. The patients, however, did not come to group to see their therapists argue or resolve their differences. Arguments between co-therapists are generally disruptive of group and should be avoided.

The question is what to do when you get really angry with your co-therapist during group. When your anger has become so obvious to the group that the group cannot really continue until some note is taken of the anger, or when resolution of the anger is likely to be rapid and satisfactory, then it is better to move openly toward acknowledg ment and resolution. If the anger is not obvious to the group, then save it until later. If your anger is obvious but rapid resolution is not possible, then deal with it as minimally as possible and work on the resolution elsewhere.

Some people, including therapists, handle anger more openly than others. If you become angry with your co-therapist during or after group, it may not be difficult to confront him or her with your anger and to resolve it. But if angry confrontation is not your style, then you are likely to have some rationalizations for not being confrontive.

Generally, these rationalizations include the fear that the relationship will break up (usually it won't); that you wish to avoid hurting your co-therapist's feelings; that you fear retaliation; and so on. Whatever these rationalizations, you (or your friends or supervisor) may raise the question of whether or not confrontation is desirable even though it is not your usual style. After all, a therapy group is involved, there is some obligation to the patients, and failure to confront your co-therapist with your anger might adversely affect the group. In addition, you or your friends or supervisor might point out that mental health professionals ought to be able to handle anger in a healthy open way, so confrontation is both the professional and the healthy thing to do.

While there are always exceptions, in general it is better *not* to try something that is not your style. If being confrontive is not your style, then it is not likely that you will do it very well. Furthermore, you risk increasing rather than decreasing the difficulties. People who are confronters do well at confronting. People who aren't, don't. Successful resolution does not always involve confrontation.

The general principle is to do what works for you, and has worked for you in the past, in dealing with your anger. If no way of dealing with your anger has really worked for you in the past, then withdrawing from the situation is probably the most responsible course. If you find that you consistently become angry with co-therapists, for whatever reason, to the point where either confrontation or breaking the relationship seem the only choices—if that keeps happening, in two or three different co-therapy relationships, then consider the possibility that co-therapy is not for you and that you and your groups would fare better if you did them solo.

Problems in the Affective Realm: Positive Feelings

Sometimes co-therapists fall in love. Maintaining professional objectivity (indeed, rationality) about someone with whom you are falling in love is at best difficult. Consequently, your assessment of any group interactions in which your loved one is involved may be clouded. In a session where a group member is exploring his sexual feelings toward your co-therapist and you know that she finds him attractive, it will be difficult for you to assess your responses as correctly as if you were not falling in love. Frequently, though not inevitably, discussion of this kind of interaction in the supervisory session leads to defensiveness, and it is usually impossible to learn anything while one is being defensive.[1]

Avoiding such falling in love with your co-therapist may require restricting your choice of co-therapist to someone with whom you are unlikely to fall in love—for most of us, a member of the same sex; or to agree beforehand that positive feelings toward each other are an important part of the co-therapy relationship and will be discussed with your supervisor. Alas, such an agreement is likely to be honored only until the strength of mutual attraction begins to transcend the group therapy situation and begins to involve your private life—that is, to the point where such an agreement begins to have importance.

---

[1]Although the example is written from the point of view of a male co-therapist and male patient both attracted to a female co-therapist, other permutations are acknowledged: the female co-therapist reacting negatively to a female patient's seductiveness toward the male co-therapist; in homosexual groups, or when both therapists are same-sex and homosexual, the negative reaction of one to a group member's attraction to his or her co-therapist. If one co-therapist is homosexual and the other not, the issue of mutual attraction between therapist and patient, whatever the feelings of the other co-therapist, is best left to a highly skilled supervisor.

Another agreement, one that is sometimes made only tacitly, is not to act on one's feelings of attraction toward one's co-therapist until after the group is terminated. That can be a difficult course of action to maintain but is both workable and prudent.

In general, solutions that prohibit, devalue, or condemn falling in love with one's co-therapist are unworkable. Solutions which *may* work involve acknowledging that these things happen, that one's judgment is sometimes impaired by one's feelings, and that one can nonetheless continue to function competently. For example, the group member who begins to explore his sexual feelings toward the co-therapist with whom you are falling in love is most likely to have some concerns about your reaction. Acknowledging your feelings without exploring them is probably a good move here, in part because it may help to validate the patient's own feelings while setting a clear example of not acting on them. "I can certainly understand why you would feel sexually attracted to her" (or him; see footnote) or some such comment accomplishes this task. The situation can be handled like any other in which the patient generates strong feelings in you: you report the feelings but don't act on them. Expressions of jealousy, however, are not likely to be perceived as therapeutic by the patient or the group. Regardless of your emotions at this point, you know that the patient is not going to act on his or her feelings, and it may be helpful to him or her and the group to know that you aren't going to act on yours either.

A related problem involves sexual attraction to your co-therapist. The distinction is between interest in a sexual companion and a life companion. Feelings of sexual attraction between co-therapists of opposite sex are not uncommon. Feelings and plans involving making one's co-therapist one's life companion are more rare. However, co-therapists do occasionally marry.

Feelings of sexual attraction become a problem in co-therapy relationships if they give rise to seductive behavior in group. Therefore, it is prudent to defuse sexual tensions between co-therapists before such tensions become so great as to unconsciously or inadvertently drive seductive behavior during group sessions. At this point in your own career you probably have developed some skill in minimizing sexual components in professional and other relationships. Use those skills here. Sometimes talking with your co-therapist about sexual interests defuses them; sometimes it explodes them; talking about feelings is not a panacea because discussion can serve as an intensifier rather than a defuser.

The conventional wisdom is that sexual affairs should await termination of the co-therapy relationship. Whatever its basis in morality, the conventional wisdom is based solidly on experience – a basis from which morality also ultimately draws its strength. Failure to deal effectively and prudently with sexual tensions between co-therapists may make it difficult to accurately interpret sexual acting-out between group members, and unnecessarily adds a challenge to the already complex and difficult task of conducting a therapy group.

It should be noted that this discussion pertains to co-therapists of equal status and power: students, interns, residents, staff members, colleagues. Supervisors who fall in love with their supervisees are at considerable risk if they begin to discuss these feelings, even if they are clearly reciprocated; the discussion of sexual attraction between supervisor and supervisee co-therapists is, simply, proscribed even if initiated by the supervisee. If you begin to fall in love with your supervisor, or feel strongly sexually attracted to him or her, don't talk about it, don't hint about it, don't act on it. It is important for both your careers that such feelings remain absolutely invisible and unacknowledged. If that becomes impossible, withdraw. Otherwise you will find that your judges are numerous and merciless.

Problems in the Cognitive Domain

Problems in this domain generally involve, or are related to, your assessment of your co-therapist's competence, both as a professional and as a person. Assessment of professional competence is based on your knowledge of your co-therapist's clinical skills, including but not limited to his or her performance as co-therapist. Such evaluation is likely to be enhanced if his or her conceptualization of what is going on in group is similar to your own and if you perceive your co-therapist as correctly or skillfully applying a technique similar to your own. Assessment of personal competence pertains to such things as being on time, remembering to bring the keys to the group room, dressing appropriately, and deftly managing problems like car breakdowns or illness in the family. The two kinds of evaluation are related: if you begin to think your co-therapist is an airhead, your assessment of his or her competence is likely to be low as well.

If your assessment of what is going on in group differs from that of your co-therapist, it will be difficult to agree on what to attend to, when to attend to it, and how to attend to it. Consider the following example:

> *Mildred:* (breaking a short silence) John doesn't bother me.
>
> *Diane* (one therapist): Who are you talking to?
>
> *Mildred:* To you, I guess.
>
> *Diane:* Why not talk to John?
>
> *Mildred:* He doesn't bother me.
>
> *Diane:* Tell that to John.
>
> *Mildred:* He heard me.
>
> *John:* What?
>
> *Mildred:* Nothing.
>
> *Diane:* Mildred, why did you suddenly announce that John doesn't bother you?
>
> *Mildred:* He doesn't.
>
> *John:* Doesn't what?
>
> *Diane:* We seem to be not getting anywhere.
>
> *Dan* (other therapist): Mildred, you really like John, don't you?

Post-group discussion revealed that Dan had assessed Mildred's opening statement as one of liking or affection, while Diane had perceived it as Mildred's attempt to deny hostile feelings for John. Which co-therapist is "right" is not the point here. There is so much discrepancy in the way each co-therapist had assessed the situation that there is little probability of them functioning as a team, or agreeing on much of what happened in group after that point. Other examples might include differences in the assessment of interactions as being angry or friendly, warm or cool, sexual or social.

This example illustrates also a group interaction that isn't going anywhere, perhaps because of the therapist intervention, or because of the low interest or intensity, or because the group is virtually para- lyzed by the tension between Diane, Mildred, and John.

When your co-therapist comes in from left field just as you feel you are getting somewhere, the effect is more marked:

> *Carolyn:* It's really hard for me to talk seriously about important things. I smile and make jokes about them.
>
> *Diane* (one therapist): Is that something you'd like to change?
>
> *Carolyn:* Yes.
>
> *Diane:* What would you like to do about it?
>
> *Carolyn:* Practice saying things that are serious and looking serious when I say them and not laughing about it.
>
> *Diane:* Would you like to practice that in here?
>
> *Carolyn:* Yes.
>
> *Dan* (other therapist): Did your parents laugh and joke about serious things?
>
> *Carolyn:* My father did, and still does.
>
> *Dan:* Tell us what he's like.

Dan has turned the focus from a potential here-and-now inter- action into one on the past—a reminiscence of Carolyn about her father. In the post-group discussion, Diane reported feeling that she was wrenched out of her frame of reference and into Dan's, while Dan reported that he felt he had prevented the group from getting into a highly artificial and frivolous kind of interaction.

Such differences in perception may indicate your co-therapist's inability or refusal to enter into your frame of reference. A tug-of-war in group is not likely to be fruitful. If you can figure out your co-therapist's frame of reference and are willing to work within it, that would be preferable to remaining silent. However, when differences of this magnitude arise during group sessions, it is usually better to back off and wait until after group to get things clarified. If such differences happen often, you may come to feel that your co-therapist is incompetent, insensitive, or both, and you may want to terminate the relationship.

In the previous example, the co-therapists were in disagreement about what was going on. Co-therapists may agree about what is going on and disagree about what to do about it. In training settings such as departmental clinics or teaching hospitals, a common disagreement occurs when one therapist wants to focus on what is being said (verbal content) while the other wants to focus on what is happening in the group (group process). The following is adapted from an inpatient group on a psychiatric ward in a general teaching hospital. The co-therapists are Penny and Denise.

Melvin: My name is Melvin, and I'm an alcoholic.

Penny: Tell us something else about you besides that you're an alcoholic.

Melvin: Ain't nothin' else to tell. I've quit now, though. When I get outta here, gonna get me a job, place to live, get my wife and kids back, ain't never gonna take another drink, no way.

Penny: Can you tell us one thing about yourself that isn't related to your alcohol problem?

Denise: What's going to happen when you get back out there and you want a drink?

Melvin: I'll just tell myself not to take one. Will power, that's all it takes.

Denise: Alcoholism is a disease, and it takes more than will power to recover from it. What else are you going to do to keep from taking another drink?

In this example, one therapist wants to focus on the patient's verbal presentation, his alcoholism. The other wants to focus on the interpersonal situation in the group and on the patient's reluctance to engage with the other group members on any issue other than alcoholism. As with previous examples, the problem here is not whether one of the therapists is correct and the other wrong, but on the magnitude of the discrepancy between what they are trying to do. The therapists in the above example stopped working together shortly after that session and have not done co-therapy together for some years, though both continue to work in the same setting.

Here is another example, from an outpatient group. The therapists are Sam and Janet, Mark is a 26-year-old part-time undergraduate student living with his parents, and Debbie is a beautiful 21-year-old university student.

Mark: I really need to be in a relationship, preferably with someone who really understands me. The medication I'm taking now keeps my obsessive-compulsive neurosis under control, and I'm only taking one pill a day for my schizo-affective disorder. I'm looking for a place to live so I can get away from my father, especially. My mother won't stand up to him. As soon as I find a place to stay, I'll get out of there and then I'll be ready to be in a relationship. (*Looks intently at Debbie*)

Debbie: Well, I certainly wish you luck. My problem is getting out of relationships, not getting into them.

Sam: Mark, you said your mother won't stand up to your father. What about you? Do you stand up to him?

In the post-group discussion, Janet said that she had been trying to formulate an intervention about the effect of Mark's presentation of himself (as mentally ill) on Debbie and other members of the group. However, Sam's questions focused instead on what Mark had said about his relationship with his father, and Janet felt it prudent to remain silent until that discussion had petered out.

Focusing on verbal content rather than group process is generally poor technique. Problems arise in the co-therapy relationship when one focuses on content and the other on process. Interventions based on verbal content tend to focus on there-and-then events outside the group or on persons who are neither present nor group members, like Mark's father. Generally, focusing on there-and-then interactions tends to decrease the emotional intensity of the group and to reduce the degree to which other group members engage in group interaction. The result of focusing on verbal content is, frequently, a low-intensity interaction between one patient and one therapist with the other group members and the other co-therapist looking on and probably bored. That is why focusing on verbal content is poor technique.

There are, however, times when focusing on there-and-then interactions leads to moments of great emotional intensity involving the entire group. A woman speaking for the first time outside of individual therapy about her childhood sexual abuse is quite a dramatic and intense moment, as is a man speaking about his lover recently dead from AIDS. Some of the most dramatic moments you will ever experience in group may come from focusing on there-and-then with individual patients rather than here-and-now with group. Thus it may turn out that what you thought was an error of focus by your co-therapist turns out very well indeed. Whether it worked or not, however, is less important than how you handle disagreement over what to focus on.

In general, problems about what to follow up on are not as difficult to resolve as problems having to do with your assessment about what is going on. Disagreements about what to focus on tend to get ideological and may boil down to the belief that "My technique is better than yours," or that "I can apply our technique better than you can." Disagreements about what is going on in group involve your assessment of reality. Disagreement about such an assessment tends to be quite threatening because ultimately it is your sanity that is being questioned.

If you find that you and your co-therapist are in constant disagreement about what to attend to, you will probably find it difficult to avoid assessing his or her competence. Repeated disagreement about procedure has a cumulative effect. For many people, respect for competence is a necessary component of respect for the person and may be a prerequisite for liking him or her. Sooner or later, if you continue to work with a co-therapist whose competence you do not respect, you may begin to feel contempt.

In such a situation, confronting your co-therapist is not likely to be fruitful. If he or she is really incompetent, there is not much that he or she can do about it. If you are convinced of his or her incompetence, there is not likely to be anything that he or she can say in a confrontation that will alter your judgment. Complaining to your supervisor about your co-therapist's ineptitude is similarly unlikely to be fruitful. If your supervisor does not share your assessment, you may find yourself defending your own competence, and against a more formidable foe than your co-therapist. If the supervisor does share your assessment of your co-therapist, it is up to him or her to do something about it.

There is, then, considerable risk in either direct confrontation or in complaining to your supervisor about your co-therapist's competence. You risk the issue of competence being turned against you, or being perceived as a malcontent, or as one who is manifesting emotional disturbance. Competence is a very sensitive issue, and students who raise it may find themselves embroiled in a political battle rather than in a struggle to develop competence in group therapy. If your co-therapist is truly incompetent, it is likely that others in the mental health care delivery system already know it, or soon will, and that they have appropriate means of dealing with it.

The present discussion is following a general outline of problems in what is going on, what to attend to, and what to do with what is attended to. There remains a consideration of disagreement about when to attend to it. The issue of timing is a technical one with which your supervisor should be of help. While you may disagree with your co-therapist about the timing of interventions and of interpretations, such disagreements are usually readily resolved in post-group or supervisory sessions. People usually talk more readily about timing than about other areas of disagreement.

For the novice group therapist, the timing problem is one of formulating an intervention and then saying it out loud. It takes a while to be able to put an intervention together. Then it takes a while longer—sometimes two or three months—to have sufficient confidence in yourself to say it before your co-therapist does. If your co-therapist is more experienced, as should be the case, the difference in timing is not a problem and will pretty much take care of itself as your experience and confidence grow.

However, if your co-therapist consistently gets there first, so that you seldom have a chance to say much, that can be a problem, especially if you are both at approximately the same experience level. As your co-therapist continues to be more verbally active and you more reticent, you will find the patients turning to him or her and beginning to ignore you; you become relegated to an assistant therapist role. The quicker and more verbally active therapist tends to be seen as the more competent, and to accept that evaluation. But the rose of quickness carries with it the thorn of impatience, and unless tended to, that thorn will prick both co-therapists.

Unless your supervisor observes the group sessions or listens carefully to the audiotape, the problem may not be readily apparent during supervisory sessions. Usually, calling the factor of timing to the attention of your co-therapist and asking him or her to wait a moment or two for you to catch up is all that is necessary. This kind of timing problem seems more formidable to the slower therapist than to the faster one. Unless the co-therapy relationship is already strained, asking your partner to slow down a little is not likely to harm the relationship.

Another problem involving timing concerns not the formulation and uttering of individual interventions but the decision as to whether to make a potentially confrontive intervention sooner rather than later. This is not the situation in which you are about to speak, only to find that your co-therapist is already saying what you were about to say. Rather, it is the situation where you realize, for example, that a patient is droning on about something and is likely to monopolize much of the session unless some intervention is made. Less experienced therapists, and people who have difficulty with even therapeutic confrontation, tend to wait until the need for confrontation is of critical importance if the session is to be beneficial. Sometimes novice therapists wait longer than that, with negative consequences. However, the point here is that therapists can disagree, sometimes vehemently, about the timing of potentially confrontive interventions.

In an era when economic and other factors are driving the mental health care delivery system toward ever briefer modes of treatment, there is considerable pressure on therapists and mental health facilities to treat as though the mind heals as rapidly as the body. Though grievous wounds to either heal only slowly, those to the mind are invisible to the eye, making the fiction of rapid healing more palatable to the healer, or at least to those providing funds for the healing. When the injuries are less deep, though not necessarily less painful, then healing can indeed be more rapid, and the economic motivation for short-term therapy may also result in improvement of clinical service delivery.

In any event, it is generally better, though difficult, to make potentially confrontive interventions sooner rather than later, and ideally the first time the occasion for them arises. Consider the following statements, all made by inpatients on a psychiatric ward of a general medical hospital during their first group sessions:

"I'm here because of nutrition." (The patient did not have an eating disorder.)

"I'm here because I have a broken leg."

"I came to the emergency room because I had a pulled muscle and they sent me over to the psychiatrist and he said I had to come into the hospital, so here I am. Nobody's looked at my pulled muscle yet."

These statements are either inaccurate or untrue, and should not

go unchallenged. Indeed, therapists' failure to challenge such statements constitutes acquiescent support for these distortions of reality.
Therapist responses might include the following:

"Would you be willing to say some more about why you were
admitted?"

"What else can you tell us about why you're here?"

"That's certainly an unusual reason for admission to a psychiatric
ward."

The last comment above is somewhat more challenging than the
others. One patient responded to it by saying "Well, there weren't any
other beds available in the hospital." At that point the therapist
prudently dropped the matter.

People differ in their willingness to engage in confrontation.
Therapists differ in their willingness to make potentially confrontive
interventions, and in their willingness to make such interventions
sooner rather than later. If there is considerable difference between
you and your co-therapist along these lines, it may be possible to
negotiate in order to reduce the magnitude of difference. If not, issues
of competence and compatibility may be difficult to avoid.

Co-therapist Problems: Concluding Comment

After reading this section, you may wonder why a co-therapist model
is recommended. The answer is that by and large it increases the
range, type, and style of expertise available to the group, and in
addition offers the advantages for training that are described in the
preceding chapter.

Developing a good co-therapy relationship may be in some ways
as difficult as evolving a good marriage, and the rewards are to some
extent analogous. However, the bonds between co-therapists are not
as firm or strong as marital bonds, nor should they be. Withdrawing
from a difficult co-therapy situation need not have the same negative
connotations as divorce. However, you may find yourself in a situation where withdrawing from co-therapy, or resigning from the group,

would have such serious consequences as to be unavailable remedies. Sometimes efforts at such withdrawal may be construed as evidence of your emotional instability. Sometimes the virtue of persevering and learning through adversity is presented by supervisors and others as sufficient reason for you to stay in a co-therapy relationship that is intolerable.

The most probable outcome of staying with a poor co-therapist relationship for a semester, school year, or clinical rotation is that neither of you will learn what you might have learned; that you will probably have had, or nearly had, some ugly confrontations; and that your patients will probably not have benefited as much as they would have had the co-therapist pairing been more compatible. Withdrawing or resigning from a poor co-therapist relationship should not be a solution of first resort, but neither should it be of last resort unless the consequences of withdrawal include a threat to your pursuit of further training for your chosen profession.

PROBLEMS WITH THE SUPERVISOR

The supervisory relationship is one in which the potential for injustice is considerable, because of the actual or perceived power differential between supervisor and student. A supervisor can, with relative impunity, make you feel quite miserable, sap your self-confidence, and challenge the strength of your grasp on reality. In addition, a poor report from a supervisor to a director of clinical training may have a significant effect on your career, while a poor rating of the supervisor by you is seldom of major consequence to the supervisor. This power differential permeates the supervisory relationship, severely limiting the choices available to the student in response to problems within it.

Most problems in the supervisory relationship involve one or more of the following:

1. The supervisor does not provide satisfactory or adequate information to you about how to do groups;

2. The supervisor is, in your perception, judgmental, rigid, insensitive, and harsh;
3. The supervisor interprets error in the application of technique as symptoms of your emotional turmoil and seeks to turn the supervisory session into a therapy session.

There are of course other types of problems in supervisory relationships and, it should be emphasized, many supervisory relationships are highly satisfactory and relatively problem-free. But this is a chapter on problems, not resources.

Early in the process of learning a new technique or treatment modality such as group therapy, students generally want quite specific information—how do you do this, what should I say when this happens, what are the consequences of this intervention, how do you make these decisions, and the like. Later on, students need (and generally want) less detailed and more conceptual supervision.

Supervisors and students may conceptualize the supervisory task differently. Supervisors are usually therapists who have been asked to assume supervisory responsibilities by virtue of their experience with groups, or with individual therapy, or sometimes because they are available and no one else is. Supervisors sometimes approach supervision in the same way that they approach therapy. They try to help the student to find his or her own answers, and they prefer not to be explicit. Thus the supervisor attempts to teach by the Socratic method, and the student perceives the supervisor as evasive, indecisive, and withholding of information.

The problem here, at least initially, is in the differing agendas that student and supervisor bring to the supervisory sessions, and the failure of either to resolve those differences during the negotiation of the supervisory contract. Such a failure may occur on the part of the student who does not yet know enough to ask for a particular supervisory style, and on the part of the supervisor who has probably had no training in supervision and may not be familiar with the relevant literature. The student may find it helpful to consult the three chapters in Hess's (1980) book on psychotherapy supervision in which the respective contributors discuss supervision from the standpoint of the trainee (Cohen 1980, Greenberg 1980, Marshall and Confer 1980).

The Socratic method, or any method that emphasizes that you find your own solutions and answers, is valid and effective in any number of contexts. Beginning the process of learning a new set of skills as complex as those required in group psychotherapy is not one of them. The Socratic method presupposes that the student has enough knowledge, experience, theory, and time to put the answers together with very little guidance or information from the supervisor. Usually, none of those prerequisites are present when the student begins the supervisory process in group psychotherapy.

The supervisor should be willing to be quite directive at first, providing information, solutions, and answers. Gradually, as the student shapes his or her own tools, the supervisor can be less active and more probing. However, since supervisors are primarily therapists or have had considerable training in therapy, they may regard an informative, didactic, directive approach to group therapy as inappropriate, and they may regard student requests for more specificity and less ambiguity as inappropriate efforts to reduce anxiety. The situation is parallel to the circumstances of the first few sessions of a new group, where patient efforts to learn the role of group member, and perception of the therapist as the expert who knows how to teach that role, are sometimes interpreted as manifestations of pathological anxiety or intolerance of ambiguity.

The best way to handle this problem is to negotiate about it with your supervisor before the supervision begins. If the supervisor is unwilling or unable to provide direction and information in the early supervisory sessions, and if you are quite new to group therapy, then seek another supervisor if at all possible.

Sometimes it is difficult to negotiate such a contract; sometimes it is difficult to find out before the supervisory relationship begins whether a supervisor's style meets your needs. If you have not yet done a group, you may not know what to ask or what to look for, and if you are new to individual therapy as well, you will have little experience with the kind of supervision that is best for you. If, on top of all this, you are new to the clinical setting in which you are working, you may not yet know whose judgment about competence to trust. In that case, all that you have to rely on is the reputation of the training program and your own assessment of the extent to which that program can meet your training needs.

A somewhat different problem is presented by the supervisor who espouses a theoretical model in which you have no interest or confidence, who guides you toward events you regard as unimportant, trivial or dull, and toward therapist interventions you would feel foolish uttering. Sooner or later in this situation, both your sanity and your aptitude are likely to be called into question, either by yourself if you are intropunitive, or by your supervisor.

Just as you may find yourself renegotiating a therapy contract in individual therapy from time to time, you may find it desirable to attempt to renegotiate the supervisory contract as issues arise that had not been anticipated in the initial negotiations. The problem of inadequate or unsatisfactory information is an example. You may attempt to persuade your supervisor that your need for greater specificity and direction is valid, stemming from clinical need rather than neurotic anxiety. Referring your supervisor to the relevant literature is, however, a risky move. Trying to tell your supervisor that your point of view is right and his or hers wrong won't get you anywhere but into trouble. But in this most ambiguous of the healing arts, there is room for more than one correct interpretation, intervention, comment, or approach. If your supervisor will allow for your point of view, he or she may be willing to be more directive for a time. But even with such a supervisor, renegotiating the supervision contract in this way may involve confrontation, which is a rather risky business because of the power differential between you. When your supervisor begins to interpret, rather than respond to, your requests, it is time to consider survival tactics.

Cruel Supervision

Sometimes a supervisor will be hypercritical, not only tearing down your every comment but also subjecting it to ridicule. This may be more common in academic settings, where work must be found for tenured faculty, than in extramural clinics where training is a secondary mission. It may appear that the supervisor is satisfying his or her own self-esteem needs by derogating the students. But there is also a tradition, more in academia and in teaching hospitals than in clinics, of being cruel to graduate students, medical students, residents, and postdoctoral fellows. Ritualized cruelty has survived from earlier times in such in such procedures as the doctoral oral examinations as practiced at some universities or by some professors, and this on occasion finds its way into supervisory relationships. It is as though the supervisor had forgotten how it feels to be a student and on the receiving end of derogatory criticism. Such people sometimes justify their cruelty on the grounds that they endured it while they were students, and now it is their turn to dish it out. Thus does the tradition survive. (There are other academic traditions, including that of the humanistic teacher.)

People who promulgate the tradition of cruelty would be unable to do so without victims. The number of willing victims is probably even smaller than the number of supervisors who seek them. The clinical settings in which such supervisors lurk may tend to funnel students or supervisees toward them. You may find yourself required by the clinic to receive supervision from a supervisor who is sadistic and who will interpret your efforts to escape as an unwillingness on your part to learn through adversity.

One solution is to call for help. If help is not available within the clinic, then go to your training director. There are, in most places, grievance procedures, but these you should consider as a last resort. Factors that tend to inhibit calling for help include fear of reprisal, fear that calling for help will be to no avail, and fear that no one else has ever been in a similar situation or could possibly believe how bad it is for you. The cruel supervisor and to some extent the system that harbors him or her, may tend to emphasize the utter uniqueness of the situation, implying or stating explicitly that you are the only one who has had this kind of trouble. Yet, once the complaint is made, you may well find that yours is only the latest in a series of such complaints, that something can be done—too slowly to be of help to you, perhaps, but still something—and that there is ample protection from reprisal. On the other hand, sometimes the good guys lose.

Another solution, not necessarily an alternative to calling for help, is to go public: to let as many people as possible know what is going on in the supervisory sessions. Publicity tends to inhibit cruelty. If the sadistic supervisor knows that what is going on in the supervisory sessions will be talked about, that knowledge may have an inhibiting effect.

The major barrier to going public is shame—what if you tell others and they agree with your supervisor? The cruel supervisor will exploit this fear to pressure you into silence. But I think there is more support now than there used to be for the trainee who talks openly of cruel supervision; the pendulum has swung the other way. There is a parallel between the situation of cruel supervision and that of the family in which abuse is going on; the strictures against disclosure are similar, but so are the support mechanisms for the individual who breaks the silence.

Most students and supervisees tend to underestimate their own power relative to their supervisors. The power of the supervisor is rarely as great as it is perceived to be by the student. The supervisor may or may not be answerable to the training director. The training director, or *someone* at the clinic, has a vested interest in maintaining good relationships with your school or training program. The school's leverage in this situation includes the threat of withdrawing its trainees, including you, from the clinic; advising students not to seek or accept appointments there; or, ultimately, complaining to the accrediting agency sanctioning the clinic. All of these are fairly powerful levers. The students are low-cost or free labor, which is provided in exchange for training and supervision. Since many clinics are funded on a per capita basis (number of patients seen or contact hours), the arrangement is mutually advantageous. There is, therefore, strong motivation in most clinical settings for maintaining good relationships with the schools that provide clinical trainees. Somewhere along the line, then, there is likely to be someone who has the responsibility for protecting you from the cruel supervisor and is willing to exercise that responsibility. It might take a while to find that person. If you find yourself needing to make such a search, it is reasonable to assume that (1) you are not emotionally defective, and (2) you are not alone; the victims of the past and those of the future send you greeting.

Supervision as Therapy

This is a problem only when one member of the supervisory dyad (usually, although not always, the student) objects to personal therapy being done during, and as part of, the supervisory session. It is not a problem if both parties agree, preferably when contracting for supervision at the outset of the relationship, that personal therapy is a legitimate part of the supervisory relationship.

It is sometimes difficult to know how to draw the line between supervision and therapy. Both are concerned with behavior change in the therapist as he or she does therapy. That behavior change represents learning. Therapy is concerned with behavior change in areas other than the application of technique or the development of a point of view from which effective therapeutic interventions can be made.

So it is legitimate for your supervisor to observe that you tend to get angry easily when, for example, attempting to deal with cold, impassive, hostile females. But it is not legitimate for him or her to wonder aloud *why* that is so, unless you have a therapy contract with him or her. Conversely, it is also legitimate for the supervisor to refuse to engage in such speculation with you if he or she believes, as I do, that therapy and supervision are incompatible endeavors.

If you object to your supervisor doing therapy on you, you may get caught in the Catch-22 of the mental health professions: your rejection of therapy is proof that you really need it and that you lack even the minimal insight or awareness that you do. If you deny, to such a supervisor, that you have major emotional problems, you are clearly using the ego defense mechanism of denial. The stronger your denial, the stronger your defense must be; and the stronger your defense, then clearly the stronger the turmoil that is being defended against and thus the stronger your need for therapy. The possibility that your rejection of personal therapy is valid may not be considered.

This can be an anguishing problem because your grasp of reality is being challenged by someone who ought to know about such things. Even if you know cognitively, or intuitively, that you are basically in good shape, a supervisor's insistence that you need therapy can generate acrid doubts.

It is therefore advisable to establish clearly in the contract you make with the supervisor the role that personal therapy is to play in the relationship. The recommendation offered here is that it should play no role at all. Your supervisor will have to make a report of some sort, an evaluation, to those responsible for deciding whether or not you can or should continue to receive training and the blessings of whatever training system you are in. If a therapy contract is included in supervision, that report may contain or be influenced by your supervisor's opinion on how well you bared your soul during supervision and the extent to which you are guilty of unresolved emotional turmoil. The reason that such information may be included in the supervisor's report is that the supervisor is an agent of the clinic, of the training institution, and ultimately of the profession you are seeking to join. His or her divided loyalties may incline him or her to report information for the benefit of others. Your personal therapist, however, is *your* agent and cannot ethically serve the interests of others as a result of knowledge about you. In a supervisory relationship that involves work on your personal issues, you do not have the same protection in terms of confidentiality that you have in relation to your own personal therapist.

Problems with the Supervisor: Concluding Comment

I have touched here on a few problems and a few solutions in the supervisory relationship. There are, of course, other problems, and they can be more severe than those discussed above. For example, your supervisor may conclude that you are incompetent, when you know damn well that you're not—or think that you are not. Or maybe he or she is a little bit right. . . . It is difficult to imagine a problem in the supervisory relationship that is not serious or potentially grave. Problems in these relationships can drive you out of the clinical setting, out of the training institution or school or degree program that you're in, and ultimately out of the mental health professions. If you have grossly misjudged the clinical setting in which you are seeking training—and that is not hard for a student to do—you may find little support from the system or from your colleagues for your position and for what you believe in. In such a situation, the available alternatives may be to conform or to leave the field. It is possible that many talented and potentially skilled therapists choose to withdraw because they are confronted with situations where to conform would be a violation not only of belief but of personal integrity. This issue is in urgent need of research.

If you are considering leaving the mental health professions because the supervision or the clinical setting is intolerable for you, consider also that each clinic is as unique as each patient who walks through its doors, and that although there are barren, dry wastelands in the interpersonal world, so are there fertile fields and green hills. Even for you.

PROBLEM PATIENTS

Problem patients are those who, after the group starts, you wish you had turned down during the screening interview. They are problems because they are disruptive of group, or because they require an inordinate and disproportionate amount of your energy, or because they consistently respond, in group, in ways that are both unpredictable and inconsistent with your theory (or your supervisor's) about how they should respond to your interventions. Problem patients may have difficulty with the structure or arrangement of the group, with functioning within the group, or with both.

Your supervisor will help you learn how to deal with problem patients. In this book, therefore, I will discuss only briefly the types of problem behavior you might encounter in the first few sessions of a group. These include late or intermittent attendance, premature self-disclosure, monopolizing the group's attention, silent unresponsiveness, and low motivation. I will discuss each of these in turn, and in the concluding comment of this section take a look at the factors which might make some patients especially difficult for you to understand and help because of personality variables.

Late or Intermittent Attendance

Coming late is disruptive at two points in a group session: initially, when no one knows whether or not to start; and midway, when, as it happens, the patient comes in. Inevitably there is a disturbance in the flow of experience of the group. If the patient does not come at all, there is only one disruption, which occurs while the group waits in the hope that the late patient will show up.

Consistent lateness and intermittent absence can be interpreted as symptoms of insufficient commitment to group or as indicative of the patient's ambivalence about attendance. Patients almost never tell you, however, that that is why they or late or why they missed a session. Generally it is that they missed the bus (again), they had to park farther away or their car broke down (again), they got lost on the way (as the humorist Dave Barry says, I am not making this up), they couldn't get off work in time. Responding to such excuses by suggesting insufficient commitment or ambivalence is a risky move early in the life of a group and early in your experience as a group therapist. The patient who is late may feel blamed or condemned, and the other group members may feel fearful that such condemnation awaits them if they mess up in some way.

How much of an issue to make of latecoming depends mainly on three factors: how much it bothers you and your co-leader; how much it bothers the group; and how much it bothers your supervisor. If you feel that it is important for patients to be prompt, and especially if you are invariably prompt yourself, it is worth making an issue of. However, if you ask patients to be on time because their being late annoys you, it is better to tell them about your annoyance than to cloak it in therapeutic concern for the patient's or the group's well-being.

But if there is an agreement about someone's coming late, groups can be quite tolerant of latecomers. If group starts at 3:30 and one patient cannot get there before 3:50, it is possible to ask the group to accept that fact. Usually, though not always, they will. The first point of disruption—waiting for the latecomer—does not occur, and the second point—the unexpected late arrival—is minimized because the lateness is expected. Latecomers who have negotiated for late arrival usually slip in as unobtrusively as possible.

You may wish to accept a patient who will have to be late for group, contingent on the latecoming being accepted by the other group members. If a group refuses a latecomer, you may have to find another group for him or her. But sometimes therapists are more inflexible than patients about such arrangements.

The intermittent attender is a somewhat more difficult problem. He or she is the patient who misses half the sessions in the first month of group, and consistently misses one meeting a month for, say, three months. If you don't take a stand, the group will do so, as cohesiveness increases. The group will attack an intermittent attender who contributes when he or she is there sooner than it will attack someone who comes on occasion, says little, and misses the following couple of sessions.

The extent to which you seek to contact the intermittent attender outside of group and review his or her commitment to group should depend on what you are comfortable with and what your supervisor suggests. A patient who is motivated to change behavior and who finds group facilitative of such change will come on time every time to the sessions, barring natural disaster. Late or intermittent attendance suggests that the patient is not as motivated as you thought during the screening interview, doesn't find group as helpful as he or she had expected, or is experiencing some difficulty beyond his or her control in getting to the sessions. Contacting the patient outside of group to find out what is going on may be helpful (to you; the patient already knows what is going on). Whether or not such seeking out of recalcitrant patients is fruitful is a matter between you and your supervisor.

Groups are generally less tolerant of intermittent attenders who know they are going to miss than of patients who know they have to be late. The intermittent attender may not ever be included in the group, and after a time becomes neither fish nor fowl, neither one of "us" nor a new group member, nor yet a stranger. It becomes difficult for the other group members to relate to such a patient except with hostility.

Other Disruptions

Two other types of disruption you may encounter early in the life of a group are the patient who, in the midst of a delicate or tense or dramatic moment, gets up to go to the toilet; and the patient who dramatically gets up and dashes out in tears.

When patients go to the toilet during group, it can be suggested to them that next time they go before group starts. However, their going may be a protective device, enabling them to withdraw temporarily from group to pull themselves together, and to re-enter without ever admitting that they could not tolerate staying. The behavior is much more frequently encountered in inpatient than in outpatient groups. Little should be made of it at first. If the pattern continues, it would seem desirable to ask the patient to sit near the door, and to leave and return as unobtrusively as possible.

Asking the patient not to leave during group may reflect your good intention to minimize the disruption, but may also put considerable strain on what is after all a rather primitive defense mechanism.[2] When the group is cohesive, when there is some interpersonal safety, then it may be possible to get the patient to look at this particular behavioral pattern. Focusing on it before the group is cohesive and safe may simply embarrass or threaten the patient to the point where unilateral withdrawal from group seems preferable to continued attendance.

The patient who gets up tearfully and runs out of the room usually causes a major disruption of group. The other group members may try to go on as if nothing had happened. If that occurs, you may have to intervene in order to get the group to acknowledge what has just occurred. This is one of those times when your own sense of reality has little to buttress it in terms of the behavior of the others in the room, and that can be a very creepy feeling.

More often, the patient's exit will stop the group. People will look at you, wanting to know what to do and what you are going to do. They may feel guilty and responsible for having driven the patient from the room. Some action needs to be taken.

When a patient leaves the room in this manner, it may look as though he or she were headed for Patagonia on a jet plane. However, only rarely does the patient leave the clinic building. Most patients head only for as quiet or private a place as they can find, and that is usually the restroom. For this reason, the co-therapist of the same sex should go looking for the fleeing patient. Walk, don't run. If he or she is not in the restroom, check other areas that are unoccupied and open. If the patient is in none of the likely places, then he or she really doesn't want to be found, and you should stop looking and return to group. If you do find the patient, you are in a one-to-one interview with someone who is upset. The patient should be encouraged to return to group, but you should not insist. If he or she won't come back this time, try for next time. Don't press, unless there is, in your

---

[2]It is generally sound practice to ask your patients to have their health checked, so that a physiological problem (as, in the present instance, a possible bladder infection) not be wrongly interpreted as a psychological one.

judgment, incipient psychosis or incipient suicidal behavior. If the patient does not want to return, try to get some indication of what he or she would be willing for you to tell the group when you return.

What the group members need to know is that the patient is all right or is being taken care of, and that they did not force him or her out. The feeling of guilt is almost always present, especially when the patient who has fled has generated a good bit of hostility first. You may have to help the group deal with its guilt before it can turn to other matters.

You may also have to attend to your own feelings of guilt and incompetence at having allowed matters to get so far out of hand that a patient would get up and leave group in tears. Replaying the tapes, if you are taping, it is sometimes possible to spot the point at which you said this thing rather than that, after which the patient rushed out of the room. Closer examination, perhaps with your supervisor, may reveal that the patient came to group halfway, or more, expecting to leave at some point. At times, however, the patient's leaving may seem to you rather clearly a result of your handling the situation poorly because of your lack of experience. Then it may be helpful to re-member that withdrawing from group is a protective mechanism that serves to keep you or the group from inflicting damage on the patient. It may be that later on, when you have more experience, you will be able to see warning signs earlier. But even when you are more experienced, you will find that patients sometimes storm out, and that not all the skill and wisdom and experience in the world could prevent them from doing so. And there is no way to avoid feeling sad when this happens.

Premature Self-disclosure

Self-disclosure is premature when it involves a greater degree of intimacy or openness than the group—or the patient—is ready for at this time. Premature self-disclosure usually consists of telling people who are strangers facts about one's past that one would ordinarily share only with close friends, other family members, or one's individual therapist. If it is going to occur, premature self-disclosure occurs in the first or second—rarely, the third—session of a group.

It tends to happen fast, and it is almost by definition unexpected. It may begin as you are surveying, at the beginning of the first or second session, how people are feeling; or it may come during a lull or pause. Suddenly, the person you would least expect it from says,

> I'd like to say something. I'm here because I need to learn how to get along with people. I ain't never been able to get along with people. Never had a date, never had sex—I'm still a virgin at 32—and besides that, I have bad thoughts about sex with my cousin. My doctor, the one who told me I needed group, told me I should talk about these things and I want to get well, so here I am.

This example is relatively mild. Others can include disclosures about recent hospitalizations, including diagnostic information; sexual deviations; or grossly deviant behavior on the part of parent or spouse or sibling, which the patient links to a behavioral deficit of his or her own.

Such premature self-disclosure, especially about so great a deviance, is frightening to a group that does not yet have sufficient cohesiveness to offer comfort to its members.

Usually, premature self-disclosure has two results. One is that the discloser does not return to group more than once after dumping the "deep dark secrets." The other is that the level of disclosure is likely to stay superficial in the group for longer than in groups where premature self-disclosure has not occurred.

It is difficult to know whether to interrupt someone who is engaging in premature self-disclosure. If you try to stop the patient, you may be cutting off something that is not only valuable but also interesting to hear; and you may be establishing a norm, for that group, that people should not talk about the ways in which they are deviant. But usually by the time you decide that the patient needs to be stopped, it is too late. On rare occasions you may be able to perceive what is happening and get the patient to postpone self-disclosure until the group is better able to handle it. Such a perception and such a postponement comprise a manifestation of rare skill and talent. The rest of us are usually going to lose a patient (the discloser) and will have a slower starting group.

The place to look for the premature self-discloser is in the screening interview. Such people sometimes fail to meet several of the criteria for patient selection outlined in Chapter 1. Look especially for diagnoses denoting psychosis or pre-psychotic personality disturbance, such as schizoid personality; excessive talkativeness; or recent hospitalization that included group therapy. If all three of these factors are present, it may be worthwhile to talk with the patient about self-disclosure during the screening interview. One possible goal of group therapy for such patients might be to learn how to modulate self-disclosure early in relationships.

Monopolizing the Group's Attention

The monopolizer is the patient who keeps the group's energy and attention focused on him or her. If this patient is not in the spotlight, he or she manages to keep you aware of that fact, and to keep you wondering what he or she is going to do next. In the early stages of group, the monopolizer is most likely to be verbally active and aggressive. Later on he or she may use other means of controlling the group interaction.

The monopolizer typically takes a great deal of time to say relatively little, building up to a statement that is genuinely poignant and then saying, "But I've taken up too much of the group's time. Go on to someone else."

The monopolizer also typically responds with empathy to what other group members say, but turns the response toward himself or herself: "That must have been difficult for you to talk about, especially since you don't know any of us all that well yet. That's helped me to get to know you, and I want you to know that I appreciate it. I used to . . ." and he's off.

One of the things that makes the monopolizer difficult to deal with is that at the same time he or she is holding onto the group's attention, this patient manages to give the impression that he or she is fragile. Deep down there is some considerable anguish. By dint of virtually superhuman effort the patient is managing to hold together while trying to enter the group, doing good in order to get the good that the group will have to offer. Put more directly, the message is *Don't interrupt.*

Whether or not you heed that message will depend on your own preferences, on how comfortable you are about interrupting someone, especially someone you don't know very well, and on your supervisor's advice. There are some tactical advantages to letting one patient monopolize the early sessions of a therapy group; if the behavior is not too extreme, it can help to get the group moving, and the silences that sometimes characterize the early sessions are both rare and brief.

However, the interpersonal effect of monopolizing conversations is probably a major factor in what brought the patient to group in the first place. Therefore the monopolizing behavior must be dealt with, and the sooner the better. Allowing the patient to engage in and continue the maladaptive behavioral pattern is likely to produce, in group, the same reaction it would outside the group: anger, attack, and withdrawal or rejection. For the patient to experience this sequence yet again, even in a therapeutic setting, is not particularly therapeutic. Group can and should offer an interpersonal context in which the patient can experience what happens when maladaptive patterns are interrupted.

That involves turning off the monopolizer. One way of doing so is to agree with the patient who acknowledges talking too much. Allow that he or she must have some need to do so, and that it may be frightening or difficult to do something different. In the very early sessions of group, it is unlikely that the other group members would be willing to offer negative feedback—for instance, to report that they are bored or irritated by the monopolizer's monologues. In these early sessions, containment may be all that you can do, perhaps by suggesting that the monopolizer limit himself or herself to one five-minute speech and guaranteeing the patient that much speaking time each session. If your co-therapist is equally inexperienced, discuss this kind of move with your supervisor before attempting it.

Your supervisor will have more specific suggestions. When you first encounter the monopolizer, during the first session or two of group, it may be best to let him or her go on for that one session and then to discuss the situation with your supervisor. The patient is not likely to generate much of an attack from the others that early in group, and waiting to talk with your supervisor may be preferable to taking on someone whose interpersonal message is *Don't interrupt*, and who knows how to make you feel awful if you try, because that patient lives there, and you don't.

Personality Variables: Concluding Comment

In this section I have described some patient behaviors that tend to be disruptive to group and are therefore a problem. I have not discussed these problems in terms of diagnostic categories except in passing. That is because my emphasis here is on patient behavior during the group sessions and on therapist and group reactions to that behavior. To be sure, there is some relationship between diagnosis and behavior, but the problem behaviors discussed above are found in more than one or two diagnostic categories. Not every patient who engages in premature self-disclosure has a schizophrenic history, not every patient who asks you to change the starting time of group to accommodate her schedule has a borderline personality disorder, and not every monopolizer is narcissistic.

Regardless of diagnosis, there are some patients who are going to be problems for you because you cannot understand them or empathize with them, or because they make you so angry so fast that it's difficult for you to be therapeutic with them.

What type of patient will be most difficult for you to work with (or easiest—but this is a chapter on problems, not joys) depends on a rather complex interplay of patient characteristics and symptomatology and your own personality. If you're a beginning therapist, you may have no idea of what type of patient you work best or poorest with. You may already be aware of the fact that some patients are easier for you to work with than others, and that the type of patient who is easiest for you is not necessarily easiest for others. You may assume that as your experience grows, and your skill, you will be able to work with a broader range of patients. However, there is considerable evidence that you won't be able to work equally well with everyone, not as a result of their pathology or your lack of skill, but as a result of the interaction between patient factors such as symptomatology and conceptions of the patient role, and therapist personality factors (Berzins et al. 1972).

The fact that you have one or two (rarely, more) people in your group whom you really can't figure out and don't like working with is not a further reflection on your competence, although that is how it may feel. Rather, it is evidence that you cannot be all things to all persons. If you have chosen your co-therapist with skill and luck, then perhaps he or she can attend to these patients, just as you attend to those to whom your co-therapist responds negatively. Sometimes the problem is not the patient, not you, and not the technique, but lies in that mysterious chemistry of interpersonal attraction of which a therapy group is but a small, if special, part.

Silent Unresponsiveness and Low Motivation

Poorly motivated and unresponsive patients are those who are not very talkative, are passive and minimally responsive in interpersonal interactions, have difficulty defining goals, and who frequently attribute their interpersonal difficulties and intrapsychic discomfort to somatic causes, to other people, or to impersonal forces far beyond their control. Seldom found in private practice, such patients populate the public clinics and hospitals.

This is actually a quite heterogeneous group. It includes people whose behavioral or emotional impairment is minimal and transient, those who live in and are damaged by life circumstances so difficult as to be almost unimaginable to young mental health professionals with graduate degrees, and people who, at the time of this writing, are described as severely and persistently mentally ill. These people have widely differing motivations for coming, or in some cases being brought, to a mental health facility.

People suffering from transient loss are sometimes puzzled by their own emotional responses to psychic injury and seek to interpret their reactions in terms of somatic impairment.

An example is the 50-year-old maintenance worker whose wife left him after 23 years of marriage, and who reported to his employer's health service with symptoms of fatigue, weight loss, insomnia, and difficulty concentrating. All physical findings were negative and the patient was referred to the mental health clinic. From the intake worker there he requested medication to help with the fatigue and insomnia. The psychiatrist, reviewing the medical findings, told him that he had a chemical imbalance resulting in depression and prescribed antidepressant medication. The psychiatrist also referred the patient for group therapy. In his first session this man attributed his difficulties to the chemical imbalance, which he said had resulted in "bad nerves," and he did not see how talking was going to help his bad nerves.

An example of a different type of problem is that of a woman in her early twenties who was referred to the clinic by her case worker. The oldest of ten children, she had dropped out of high school to help raise her younger siblings and to provide support of various kinds to the farmhands during the growing seasons. She had two children of her own and provided for them, along with her own siblings and the three children of her next-younger sisters. The client had become increasingly resentful of her sisters, who did not help with child care, cooking, or other household chores, and had suddenly one day refused to provide services except child care for her own children. It was this refusal and the subsequent family conflict that had led to the mental health referral and subsequent referral for group.

A third example is that of a man in his early forties who worked as a part-time warehouseman for a local clothing manufacturer. He had been troubled by delusions of reference for about ten years, following a homosexual approach by another man, which he had promptly rejected. At times the delusions were so troubling that he could not work at all; he was supported by his wife, who worked as a hairdresser. The treating psychiatrist at the mental health center had tried a variety of medications, none of which seemed to affect this man's delusions. Concluding that the patient spent too much time home alone brooding, the psychiatrist recommended group therapy.

The behavior of these three patients in group was remarkably similar. All three came in, sat silently, said little or nothing, and left. What they had in common was a discrepancy between what the clinic and the group was prepared to offer them and what they wanted or needed. The man in the first example needed more and different orientation and preparation for group therapy before he would be able to participate in and benefit from it. He wanted a quick and magical solution, preferably one that would entail the return of his wife. The group offered exploration of interpersonal coping strategies. The young woman wanted more help from her siblings and support from her family than she was getting, or she wanted freedom from the crushing burden of obligation and work placed on her by her mother's fecundity. The group offered an opportunity to explore new ways of handling anger. The patient of the third example wanted nothing at all from the clinic or the group. He would have been content to remain at home, watching television and peeping out fearfully from time to time at the neighbors as they left for and returned from work each day. The group offered an opportunity to engage in interpersonal interaction and to re-evaluate his delusions of reference.

There was, then, a significant difference between what these patients wanted and what the group therapists were offering or attempting to provide. The problem here is not the impassive silence of the patients or their apparent lack of motivation. Rather, it is in the discrepancy between the services they were seeking (or, in the last case, seeking to avoid) and the services they were receiving. It is possible that a more careful screening interview would have revealed this discrepancy in expectations, resulting in the patients' agreeing that they needed and should therefore seek the very services that the group would provide.

However, this is frequently a difficult and lengthy negotiation because it involves major shifts in the patient's conceptualization of what is going on, including changes in the patient's ideas about the magnitude of emotional pain or behavioral deficit, the root causes of that pain or deficit, and therefore the most effective remedies. Such a negotiation cannot usually be accomplished in a single screening interview or two, but may require more extensive individual therapy. However, even then the problem may remain that what the patient wants is rapid symptom relief, or to be let alone, and what the clinic offers is insight, understanding, and the development of new interpersonal skills.

It is the discrepancy between what the clinic offers and what the patient wants that leads some patients to be labeled, usually informally, as problem patients lacking in motivation and that leads some patients to a sullen silent demeanor in group therapy.

It is doubtful that there are *any* people who are truly unmotivated. Clinic patients who are regarded by staff as unmotivated are not motivated in the way that staff think they should be, or are not motivated to do the things that staff thinks they should want to do. In terms of group therapy, such patients may not be motivated to use the group experiences to help them to make behavioral changes that the therapists, but not the patients, regard as desirable.

The problem of the silent or unmotivated group member, then, is usually a problem in the contract between the patient and the clinic for the provision and receipt of mental health services. That is a difficult problem for even an experienced group therapist to resolve, either in the screening interview(s) or during group sessions. The probability is low that patient will benefit from group therapy under these conditions. At the time of this writing, the difficult problem of whether to deny services to patients who do not want clinic services and therefore have quite poor prognoses has not yet been resolved.

If you and/or the mental health service delivery system in which you find yourself are committed to offering group therapy services to such patients—that is, if you do not wish to or cannot exclude them from the group by screening them out—then it may help you to be more patient with them, and to avoid pushing them toward an outcome they do not want, by defining the problem as one in the interpersonal contract between you and the patient or perhaps between the clinic and the patient. Such an interpersonal approach may, over time, be more satisfactory and helpful to the patient than the more judgmental and typically fruitless approach of seeking to motivate or remotivate the patient to want what you think is best.

13

Inpatient Group Therapy

Inpatient group therapy is in many respects different from outpatient group therapy. Indeed, the difference is so great that inpatient group therapy—or rather therapies, for here too there are many techniques—may be regarded as an altogether different endeavor. The major difference between the two is the inpatient status itself. That status involves a major disruption in the life of each patient in the group. Admission to inpatient status constitutes a nadir in the lives of most people, as Goffman (1959) argued eloquently in his classic study. Differences between outpatient and inpatient groups involve the severity of disturbance of each patient, the structure and purpose of the groups, the roles required of the group leaders, the length of the sessions, the relationships of the patients to each other outside the group, and other differences which depend in part on the type of inpatient facility in which the group is offered.

Despite the ranges of psychopathologies, the plethora of techniques, and the gamut of purposes, inpatient group can generally be classified as to the length of hospitalization and the level of functioning of the patients. In this chapter I will discuss the short-term inpatient group characteristic of psychiatric wards of general hospitals, private psychiatric hospitals, and other brief inpatient facilities.

A short-term or brief (the terms are used here interchangeably) inpatient group is defined as one that is open; new members may come in at any time and current members leave as soon as they are discharged from the hospital. No two sessions of the group will necessarily have the same membership. In some settings, the therapists may also change from day to day. Because of these changes in both membership and leadership, Yalom (1983) has suggested that brief inpatient groups be regarded as meeting only once. Nearly every session of the group seems like—and, to the experienced group leader, feels like—the first session of a new group. There is little opportunity for the group to move through the stages of group development and cohesiveness generally remains low (Leszcz et al. 1985, Maves and Schulz 1985). Brabender (1985, 1988) has proposed a short-term inpatient group model in which group membership is stable over eight sessions (two weeks), which seems like a very desirable arrangement but which might prove very problematic as rapid turnover and very short lengths of stay become more and more typical of inpatient psychiatric hospitalizations.

THE PURPOSE OF INPATIENT GROUPS

In discussing the purpose of any psychotherapeutic endeavor, it is instructive to look both at what the institution is seeking to provide and what the patients are hoping to obtain. Leszcz and colleagues (1985) compared the evaluations by patients of two inpatient groups, one unstructured and heterogeneous and the other structured and homogeneous. Both groups were voluntary, though the student may find that the term *voluntary* pertaining to psychiatric inpatients is sometimes an oxymoron, a factor taken into account by these authors in their discussion of the results. Leszcz and colleagues conclude:

> [The] goals [of acute inpatient group psychotherapy] include decreasing the patient's sense of isolation and estrangement, and initiating a process in which verbalization and personal engagement are experienced as helpful and therapeutic. Further goals include helping the

patient make more sense of his interpersonal environment and the large part he plays in it, both within the hospital and outside of it. This can be done in a way that begins to educate him regarding possible alternative ways of perceiving his world and behaving within it. The aim of major characterological change through the acquisition of insight on a genetic basis is not suited for the clinical reality of the acute inpatient unit, and will likely be confusing and demoralizing for both the patient and therapist. Last, but perhaps most importantly, the group psychotherapy experience should be a sufficiently successful and hopeful one to encourage the patient to continue in posthospitalization treatment as may be required, in order to carry on with a process of treatment that is often begun but rarely completed in hospital. [p. 431]

Cost-containment pressures tend to lead inpatient facilities to seek ways to reduce length of stay as much as possible. Under these conditions, one purpose of an inpatient group is to facilitate the patient's return to the community as rapidly as possible. Hence, the most important question is, "What has to change before the patient can be discharged?" The answer frequently includes medication-induced changes in the patient's behavior. It also includes change in the patient's living arrangements outside the hospital: in marital status, job, geographic location, and the like. In these instances, the purpose of group is to help the patient define what needs changing, to define change in ways that can be rapidly accomplished, and to evaluate some possible consequences, both positive and negative, of making the needed changes.

These institutional purposes of group are somewhat different from those discussed by Leszcz and colleagues. Differences in patient and staff perceptions, needs, goals, and acculturation have been documented by Kahn and his associates (1992). There is, however, a confluence of purpose since voluntary patients usually want their hospital stays to be as brief as possible. To the extent that such patients can begin, in group, to identify and plan for life circumstance changes that facilitate early discharge, patient and institutional goals are similar.

A 66-year-old woman was admitted to the psychiatric unit of the hospital with symptoms including hallucinations and severe depression. She had been living alone for some years in a lonely house trailer in a rural area. She had had very few human contacts, and was in effect living in circumstances of sensory deprivation so severe as to virtually guarantee the development of visual and auditory hallucinations. In hospital, her recovery from these symptoms was rapid. Group therapy helped her to realize that human contact was preferable to interpersonal isolation even if it meant that she was somewhat more dependent on her daughter than she had been. She began, albeit reluctantly, to explore alternative living arrangements and was discharged as soon as these were completed. Factors that led her to choose and to maintain the interpersonal isolation that precipitatea the hospitalization were not explored.

Usually the patient's own coping mechanisms are in need of change as well. Such changes usually require considerably more time than changes in behavior resulting from the administration of medicines, and are not likely to occur as a result of participation in a short-term inpatient group. Such groups may serve a number of purposes, but the facilitation of change in behavior is not usually one of them. The goals of inpatient group most frequently include modification of the acute symptom picture in order to facilitate rapid discharge, and bolstering the patient's willingness to continue therapy outside the hospital.

The situation with involuntary patients is somewhat different. Here, too, the goal of the institution is likely to be early discharge because of cost-containment pressures. Disposition is usually a more difficult problem than for the voluntary patient, since the involuntary patient may be more or less actively opposed to whatever the mental health care delivery system is trying to impose on him or her. For the group therapist, the focus of therapy may involve attempts to reduce the discrepancy between the patient's agenda and that of the institution—an issue similar to that described in the preceding chapter with regard to difficult or unmotivated patients. Beginning therapists frequently assume that health or being well is a self-evident desirable goal and that patients want to get help in order to attain that goal. Consequently, new therapists are sometimes puzzled by the vehemence with which their offers of help are rejected even by involuntary patients.

One reason for this rejection may be that for some patients, *help*, as in *let me help you*, is associated with grievous threats to the patient's autonomy, identity, and very sense of existence. In these instances, *help* means invasive control by another person. The paradigm is that of the well-meaning and earnest young mother forcing some dark green goo into the mouth of her young infant and solemnly assuring the infant that it tastes good. Some patients react to proffered help as though it were dark green goo being forced into their mouths.

For these patients, the urgent work of the short-term inpatient therapy group involves an exploration and perhaps renegotiation of the treatment contract between the patient and the institution, and perhaps some exploration of more adaptive consequences of getting better and accepting help.

Another purpose of short-term inpatient groups, with both voluntary and involuntary patients, is to help the patient identify strengths and resources: what is working rather than what has broken down. In the inpatient group therapy literature this is sometimes referred to as strengthening existing ego defenses (Marcovitz and Smith 1983) or improving coping skills (Kanas 1991).

All of this boils down to two functions or purposes for short-term inpatient groups. One is to facilitate the disposition process: to help get the patient out of the hospital as rapidly as possible. The other purpose, more limited, involves reaching through the walls of terror and despair, isolation and rage, and helping the patient to see, if only for a brief moment, that he or she is not alone facing the demons of madness and oblivion. If for one minute out of an hour's group session you can be in contact with, in human touch with, a person otherwise totally absorbed in those internal battles, then you have not solved the world's ills, but you will have done a great thing.

THE SELECTION OF PATIENTS

On psychiatric wards where a group therapy program is already established, the student therapist is not likely to be consulted about the selection of patients for group. On wards where there is no established group program, or hardly any, the student may be given carte blanche, and may find that supervision is minimal or difficult to arrange.

In either case, there are some selection principles; or, to be more precise, the student will find it helpful to know what selection principles are being used, because selection criteria and procedures strongly influence what happens in group. Of critical importance is the principle that the group leaders are the final arbiters of admission to the group. On some wards, the attending physician may assign group in the same way that drugs are prescribed, and the group leaders lack veto power. The student would do well to avoid the latter situation, since it allows for the possibility of patients being in the group whom the group leader does not want there. If the group leaders cannot control access to the group, then they have such low power and the group such low status that it is unlikely anything therapeutic can occur during the group sessions.

Patients on general hospital psychiatric wards and on the admissions wards of longer-term hospitals tend to vary widely in age, intelligence, race, and diagnosis. Homogeneity of background is seldom attainable despite some evidence of its value (Kanas 1991). Kahn (1986) has summarized the arguments for and against homo- or heterogeneity in inpatient groups and offers some principles for assignment of patients to group.

Patients who are floridly psychotic are not likely to benefit from group therapy. Their presence usually impairs the ability of the group and its leaders to function effectively. Some group leaders allow acutely disturbed patients to attend group, in the belief that the less disturbed patients will have a calming effect upon them. However, a less severely disturbed patient placed in the same group as one who is more or less literally climbing the walls will frequently become more upset, and the agitated patient will not become calmer. In the psychoses, interpersonal influences are at best minimal.

Homogeneity in terms of severity of pathology is therefore what should be sought after. Yalom's (1983) suggestion of high- and low-functioning groups is commendable, though his suggestions as to how the low-functioning group should be conducted have not met with universal approval (Kibell 1993). However, patients who are highly agitated should not be referred for or accepted in even the low-functioning group. Patients who are so extremely withdrawn as to be nonresponsive to environmental stimuli should also be excluded—whether such behavior is attributed to the apathy of depression or that of schizophrenia. Patients with impaired consciousness should also be excluded, whether the impairment results from some intrinsic process such as injury or disease, is a side effect of medication or other therapies, or is a result of intoxication. However, patients who are disoriented as to time, place, and person can be considered as possible candidates for group if they are not agitated, if their disturbance is not associated with impaired consciousness, and if the severity of deficit is consistent with the general level of pathology of other members of the group.

Another criterion for exclusion involves the willingness of the therapists to tolerate behavior they find upsetting or disturbing. Some psychiatric inpatients are not merely unpleasant but intolerably so. In some cases that might be why they are inpatients. Such patients may be skilled in getting others to respond to them with anger and rejection, and it is not always possible for therapists to avoid responding to them in the same way.

The rationale for admitting such a patient to group therapy is that the group offers an opportunity to explore alternative ways of relating that do not generate so much hostility. However, change in behavior is seldom a viable goal for short-term inpatient groups. What tends to happen is that the group interaction intensifies both the maladaptive behavior and its reciprocal: the patient succeeds in getting people angry, and the other group members tend toward silent passive observation of the battle between the offensive member and the therapist. Good seldom comes of this.

Patient Selection: High-functioning versus Low-functioning Groups

It is possible but unnecessary to develop a set of criteria for determining whether a patient should go into the high- or low-functioning group. There is on most psychiatric wards a consensus among ward personnel about who is high- or low-functioning. Students are not usually called upon to make that determination, but staff members just beginning to do groups may be. Some patients will clearly belong in the high-functioning group; others, clearly in the low. For some patients it will not be clear at all as to whether they should go into the high or low group, and for such patients it probably does not matter which group they are assigned to. If it becomes evident that an assignment error has been made, then put the patient in the other group. If the group therapists are not sufficiently familiar with the patients to make the determination, then ask the ward personnel, who know the patients best.

If there is only one group on the ward or in the psychiatric unit, the problem is somewhat different and pertains to the maximum level of disturbance, or minimum level of functioning (the two are not always the same) that the group, and the leaders, are willing to accept. If there are two groups, high and low, it is possible that some patients who would not be in group at all if there were only one group would be eligible for the low-functioning group. That is, having high- and low-functioning groups on the same unit lowers the threshold for admission.

Pre-group Screening

In the present era of very short term hospitalizations, there is no time for exhaustive pre-group screening. In some inpatient settings, psychiatric and other (e.g., residential substance abuse treatment facilities), every patient admitted to the unit is expected to attend group therapy sessions and some administrative action is required if the patient is to be exempted. In such settings the therapists lack veto power over group membership, as do the members themselves. The result is likely to be a host of problems having more to do with administrative policies than with patient benefit or the technical skill of the therapists, and the student is advised to avoid such settings if at all possible. Some screening is desirable. A patient should not automatically be referred for group upon admission to the ward unless the ward or the facility is highly selective in its admissions.

When a patient is first admitted to the ward, a process of assessment begins. This process has both formal and informal components. The formal assessment will consist, at a minimum, of the admitting physician's physical and mental status examinations. At all accredited hospitals these examinations must be performed within twenty-four hours of admission. Formal assessment may include psychodiagnostic testing and other procedures. Informal assessment is the subjective judgment of the staff and other patients about the magnitude of disturbance of the newcomer. Although it is based on first and therefore superficial impressions, this informal assessment strongly influences how others on the ward begin to relate to the new patient.

In the screening process, the group leaders should if possible avail themselves of both the formal and the informal assessments of the patient. The most important question to ask is probably some variant of the general form,"Is this patient too disturbed or disturbing to be in group?" Whether the patient can benefit from group is frequently more difficult to ascertain from the formal assessment process. The informal process, perhaps codified as *clinical judgment* by mental health professionals, may provide more useful information. First impressions are important because they guide the initiation of interaction. But first impressions are seldom codified in admission assessment procedures.

The screening interview itself should be as brief and succinct as possible. It need not be held in an interview room. An informal brief conference in the day room, or wherever the patient may be found, has much to commend it. The patient is in a situation where he or she has very little freedom or autonomy. Patients are summoned hither and thence. Things are done to them about which they may be informed but are seldom asked. Coming to the patient, rather than *summoning* him or her to yet another conference with strangers, is at least courteous and perhaps less frightening, and allows the patient rather more autonomy — it is easier to refuse and walk away in a day room than in an interview room — and may enhance, however slightly, the patient's feeling of being in control of *something*.

Your task during the screening interview is to provide the patient with enough information about group therapy and its benefits to persuade the patient that attendance is likely to be a good thing. At the same time, you're making your own informal assessment of whether or not the patient should be in your group. Because it is at best awkward to do a screening interview and then tell the patient not to come to group, it is prudent to be fairly certain, based on other available information, that you will accept him or her prior to initiating the screening interview.

The screening interview, then, is a complex task that must be accomplished in a relatively short time. What happens in the screening interview will influence, if not determine, what the patient will do in group — how active and how appropriate he or she is likely to be — and is therefore of considerable importance for patient participation and benefit in group therapy. Therefore, if you don't have much experience with brief inpatient group therapy, you should let someone else do the screening interviews while you observe for a time. Unless you are a gregarious sort of person who meets people easily, consider practicing screening interviews with a colleague until the interactions go smoothly and the way you want them to go.

Here's an example of how such an interview might go:

Therapist: Hi. I'm Dr. Houshmand and this is Ms. Dugan. We're group therapists, and you've been referred for group therapy. Have you ever been in group therapy before?

Patient: No.

Therapist: Group therapy is a meeting where we talk about what needs to change before you leave the hospital, so that you don't go back into the same situation you were in when you came. Sometimes that means looking at relationships with other people and what needs to change there, and what happens when you make those changes. Group is a place where you get help from other people and you also have a chance to help others.

Patient: Hunh.

Therapist: The group meets at 12:30. You don't have to come, but most people who come find it helpful. We'd like for you to come.

Patient: OK, I guess.

Therapist: Wonderful! Do you have any questions about group therapy?

Patient: What am I supposed to talk about?

Therapist: Well, you can talk about whatever's on your mind. For most people that means what needs to happen so they can get out of the hospital, but sometimes it means talking about other things too.

Patient: Who's going to be there?

Therapist: Ms. Dugan and I, of course, and some of the other people from the unit. People you've already met. What you talk about in group doesn't get talked about with other people on the ward who don't come to group.

Patient: OK, I guess.

Therapist: Great! See you then.

For patients who are more disturbed, a briefer introduction might be appropriate. For people who are more anxious and have many questions, a more lengthy discussion might be required. Answer all of the questions the patient asks, if you know the answers and are not uncomfortable with giving them, and if they do not involve breaching professional ethics or confidentiality. It is rare that therapists get quizzed about group during a screening interview.

In general, group should be presented as a place or means for patients to get some help in obtaining the benefit that they came to the hospital for. If you suggest that the group is a place to talk about problems, you'll have difficulty with the patient who feels that he or she has no problems. The patient who denies needing help can be asked why he or she is in the hospital, and that can sometimes lead to a brief discussion of what group might be able to offer.

The question may arise of how much coercion to use to get a recalcitrant patient into group. A therapist on a locked ward is perceived by the patient who has no key as quite powerful. Anything the therapist does, including the issuance of such a relatively mild invitation as "We'd like for you to come to group" may be experienced as a coercive demand because of the power differential between therapist and patient. That may be undesirable, but it is also unavoidable. What *is* avoidable is linking attendance to ward privileges, pass cards, and the like by the person who has the authority to give or withhold such privileges. This kind of coercion is seldom fruitful and frequently signifies negative countertransference. Patients should have the right to refuse group. If moderately strenuous efforts at verbal persuasion are not successful, more vigorous efforts may produce the patient's presence but not participation in group therapy.

Screening interviews may last a couple of minutes, or they may last for 45 to 60 minutes if you let them. Sometimes patients are eager to tell their stories, to begin sorting out what has happened to them, to have some interchange with a safe professional. In such instances, the therapeutic work that involves disclosure begins in the screening interview and is continued in the group session. When that occurs, you also have a considerable opportunity to talk further with the patient about what happens during group sessions, and to begin to help the patient focus on here-and-now interactions as you will do in the group. If the patient needs to say more words than you or the group will be able to tolerate—that is, if the patient seems like a potential monopolizer—this is the time to begin putting some boundaries around the torrent of words and to see how well that containment is tolerated by the patient. The novice group therapist might say,

"But what if every screening interview takes an hour?" Fear not: that won't happen, unless you are in a *very* unusual facility.

TECHNIQUE: SOME GENERAL CONSIDERATIONS

The three tactical goals of the inpatient group therapist are (1) to reduce anxiety; (2) to initiate, facilitate, and encourage communication; and (3) to support, reinforce, and consensually validate those aspects of a patient's experience that are not psychotic.

These tactical goals hold true for each group session, and through the series of sessions across the life of a group. In an inpatient group, what you are frequently faced with is, in effect, a series of initial group sessions. This is due primarily to the relatively rapid turnover in group membership. Even in a group that meets daily, it is rare to have the same membership on more than two successive days. It may be possible on occasion to facilitate communication among the patients and even to seek some validation by the group of the healthy aspects of a patient's experiences, but for the most part you will be dealing with the reduction of anxiety and concomitant reduction in the severe interpersonal isolation associated with major mental illness.

The magnitude of anxiety of an inpatient group differs from that of outpatient groups. It is the difference between the Himalaya and the Allegheny mountains. In both inpatient and outpatient groups, some of the anxiety of the initial group session is situation specific: the anxiety stemming from being in a new situation with strangers, not knowing what is expected or what to do or what will happen, fearful of being judged and of other people. These are not uncommon anxieties about group. In addition to the anxiety generated by the situation, there are the anxieties each patient brings to the session: anxieties stemming from the patient's assessment of the world and of his or her ability to survive in it. In inpatient groups, that anxiety is frequently so overwhelmingly negative as to be intolerable.

There are many ways of categorizing, conceptualizing, and accounting for deviant behavior—for instance, as primarily of biochemical etiology, as representing learning deficits, or as the result of environmental deprivation or psychic trauma. Each view is fruitful in some context. For group therapy, which is above all interpersonal, the most fruitful way of conceptualizing psychosis is as a disturbance in interpersonal behavior, an impairment of the desire or ability to relate with other people. From this view, which is an extension of the interpersonal theory discussed in Chapter 8, death and madness are solitary experiences; joy can never be attained in isolation; interaction is both healthy (or health-producing) and potentially joyful. This argument has been most cogently advanced by Pesso (1973), who has recently added to his theory the concept that meaning stems from interaction (Howe 1991).

It follows that the task of the group therapist is to facilitate interaction among patients. The first barrier to interaction is anxiety. The anxiety of the psychotic patient frequently, although not always, stems from his or her assessment of the world as an unsafe place, and of his or her ability to survive in it as not equal to the task. It is as though the patient says, There is no safety in this world, only danger, and I am not strong enough to resist the danger. Therefore I will be (am being, have been) overwhelmed by my enemies, or by evil. . . .

This is an intolerable way to live. Some psychotic behavior may be understood as the patient's effort to seek a safe place within himself or herself, or within his or her own fantastic re-creation of reality. Thus some psychotic patients relate to themselves rather than to other people, and lose the consensual validation of reality that keeps us sane.

Before healing can occur, the patient must have a safe place to experience himself or herself. To provide such a place is sometimes a difficult and challenging task for the group leader. Yet anxiety will generally diminish in proportion to the degree that group is seen as a safe place.

A number of factors will facilitate establishment of the group as a safe place. One is the environment. The group session should, if possible, be held in a quiet place, away from patients who are screaming or pounding. The group members need to be sure that there is no danger of physical violence during the group session, especially if there is or has been physical violence on the ward. The group room must be protected from intrusion, either by aides summoning patients to other activities (a frequent type of intrusion) or by patients wandering in. Locking the door to the group room, however, is not a good solution because it makes prisoners of all those group members who lack keys.

The careful selection of patients is a second factor that facilitates establishment of the group as a safe place. The range and severity of pathology observable in the dayroom at any one time is likely to be quite wide, and disoriented or loudly hallucinating patients are often in the same room with patients for whom such behavior is very frightening. Such a situation is less common in private psychiatric facilities, but so is training in group therapy. Exclusion from group of patients with marked degrees of agitation may be reassuring on several counts to the group members—including some evidence that the staff does not, after all, regard all patients as equally crazy. As noted above, homogeneity in severity of pathology is desirable in inpatient groups.

But the group leader is the most important factor in establishing and maintaining the group as a safe place. The group leader should ideally be perceived as powerful, benevolent, fair, and just: powerful, to banish the patient's internal demons and to vanquish those external demons that make a psychiatric ward, especially an admissions ward in a large psychiatric hospital, such a frightening place; benevolent, to meet the patient's interpersonal needs without demanding intrusive control; and fair and just, to be honest and firm without being vindictive.

The group leader, then, must act the role of a powerful and benevolent quasi-parent, the role of one who, in terms of the leadership styles described in Chapter 12, is active rather than passive, cue-emitting rather than cue-suppressing, and authoritarian rather than collegial—an active, controlling and at times quite directive and assertive group leader. Being overassertive is, in this context, less of an error than being underassertive. Novice group therapists tend not to

function assertively in groups initially, even when suited by personality to do so. Clinicians coming to group therapy after training and
experience in individual therapy typically have considerable difficulty
shifting to the more active and process-oriented role. The reticence of
the novice group therapist arises at first from uncertainty and lack of
confidence, and sometimes also from habits developed in individual
therapy. Therefore, groups in short-term inpatient psychiatric units
are not good places for novice co-therapist pairs to begin doing groups.
The student doing his or her first group should seek a more experienced therapist as co-leader.

   One other general consideration should be mentioned before we
look at some specific techniques. That is the issue of confidentiality. A
patient may ask, on occasion, that something he or she says in group
remain confidential; or patients may ask whether what is said in group
will reported back to the doctors or the ward personnel. Patients
should be told the truth. The truth in this instance is that what
patients say in group may in fact be reported back in some detail, and
documented in the chart notes, with due protection for the identities
of the other patients. There can be no confidentiality on an inpatient
psychiatric service.

   What you can offer the patient, and request from the other group
members, is *privacy*. In this context, privacy means that you will
discuss the patient only with those other mental health professionals
who have some need to know, and who themselves are ethically
bound to respect the privacy of the patients in their care by avoiding
extramural disclosure of patient information. At the time of this
writing, the blatant breach of professional confidentiality entailed in
the reporting requirements of third-party payers has not been ade-
quately resolved. It seems that patients are willing to tolerate intru-
sions into their privacy in order to obtain third-party reimbursement
for their therapy.

   Since you cannot promise confidentiality, there are some things
that patients might want to talk about, in confidence, that they are
not going to discuss for fear that you will report the discussion to
others. That is a real and necessary limitation of inpatient group

psychotherapy—and, for that matter, of individual psychotherapy as well. Sometimes it is possible to negotiate with the patient about the kind and amount of information that will be reported to others. Such negotiation is most easily accomplished in individual psychotherapy. It is more difficult in an outpatient group, and virtually impossible to accomplish in an inpatient group. The patient may choose to remain silent, and it is important for the therapists, and the rest of the group, to respect that silence. If the patient chooses to proceed without a guarantee of confidentiality, the type of material that is most likely to emerge tends to pertain to the relationship between the patient and the ward physicians or staff. Sometimes, however, what emerges is highly personal and idiosyncratic.

The issue becomes particularly critical if you suspect that a patient would talk about contemplated suicide or homicide if granted a guarantee of confidentiality. There may be some valuable information which you will have to forgo. You need not hear from the patient's own lips that he or she is contemplating suicide before you take appropriate action.

TECHNIQUE: STARTING THE GROUP

Even if you yourself have done all of the screening, it will still usually be helpful to reintroduce yourself and make some brief statement of what the group is about. An exception is if you are the physician in charge of all the patients in the group, so that your name and face have some salience for them beyond what is involved in the group.

There is no particular formula for describing what the group is about. You will have to find words that suit you, given the purpose of group and the emphasis on interpersonal issues suggested above. One example of this type of introduction is this:

> I'm Dr. Egglesworth. This is a group therapy session. It's an opportunity to talk about what brought you to the hospital and what needs to change before you leave so you don't go back into the same situation

you were in when you came. Group can help you to understand people better—how they see you, why they react to you the way they do, how you influence other people's reactions to you, that sort of thing. It's also an opportunity for people to help each other.

We have some new members here today, Lynne and John. I'd like for everyone to say a word or two about how you're feeling right now, how it feels to be here in this room, and also please tell us one thing about yourself that you're comfortable with telling us, that you'd like for us to know about you.

A more succinct introduction is, "Group therapy is where you talk about your problems. We're here to talk about your problems. Who wants to start?" Such an introduction has the advantage of being brief. However, it is likely to be followed by silence. An invitation to talk about one's problems in a group full of strangers is not likely to be accepted. It is necessary to start with small and relatively safe disclosures and gradually build on them. In addition, many patients do not perceive *talking about* as particularly fruitful; nor do they necessarily conceptualize what is happening to them as *their* problem. Initially, patients may not anticipate that talking in a therapy group will be of much benefit to them, and a simple invitation by the group leader to begin is not likely to be fruitful.

Another way that inpatient groups sometimes start is that the patients begin to complain about conditions on the ward, or about the incompetence of their doctors, or the side effects of their medicines. Such complaints should be listened to attentively, at least at first. The possibility that such complaints may have some validity should be acknowledged ("Yes, the dayroom is noisy when both televisions are going full blast"), though comments about staff competence are best left unacknowledged, whatever your private agreement with such comments may be.

Sometimes, after a patient has complained bitterly about conditions on the ward, or the noise, or the food, and so forth, it is possible to ask, "How would you like for us here to help? What would you like for us to do?" The patient may well say, "Make them serve better food." You might then ask, "Do you really think I can make them do that?"

which brings the focus of the interaction into the here-and-now. If the patient honestly answers in the affirmative, then a simple "I can't do that" is in order. But much more frequently the patient will acknowledge that the request is inappropriate or is not aimed at the therapist or the group, and the door is opened to explore the function and interpersonal consequences of making requests that the patient knows cannot be met by the people with whom he or she is talking.

The amount of verbal activity in an inpatient group will probably vary considerably from one session to the next, as will the amount of interaction. In general, the interactions are one-to-one: patient–therapist, patient–therapist. Sometimes it is as though there were no others in the room but you and the patient. No one listens or attends to what is going on except you and the patient who is speaking or has your attention at the moment. That is the interpersonal isolation mentioned above.

Inexperienced therapists sometimes invite patients to address each other, in the belief that such instruction will facilitate interpersonal interaction. "Mrs. Fisher, how does Ms. Sykes look to you today? Tell her now, look at her, and tell her." Mrs. Fisher may indeed comply, but the interaction is most likely to be farcical or wooden. Patients aren't going to give a damn about each other's opinions until they are ready to. They are not going to be ready until group is a safe place. One way to begin making group a safe place, in this context, is to facilitate the type of interaction that most readily presents itself: one-to-one.

This is a tactical suggestion. Since all that you are likely to get anyway with such an inpatient group is a series of one-to-one interactions, patient to therapist, you may as well go ahead and engage the patients one to one, as fully as possible or appropriate. If you can get a patient to interact with you, that is better than the patient remaining silent and withdrawn. Further, if you engage with the patient and the engagement is both meaningful and satisfactory to him or her, the chances that he or she might be willing to engage with another patient are enhanced.

Engagement, here, requires that you take a stand. The impersonal approach favored by some physicians and some psychotherapists is not likely to be fruitful. There is no safety with someone who is impersonal, and such a stance is not likely to reduce anxiety in this context. (In other types of interaction, such as physical examinations of the patient, and perhaps at times during individual psychotherapy, an impersonal approach might be anxiety-reducing.) Taking a stand involves allowing your opinions to be known; that is, it involves therapist self-disclosure. Such self-disclosure should be limited to opinions and/or feelings that (1) have direct relevance within the patient's frame of reference and (2) pertain to here-and-now interactions in the room with people who are physically present. The following examples illustrate this point:

Patient: Tell me, doctor, do you believe in ESP?

Doctor: No, I don't. Some people believe in it. I don't share their beliefs.

Patient: Well, I believe in ESP. There is something about you, an aura, that I knew, I knew at once that you would not knowingly do me harm.

Doctor: I think that what you are saying is that you feel that you can trust me.

Patient: Yes.

Doctor: I'm glad you feel that way.

In this example, the first thing to note is that the therapist gave a direct answer to the question. His answer was as clear and unequivocal as he could get it. He also said something about himself, his beliefs, and about how he handles differences of opinion. The patient's next comment does not make much literal sense. The therapist took it symbolically, and translated[1] the comment into language that is less

---

[1] *Translation* refers to saying the same thing in different words, taking care to leave the meaning intact. *Interpretation* involves placing a different meaning on what the patient is saying or doing. An interpretive comment, in the above example, would take note of the patient's reaching out, or perhaps of the significance of the aura.

idiosyncratic and closer to consensual meaning. He then again took a stand ("I think that . . .") in the process of checking whether or not his translation was correct. His final statement is again a personal one ("I'm glad . . ."), but still limited to that particular patient at that time.

Another example of how this interchange might have been handled:

> *Patient:* Doctor, do you believe in ESP?
>
> *Doctor:* You want to know if I believe in ESP.
>
> *Patient:* Yes, I do.
>
> *Doctor:* Why is it important for you to know that?
>
> *Patient:* Because I just wanted to—I thought that—
>
> *Doctor:* I wonder if anyone else in the group believes in ESP?

In this example, the therapist first repeats the patient's question, although he heard and understood it quite well. His repetition is simply a device to buy time while he tries to think of what to say next—and then he dodges the question by responding to it with another. Answering a question with a question is poor technique. It is obstructive rather than facilitative. Finally, the therapist diverts the question clear away from himself and onto the group, so that the thrust of the patient's effort to engage him one-on-one is thwarted and diffused. It is as though the patient reached out and found only a phantom. The therapist's rationale for diverting the question to the group was that he was trying to draw others in, and to employ the therapeutic factor of universality. That is a reasonable enough move, but it should have followed rather than preceded his interaction with the patient.

The patient's questions at times will generate real questions for the therapist, for which he or she will want answers. It is still important to answer the patient first, and directly, before posing questions of your own. In the second example, both of the therapist's questions could have been asked after an interaction such as the first example took place.

If a patient asks a question, answer it. If you don't know the answer, say so. If you don't want to answer it, say that too. Then ask your questions.

Your answers should be brief. The best therapist intervention is a short one. That is especially true when anxiety is high, as it almost always is in inpatient groups. Cognitive complexity and anxiety appear to be negatively related: the higher the anxiety level, the simpler the cognitive functioning of the patient (and the therapist). Patients are not likely to be able to follow long, involved, complex statements, delivered in compound sentences (like this one), intended to provide complete and structured responses, in the belief that such full responses will be anxiety-reducing. Short, declarative sentences are more likely to be understood. Your comments should be brief, simple, concise, concrete, and refer to observable behavior. The simplicity referred to here is *grammatical*, not intellectual. A succession of grammatically simple sentences may refer cumulatively to complex conceptualizations.

To start a group session, then, engage the patients one at a time. Which patient to engage first is as difficult a decision to make as in an outpatient group. The principles that apply there do not necessarily apply in inpatient groups. The patient who, in an inpatient group, looks most eager to talk may be manic, or so tenuously in contact with reality that engaging with him or her at the very start of the group session will make things more rather than less difficult. The patient who looks most frozen, frightened, or apathetic may well be most in need of being reached out to. The best procedure to follow is to use your common sense, and to attempt to engage the patient who looks both in need of being reached out to and most likely to respond. If you are not sure of who that might be, start with the patient with whom you have the best eye contact. If you don't have good eye contact with anyone (not an unusual circumstance), start with the person sitting next to you. That is not a good idea in an outpatient group, but with inpatients you have to put more energy into the interactions than with outpatients. When starting an inpatient group session, which is sometimes quite draining of the therapist's energy, it may help to remember that you have many interpersonal resources, and that's one reason you are there; the group members may have *no* interpersonal resources, and that is one reason they are inpatients and you're not. So it's up to you to supply the energy and momentum to get things started.

Once again we have reached the moment, at the start of a group, when it is up to you to *do* something. You are the therapist, and you feel, more or less strongly, that all depends on you and that you are supposed to know what to do. But nothing in the books you have read is quite like the situation you are now facing, and you don't know what to do. You turn to the patient sitting next to you and you see the eyes that are dim or blank or vacant, the bent shoulders and the gnarled, nicotine-stained hands. You think, "Oh Lord, how can I reach this person? What will I say?" and you have only the vaguest road map: reduce anxiety, make the group a safe place, facilitate interaction. You hear a voice—it is yours, but it sounds remarkably like your supervisor's—saying, "Mr. Lang, what would you like to tell us today?" Miraculously, the blank, dim eyes look up, and for a moment, just a moment, there is a glimmer in them, of fear, of uncertainty, of—shrewdness.

"I'd like to go home," says Mr. Lang, and the group is started.

Time Structuring

At some point a patient is likely to indicate that he or she is not quite ready to respond at just that moment or, having gotten this far, is not ready to talk further. It is as important for the therapist to know when and how to disengage as to engage with patients. When a patient is saying *not yet*, it is important to let him or her know that (1) you will get back to him or her and (2) you will do so in some specified time. "We'll come back to you in five minutes" is generally a useful and helpful comment because it lets the patient know that there will be time to think, followed by an opportunity to continue participation. Patients sometimes indicate that while they are not ready to talk today, they may be ready tomorrow (or next time the group meets).

Then it is easier and, in a sense, mandatory, to start the next session by inviting those patients to begin.

Structuring in general tends to reduce anxiety because it makes the immediate future more predictable. The more predictable the future, the less anxious the patients. The less anxious the patients, the more likely they are to benefit from group.

Verbal and Nonverbal Communication

A major problem in many publicly funded inpatient facilities is that most patients are neither practiced nor skilled in talking about affect or about the relationship between affect and behavior, while psychotherapies are by definition primarily verbal. The therapist who inquires, "How did you feel about that?" is likely to get a reply like "Fine," or "All right," rather than a verbal report of affect. Similarly, patients learn (but are seldom taught) that the term *sick* in a psychiatric facility refers to behavior rather than to physical illness. Until they learn this difference, patients may respond with confusion to this novel use of the term. Although these differences between patients and therapists in communicative styles is probably most marked in long-term treatment facilities, they may be characteristic of other inpatient settings as well.

Both social class (Hollingshead and Redlich 1958) and personality factors (Berzins et al. 1972) point in the same direction regarding the expression of affect for many patients in publicly funded inpatient units: feelings lead to action, not talk. Since most of the psychotherapies, including the group psychotherapies, facilitate talk rather than action, patients in such settings are being asked to commit themselves in an arena in which they may have little investment, little skill, and little esteem. The attempt to get inpatients to talk about feelings is frequently an inappropriate technical goal.

Nonetheless, patients do experience and do communicate affect, if not verbally then nonverbally. The cues are different, perhaps more ambiguous, perhaps muted, but they are present. In inpatient groups, the non-verbal presentation of self may be of considerably greater importance than the verbal interaction. To the extent that nonverbal presentation is form, and verbal interaction is substance, *there may be no meaning in the substance*, and form may be the entirety of the communication. The interpersonal message is entirely in the process and not at all in the content. Thus the patient who babbles incoherently may be trying to reach out, to make contact. The response to such a patient—"I'm sorry, I can't understand you"—takes form for granted and assumes that there must be some meaning in the substance.

How do you determine what might be an appropriate response here? By looking at the patient, and what he or she is *doing*, rather than by listening to what he or she is saying—by attending to process rather than to content. Hence, what you attend to is the patient's tone of voice, to the affect conveyed by that tone, and to the interpersonal response of the group to the incoherent patient. Perhaps the surest guide as to what to do is your own internal, subjective response to the patient. He or she may want comforting in some way; or perhaps the babbling is intended to provoke rejection. Offering reassurance—a smile and a nod, and perhaps "It's OK, it's all right, I understand that you're feeling anxious right now" is a response to the non-verbal aspects of the patient's communication. To the extent that you can respond along the same communicative dimensions, non-verbally, that the patient is using, your chances of reaching him or her are enhanced.

The babbling patient is more likely to be encountered on wards other than short-term admissions service units. On such units, silence, monosyllabic replies, and confused looks are common responses to therapist attempts to get patients to talk about their feelings. It is then more difficult to find out how to reach them on an affective level.

The question is whether the therapist should even try to deal with patients' feelings in this type of group. The answer is yes, but only to the extent that the patient's feelings stem from or are impairing his or her ability to function in the group. You are not aiming for the development of insight, or even significant behavior change. You are aiming for the reduction of anxiety, the facilitation of communication, and the reinforcement of adaptive and nonpsychotic behaviors. One of the first steps in the reduction of anxiety may involve the patient's perception that he or she is understood, and that the understanding does not provoke hostility or rejection.

Nonverbal communication involves the emission of quite small behavioral cues. For the frightened paranoid patient, for example, the smallest smile of acknowledgment may be sufficient reassurance that the patient's fear has been seen and understood and that it will be responded to gently. For the depressed patient, perhaps a look of kind concern and a shift in body posture, attentive and receptive, may be meaningful and effective. It is impossible to prescribe what will work with which patient, or within which patient type.

How, then, is the novice therapist to learn? Preferably by watching a more experienced therapist lead the group, and by talking together afterward. And by attending to the nonverbal domain; by attempting to convey nonverbally the attitudes of acceptance and understanding, of recognition without revulsion, and of confidence in the patient's abilities, with your help, and that of the group, to successfully combat the demons of madness.

References

Alfred, A. R. (1992). Members' perceptions of co-leaders' influence and effectiveness in group therapy. *Journal for Specialists in Group Work* 17: 42–53.

Alonso, A. (1992). Personal communication.

Alper, V. S., and Kobos, J. C. (1988). Cotherapy in psychodynamic group therapy: an approach to training. *Group* 12: 135–144.

Anderson, B. N., Pine, I., and Mee-Lee, D. (1972). Resident training in cotherapy groups. *International Journal of Group Psychotherapy* 22: 192–198.

Armstrong, S. W., and Rouselin, S. (1963). *Group Psychotherapy in Nursing Practice.* New York: Macmillan.

Battegay, R., and von Marschall, R. (1978). Results of long-term group psychotherapy with schizophrenics. *Comprehensive Psychiatry* 4: 349–353.

Beck, A. P. (1983). The participation of leaders in the structural development of therapy groups. In, *Advances in Group Therapy: Integrating Theory and Practice*, ed. R. Dies and K. R. MacKenzie, pp. 137–138. New York: International Universities Press.

Berman, A. L. (1975). Group psychotherapy training. *Small Group Behavior* 6: 325–344.

Berne, E. (1966). *Principles of Group Treatment.* New York: Grove.

Berzins, J. I., Friedman, W. H., and Ross, W. (1972). Toward patient–therapist matching. Unpublished manuscript.

Bion, W. R. (1961). *Experiences in Groups.* New York: Basic Books.

Bloch, B., and Crouch, E. (1985). *Therapeutic Factors in Group Psychotherapy.* Oxford, England: Oxford University Press.

Bowers, W., and Gauron, E. F. (1981). Potential hazards of the cotherapy relationship. *Psychotherapy: Theory, Research and Practice* 18: 225–228.

Brabender, V. (1985). Time-limited inpatient group therapy: a developmental model. *International Journal of Group Psychotherapy* 35: 373–390.

———— (1988). A closed model of short-term inpatient group psychotherapy. 38th Institute on Hospital and Community Psychiatry (1986, San Diego, California). *Hospital and Community Psychiatry* 39: 542–545.

Carson, R. C. (1969). *Interaction Concepts of Personality.* New York: Wiley.

Cartwright, D. (1968). The nature of group cohesiveness. In *Group Dynamics: Research and Theory*, ed. D. Cartwright and A. Zander, pp. 91–109. London: Tavistock.

Clarkin, J. F., Marziali, E., and Monroe-Blum, H., eds. (1992). *Borderline Personality Disorder: Clinical and Empirical Perspectives.* New York: Guilford.

Coche, E. (1977). Supervision in the training of group therapists. In *Supervision, Consultation, and Staff Training in the Helping Professions*, ed. F. W. Kaslow (pp. 235–253). San Francisco: Jossey-Bass.

Cohen, L. (1980). The new supervisee views supervision. In *Psychotherapy Supervision: Theory, Research, and Practice*, ed. A. K. Hess, pp. 78–84. New York: Wiley.

Davis, F., and Lohr, N. (1971). Special problems with the use of co-therapists in group psychotherapy. *International Journal of Group Psychotherapy* 21: 143–158.

Dick, B., Lessler, K., and Whiteside, J. (1980). A developmental framework for cotherapy. *International Journal of Group Psychotherapy* 30: 273–285.

Dies, R. (1980). Group psychotherapy: training and supervision. In *Psychotherapy Supervision: Theory, Research, and Practice*, ed. A. K. Hess, pp. 337–366. New York: Wiley.

———— (1983a). Bridging the gap between research and practice in group psychotherapy. In *Advances in Group Psychotherapy: Integrating Research and Practice*, ed. R. Dies and R. MacKenzie, pp. 1–26. New York: International Universities Press.

———— (1983b). Clinical implications of research on leadership style in short-term group psychotherapy. In *Advances in Group Psychotherapy*, eds. R. Dies and K. R. MacKenzie, pp. 27–78. New York: International Universities Press.

Dies, R. R., and Cohen, L. (1976). Content considerations in group therapist self-disclosure. *International Journal of Group Psychotherapy* 26: 71–88.

Freud, S. (1922). *Group Psychology and the Analysis of the Ego*. London: Hogarth.

Fried, E. (1971). Basic concepts in group psychotherapy. In *Comprehensive Group Psychotherapy*, eds. H. I. Kaplan and B. J. Sadock, pp. 47–69. Baltimore: Williams & Wilkins.

Friedman, B. (1973). Cotherapy: a behavioral and attitudinal survey of third-year psychiatric residents. *International Journal of Group Psychotherapy* 23: 228–234.

Goffman, E. (1959). *Presentation of Self in Everyday Life*. Garden City, NY: Doubleday Anchor.

Greenberg, L. (1980). Supervision from the perspective of the supervisee. In *Psychotherapy Supervision: Theory, Research, and Practice*, ed. A. K. Hess, pp. 85–91. New York: Wiley.

Grinker, R. R. (1977). The borderline syndrome: a phenomenological view. In *Borderline Personality Disorders*, ed. P. Hartocollis, pp. 159–172. New York: International Universities Press.

Hall, C., and Lindzey, G. (1970). *Theories of Personality*, 2nd ed. New York: Wiley.

Heitler, J. B. (1973). Preparation of lower-class patients for expressive group psychotherapy. *Journal of Consulting and Clinical Psychology* 41: 251–260.

Hellwig, K., and Memmot, R. J. (1974). Co-therapy: the balancing act. *Small Group Behavior* 5: 175–181.

Hess, A. K., ed. (1980). *Psychotherapy Supervision: Theory, Research, and Practice*. New York: Wiley.

Hess, A. K., and Hess, K. A. (1983). Psychotherapy supervision: a survey of internship training practices. *Professional Psychology* 14: 504–513.

Hollingshead, A. B., and Redlich, F. C. (1958). *Social Class and Mental Illness*. New York: Wiley.

Howe, L. P. (1991). Origins and History of Pesso System/Psychomotor Therapy. In *Moving Psychotherapy*, eds. A. Pesso and J. Crandall, Cambridge, MA: Brookline Books.

Kadis, A. L., Krasner, J. D., Weiner, M. F., et al. (1974). *Practicum of Group Psychotherapy*. 2nd ed. New York: Harper & Row.

Kahn, E. M. (1986). Discussion: inpatient group psychotherapy: which type of group is best? *Group* 10: 27–33.

Kahn, E. M., Sturke, I. T., and Schaeffer, J. (1992). Inpatient group processes parallel unit dynamics. *International Journal of Group Psychotherapy* 42: 407–418.

Kanas, N. (1991). Group therapy with schizophrenic patients. *International Journal of Group Psychotherapy* 41: 33–48.

Kaplan, H. I., and Sadock, B. J., eds. (1972). *The Origins of Group Psychoanalysis*. New York: Jason Aronson.

Kibell, H. D. (1993). Inpatient group psychotherapy. In *Group Therapy in Clinical Practice*, eds. A. Alonso and H. Swiller, pp. 93–112. Washington, DC: American Psychiatric Press.

Klein, R. H., Bernard, H. S., and Singer, D. L., eds. (1992). *Handbook of Contemporary Group Psychotherapy: Contributions from Object Relations, Self Psychology, and Social Systems Theories*. Madison, CT: International Universities Press.

Lakin, M. (1985). *The Helping Group: Therapeutic Principles and Issues*. Reading, MA: Addison-Wesley.

Leary, T. (1957). *Interpersonal Diagnosis of Personality: A Functional Theory and Methodology for Personality Evaluation.* New York: Ronald.

Leszcz, M., Yalom, I., and Norden, M. (1985). The value of inpatient group psychotherapy: patients' perceptions. *International Journal of Group Psychotherapy* 35: 411–433.

Lewin, K. (1947). Frontiers in group dynamics, I: concept, method, and theory in social science: social equilibrium. *Human Relations* 1: 5–40.

Lieberman, M., Yalom, I., and Miles, M. (1973). *Encounter Groups: First Facts.* New York: Basic Books.

Linehan, M. M. (1987a). Dialectical behavior therapy: a cognitive behavioral approach to parasuicide. *Journal of Personality Disorders* 1: 328–333.

_____ (1987b). Dialectical behavior therapy for borderline personality disorder: theory and method. *Bulletin of the Menninger Clinic* 51: 261–276.

Lonergan, E. (1982). *Group Intervention: How to Begin and Maintain Groups in Medical and Psychiatric Settings.* Northvale, NJ: Jason Aronson.

Marcovitz, R. J., and Smith, J. E. (1983). An approach to time-limited dynamic inpatient group psychotherapy. *Small Group Behavior* 14: 369–376.

Marshall, W. R., and Confer, W. N. (1980). The phenomenology of being a supervisee. In *Psychotherapy Supervision: Theory, Research, and Practice,* ed. A. K. Hess, pp. 92–100. New York: Wiley.

Maves, P. A., and Schulz, J. W. (1985). Inpatient group treatment on short-term acute care units. *Hospital and Community Psychiatry* 36: 69–73.

McMahon, N., and Links, P. S. (1984). Cotherapy: The need for positive pairing. *Canadian Journal of Psychiatry* 29: 385–389.

Monroe-Bloom, H. (1992). Group treatment of borderline personality disorder. In *Borderline Personality Disorder: Clinical and Empirical Perspectives,* ed. J. F. Clarkin, E. Marziali, and H. Monroe-Bloom, pp. 288–300. New York: Guilford.

Paulson, I., Burroughs, J. C., and Gelb, C. B. (1976). Co- therapy: what is the crux of the relationship? *International Journal of Group Psychotherapy* 26: 213–224.

Pesso, A. (1973). *Experience in Action*. New York: New York University Press.

Piper, W. E., Doan, B. D., Edwards, E. M., and Jones, B. D. (1979). Cotherapy behavior, group process, and treatment outcome. *Journal of Consulting and Clinical Psychology* 47: 1081–1089.

Poey, K. (1985). Guidelines for the practice of brief, dynamic group therapy. *International Journal of Group Psychotherapy* 35: 331–354.

Powdermaker, F., and Frank, J. (1953). *Group Psychotherapy: Studies in Methodology of Research and Therapy*. Cambridge, MA: Harvard University Press.

Rice, D. G., Fey, W. F., and Kepecs, J. G. (1972). Therapist experience and "style" as factors in co-therapy. *Family Process* 11: 1–12.

Rosenbaum, M. (1978). Organization of the group and the first group meeting. In *Group Psychotherapy: Theory and Practice*, eds. H. Mullan and M. Rosenbaum, pp. 94–114. New York: The Free Press.

Russell, A., and Russell, L. (1980). The uses and abuses of co-therapy. *Advances in Family Psychiatry* 2: 401–410.

Rutan, J. S., and Stone, W. N. (1984). *Psychodynamic Group Psychotherapy*. Lexington, MA: Collamore.

Shaffer, J., and Galinsky, M. D. (1974). *Models of Group Therapy and Sensitivity Training*. Englewood Cliffs, NJ: Prentice-Hall.

Silverstein, H. G. (1981). *Group therapists' attitudes toward co-therapy and intimacy*. Doctoral dissertation, Temple University, Philadelphia.

Strassberg, D. S., Roback, H. B., and Anchor, K. N. (1975). Self-disclosure in group therapy with schizophrenics. *Archives of General Psychiatry* 32: 1259–1261.

Sullivan, H. S. (1954). *The Psychiatric Interview*. New York: W. W. Norton.

Toseland, R., and Siporin, M. (1986). When to recommend group treatment: A review of the clinical and the research literature. *International Journal of Group Psychotherapy* 36: 171–201.

Van Atta, R. E. (1969). Co-therapy as a supervisory process. *Psychotherapy: Theory, Research, and Practice* 6: 137–139.

Weiner, M. (1974). Genetic versus interpersonal insight. *International Journal of Group Psychotherapy* 24: 230–237.

Wolf, A., and Schwartz, E. (1972). Psychoanalysis in groups. In *The Origins of Group Psychoanalysis*, eds. H. I. Kaplan and B. Sadock, pp. 41–91. New York: Jason Aronson.

Yalom, I. (1983). *Inpatient Group Psychotherapy*. New York: Basic Books.

_____ (1985). *The Theory and Practice of Group Psychotherapy*, 3rd ed. New York: Basic Books.

Index